T0355574

THE KING'S PEACE

THE KING'S PEACE

Law and Order in the British Empire

LISA FORD

HARVARD UNIVERSITY PRESS

Cambridge, Massachusetts, and London, England

2021

Library of Congress Cataloging-in-Publication Data
Names: Ford, Lisa, 1974– author.
Title: The king's peace : law and order in the British Empire / Lisa Ford.
Description: Cambridge, Massachusetts : Harvard University Press, 2021. |
Includes bibliographical references and index.
Identifiers: LCCN 2021003232 | ISBN 9780674249073 (cloth)
Subjects: LCSH: Sovereignty. | Great Britain—Colonies—Administration. |
Great Britain—History, Military—18th century. | Great Britain—History,
Military—19th century. | Great Britain—History—1714–1837.
Classification: LCC JV1060 .F67 2021 | DDC 909/.097124107—dc23
LC record available at https://lccn.loc.gov/2021003232

For Mary

Contents

THE KING'S PEACE

INTRODUCTION: THE KING'S COLONIAL PEACE AND ITS LEGACIES

Historians love to write about war, but "the peace" deserves more of our attention.[1] "The peace" is something we notice in its absence, in the wee hours of Sunday morning when our neighbors are disturbing it. We lie awake wondering whether to call the police—an armed, paramilitary force in the service of the state. Centuries of jurisprudence and practice are bound up in that impulse. It should give us pause.

We should pause because the details of the peace mark the limits of our citizenship and subjecthood. People in most liberal democracies cannot march or even gather in large numbers in a public place without a permit. When I was growing up in Queensland, Australia, in the 1980s, a notoriously corrupt police force was authorized to charge groups of three or more perfectly orderly people with disturbing the peace. In the United States today, most marches, however peaceful, are closely guarded by police with military-grade weapons. Indeed, in gun-saturated America, African American adults and children alike have reason to fear the use of deadly force by police in the course of routine traffic stops, for nonviolent crime, or even for playing cops and robbers at the park. Native Americans and Aboriginal Australians are more likely than most people in the world to end up in a jail cell for appearing drunk and disorderly in public—a common breach of the peace. Aboriginal Australians are more likely than most people in the world to die there.[2] The Indian state stands by while citizens violently breach the peace of Muslim minorities and has kept other regions of the diverse federation under martial law for generations in defense of everyday order. In the modern world, the blurred line between order and disorder resolves consistently into differences of race, religion, gender, and wealth—parameters that bound everyone's liberty.

The peace deserves our attention because, as a legal idea, it comprehends all of the mysteries of medieval and early modern state-making in the British Isles, and many of the deepest constitutional questions about empire abroad—mysteries that were hotly debated in the local and global cataclysms of the seventeenth and eighteenth centuries. Though the "king's peace" is a vague term that has long "passed into common use as a kind of ornament of speech, without any clear sense of its historical meaning," it invokes the sovereign's authority to order people in and sometimes beyond the realm.[3] When we think of the state's capacity to curb everyday disturbances by brawlers and revelers, we are thinking both of a series of porous, public performances and of key sticks in the "bundle of rights" constituting the authority to rule.[4] These were sticks gathered by the English crown and disputed by subjects over centuries as kings progressively declared their power to order roads, borders, waterways and tidewaters, chartered towns and colonies.[5] Gradually the sovereign came to be understood as the protector of the realm, preserving the life and property of his subjects by keeping the peace. He might do this by administering justice according to law (through judges and magistrates wielding delegated power), or by suspending courts and raising armies to protect the polity from internal rebellion or external attack. States still announce their arrival in international law by securing the willing or terrified adherence by citizens and subjects to the rituals of everyday order. Then and now the parameters of the peace define modern sovereignty.

But those parameters have shifted. Two seventeenth-century kings lost their thrones and one his head in disputes over when they might raise armies to bring England to order. In the late eighteenth century, George III lost thirteen American colonies not only because Parliament asserted its power to tax, but because his own power to keep the peace in unruly American port towns, Indian Country, and Quebec was deeply disputed. Such restraints are laughable in the twenty-first century. Their unraveling cannot be understood without empire.

The King's Peace tracks the changing parameters of colonial peace-keeping in the Age of Revolutions, and through it, the fraught transformation of the British imperial constitution.[6] It does this by exploring a series of contests about who got to keep the peace over whom and where in Massachusetts, Quebec, Jamaica, Bengal, and New South Wales between 1764 and 1836. These contests exemplify (but do not exhaust) the shifting foundations of imperial order. Disorders in Massachusetts and Quebec catalyzed metropolitan debate about the governance and political economy of empire. In tandem with new conquests in India, American chaos helped to precipitate a sudden shift from colonial self-government to autocratic rule, the single most important change in the governance of the empire since its inception. Meanwhile, Jamaica's peculiar dependence on unspeakable cruelty, imperial military power, and martial law generated techniques of racialized peacekeeping that spread throughout the empire. The island's uncivil peace also fed the shift to autocracy by prompting evangelical reformers in the British Isles to argue that crown government alone could tame the moral and legal disorder of slavery.[7] With few exceptions from 1773, new colonies in the British Empire, slave and free, were ruled directly by autocratic governors-in-council, exercising the power of the British crown.[8]

This book also explores the unfolding of some of the earliest experiments in autocracy. The first of these was partial and peculiar. In 1773, Parliament intervened to give the king some control over the enormous and growing power wielded by the East India Company in the name of the Mughal Emperor. This intervention carried all the license of imagined foreign tyranny. The Regulating Act of 1773 refined a model of gubernatorial autocracy already established in the Indian subcontinent by the East India Company. The act established a governor-general-in-council and made it answerable (albeit temporarily) to a crown appointed supreme court. From 1784, governors-in-council were overseen by the king's privy councillors, though on paper they ruled for and were employed by the Company.[9] Quebec was the second constitutional experiment. The Quebec Act of 1774 removed all hope that the province would receive the legislature promised by the Proclamation of 1763, instead establishing a governor who ruled in council without an elected legislature until 1791.[10] The third departure was quirky and important for other reasons. The convict colony of New South Wales was established in 1788 with a crown-appointed naval or military governor and military-style courts. There, the governor ruled without a council until 1824.

These experimental constitutions were not the first of their kind: early efforts to eviscerate Jamaica's assembly and Sir Edmund Andros's brief reign in New York and New England demonstrate the appeal of prerogative rule in restoration England, while eighteenth-century garrison governments in the fortresses of Gibraltar and Minorca remind us that many imperial outposts operated perennially under some species of military rule.[11] Nevertheless, the constitutional settlements in Quebec, Bengal, and New South Wales marked the advent of a new kind of empire. In Bengal and New South Wales that constitutional shift blossomed into experimental modes of policing and the militarization of the colonial peace in the early nineteenth century. All showcase sudden and massive legal divergence between the center and periphery of empire—divergence that changed empire and shaped modern states.

Eighteenth-century legal divergence unfolded within new and old constitutional praxes. It invoked, directly or indirectly, the only stable constitutional principle of empire—that colonial law should not be repugnant to metropolitan law unless local circumstances demanded it. Of course, this principle could be deployed to set powerful limits on colonial courts and legislatures. It carried within it implicit metropolitan power to review law, appeal decisions, and supervise colonial government—to limit what could be done to the king's subjects and their interlocutors in the defense of the peace.[12] Most of the time this maxim had a very different effect, authorizing the bastardization of basic procedural safeguards and, with it, the transformation of subjecthood. Until the end of the eighteenth century, the ramifications of this rule of colonial legal exception were nowhere more evident than in the horrifying details of British new-world slavery.

Legal divergence had more recent drivers, too. With the exception of New South Wales, after 1750 new colonies were conquered from or ceded by other empires. After 1783, sometimes by default, and increasingly by policy, the empire and its delegates elected to maintain

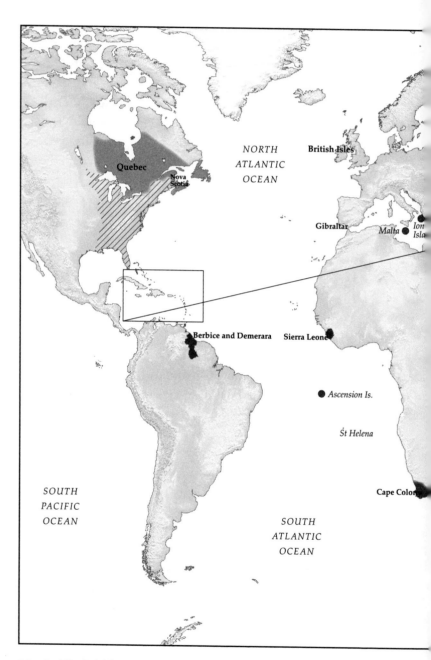

NORTH ATLANTIC OCEAN

British Isles

Quebec

Nova Scotia

Gibraltar   Malta   Ion Isla

Berbice and Demerara   Sierra Leone

Ascension Is.

St Helena

SOUTH PACIFIC OCEAN

SOUTH ATLANTIC OCEAN

Cape Colon

Map I.1 The British Empire to 1815. © Lisa Ford

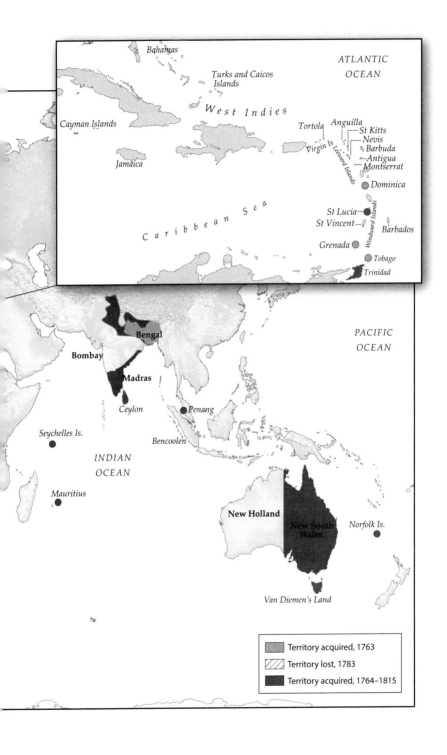

Bahamas

Turks and Caicos
Islands

ATLANTIC
OCEAN

W e s t   I n d i e s

Cayman Islands

Tortola Anguilla
Virgin Is St Kitts
Nevis
Barbuda
Antigua
Montserrat

Jamaica

Dominica

C a r i b b e a n   S e a

St Lucia
St Vincent

Grenada

Barbados

Tobago

Trinidad

Bengal

Bombay

PACIFIC
OCEAN

Madras

Ceylon

Penang

Seychelles Is.

Bencoolen

INDIAN
OCEAN

Mauritius

New Holland

New South
Wales

Norfolk Is.

Van Diemen's Land

Territory acquired, 1763

Territory lost, 1783

Territory acquired, 1764–1815

and adapt inherited legal regimes. Some of these were European colonial legal systems; others were older, like Mughal law in Bengal.[13] This shift was bolstered by the very latest restatement of imperial constitutional law. Sweeping aside arguments made by British colonists about their birthright to self-rule, but also reinforcing powerful parliamentary limits on the prerogative, *Campbell v. Hall* (1774) pronounced that the king (or his delegate) could settle whatever law and government he wanted in a conquered colony, so long as he adhered to nebulous "fundamental principles." Once he had done so, he was bound by that settlement unless Parliament legislated a new colonial constitution.[14] Within these parameters, coercive peacekeeping measures proliferated after 1800.

Powerful governors (the king's representatives in the colonies) argued repeatedly that the colonial peace was exceptionally disorderly because of some combination of people, place, and geopolitics. As the American Revolution receded and the French and Haitian Revolutions erupted, the world, unsurprisingly, seemed like a disorderly place. The demographics of late eighteenth-century empire shifted too, as many new colonies had large, nonwhite populations.[15] In the revolutionary Caribbean, many residents of Britain's new conquests shared the double infamy of being predominantly free-Black and French-speaking. Racially diverse colonies were acquired at a time when new-world slavery and orientalism combined and hardened to mark their inhabitants out as morally and intellectually unequal to the full benefits of British subjecthood. So, a very important strand of history and theory rightly stresses the centrality of racism and ethnocentrism to the changing parameters of colonial law.[16]

These circumstances combined with new modes of governance to hasten the collapse of the recent and unstable constitutional settle-

ment reached after the Glorious Revolution. This shift told in
bodies. The Victorian "jurisprudence of emergency" and the proliferation of martial law that has so fascinated historians since 2001
took root in fissures created by eighteenth-century shifts in the constitutional parameters of the colonial peace.[17] However, the transformation of the imperial constitution was not only about race. So
much is clear from the fact that the British Parliament spearheaded
a syncopated unraveling in the British Isles. In the eighteenth
century, it frequently legislated to allow coercive policing, culmi-
nating in the suspension of habeas corpus for years during the
American and Napoleonic Wars.[18] Though passed by Parliament,
these laws empowered the Privy Council or a secretary of state to
order imprisonment without bail on suspicion of treason: Parliament emboldened the crown.[19]

This book forms one strand of a much larger tale about the rise
of the crown and the modern police state. But the process of imperial transformation matters too. To understand it, we have to ex-
amine the colonial peace at multiple scales. As Lauren Benton and
I have demonstrated elsewhere, case law and treatises did not define the jurisprudence of empire.[20] Because it was such a porous and
messy business, suspended between law, performance, and practice,
this is especially true of colonial peacekeeping.[21] To understand its
workings, we must pay attention to the local: tracing the shifting
parameters of the colonial peace requires the repeopling of the history of the imperial constitution, following the lead of New Imperial Histories by recovering multiple perspectives from the truncated
archive.[22] Colonial archives abound with controversies about the
peace. Every episode traced here brims with alternative visions of
order, curated for the consumption of magistrates, governors, administrators, or publics, but there for all to see. A crowd gathered

outside a smuggler's house in Boston in 1766 had very clear ideas about the boundary between peace and riot. Some even claimed to keep a people's peace against the crown. Thomas Walker and Mr. Livingstone, both justices of the peace, held opposing ideas about order in Montréal in 1764; one mobilized Protestants against military tyranny, which the other cast as the stirrings of sedition. Trelawny Town Maroons thought magistrates in Montego Bay breached a different kind of peace when they ordered two Trelawny townsfolk to be whipped like slaves in the jail yard in 1795. These acts of protest looked like war to Governor Balcarres—an interpretation that was contested by planters, pundits, and parliamentarians. Brahmins and other notables were outraged by their incarceration by the lawless rabble entrusted with peacekeeping in Hooghly in 1809, though the pikes and peons who arrested them thought local elites were purveyors of disorder. Free men trying to make their way in New South Wales in the 1830s described draconian anti-bushranger laws as the height of arbitrary government, and the new civilian governor agreed. However, country magistrates and accomplished judges defended such laws as vital elements of the convict peace.

These different perspectives were not curiosities. They were repeated and weighed carefully in the colonies and the metropole. Told right, small stories about peacekeeping could affirm or undermine sweeping claims about political economy and good government; they could even topple ministries.[23] This was so because the shifting parameters of the colonial peace raised fundamental questions about empire, changing the course of colonial governance. The evolving peace altered the privileges and obligations of colonial subjects, regardless of their race. It reshaped the imperial constitution, and lodged the crown squarely at its center.

Constituting Subjects

The transforming peace reshaped British colonial subjecthood in the Age of Revolutions, multiplying its gradations and winnowing its bounties. British subjecthood was a fluid category, as Hannah Weiss Muller has demonstrated. Since England's seventeenth-century revolutions, contract theory had conjured subjects who had some say in their subjection to the king; in Locke's famous formula, men traded their natural liberty for the king's protection (the peace). But when subjects might renounce allegiance, how they became subjects, what they gave up for that protection, and what they gained in return remained highly uncertain, particularly in the washing machine of empire. *Calvin's Case* (1608) famously gave Robert Calvin—a Scot born *after* James VI of Scotland had become James I of England—the rights of a freeborn Englishman. James VI was James I, so Calvin's personal allegiance to James entitled him to the benefits of subjecthood in both of James's realms. This was, as Muller points out, an inclusive definition of subjecthood that had important ramifications for the eighteenth-century empire, but it did not answer the important question of what happened to people already living in a colony at the time of conquest or whether, indeed, anyone could shift their allegiance from their "natural" king to a foreign invader.[24]

Two domestic revolutions later, the privileges and burdens of British subjecthood were no more certain. The cacophony of constitutional crises filled subjecthood with claims and counterclaims that ranged from the plausible to the absurd.[25] All of this noise yielded little in the form of justiciable privileges. Like Magna Carta, the 1628 Petition of Right and the 1689 Bill of Rights were little more than an amalgam of "vague constitutional clichés" that, among other things, suggested that freeborn Englishmen had a right to petition, and should not be cruelly punished or incarcerated arbitrarily. They also enjoined the crown not to raise armies in peacetime, suspend laws, or raise taxes without the consent of Parliament.[26] By the mid-eighteenth century, in return for their allegiance, free subjects might plausibly expect the king (through officers of the crown) to hear their complaints, and attempt to ensure that they were governed by properly administered laws and disciplined by civilian courts.

However, the exigencies of empire rendered these privileges unstable. In the American northeast, the vagaries of subjecthood bloated into exorbitant and disorderly claims. It was quite clear to everyone, including some among Boston's elite in the 1760s, that white Protestant men claiming excessive liberties strained against the obligations owed to their monarch, and chipped away at imperial order. Such men demonstrated their republican proclivities nowhere more clearly than in their war with Governors Bernard and Hutchinson about the nature of the king's prerogative to keep the peace. For this reason the liberties claimed by Boston's mobs epitomized the unsustainability of compromises about military power, civilian order, and basic civil rights worked out in the colonies after the Glorious Revolution. Protestant Bostonians' contempt for rules that did not suit them and their inflated notion of birthrights demonstrated the urgent need to reset colonial expectations by shifting the boundaries of the colonial subjecthood in defense of the colonial peace. But if the extravagant rights claims of eighteenth-century Protestant men were the problem, the demographic diversity of the post-1763 empire offered a solution.

Uncertainties about the allegiances and liberties of vulnerable subjects in newly conquered colonies carried the promise of a new imperial order. Muller has tracked the creativity and liberality of eighteenth-century administrators and legislators, who welcomed Catholics of all colors, even French ones, to transfer their allegiance to the British king. They did this by yielding, piecemeal, to myriad claims for privileges and immunities, including partial exemption from the Penal Laws that limited Catholic civil rights in Britain.[27] However, that account does not begin to exhaust the significance of subjecthood in La Paix Québécoise. When calling for their partial emancipation, Quebec's first governor, James Murray, passionately extolled the virtues of French Canadians and sought to bind them to the British Empire. But Murray had other motives too. As a minority of Protestant "Old Subjects" wielded its new judicial powers in opposition to the hybrid military-civil government, Murray scrambled to stop Quebec from getting a legislature in order to preserve crown authority in the colony. His defense of Canadians against Protestants— taken up by his successor Guy Carleton—made limited Catholic subjecthood the foundation stone of a new sort of crown colony. It underpinned a watershed in thinking about colonial constitutions that waxed and waned in Canada, but shaped empire for generations.[28]

The full significance of that watershed becomes apparent only when we put it in imperial context. The Quebec Act of 1774 was not just an incorporative solution for the nearly 70,000 French Canadians; it also cast jurisdiction over a huge swath of Indian Country. Settlers and traders there would be ordered, henceforth, by a governor-in-council. A few thousand French Canadians of dubious affiliation lived in Indian Country, but the chief problem there was Protestant British Americans squatting and cheating their way westward from the east. The Quebec Act ensured that they too would have a new relationship with the king, as would almost every new colonial subject from 1774 until the end of empire.

Slaves changed colonial subjecthood too, but in a much longer time frame. Struggles about the slave peace in Jamaica in the late eighteenth century did not embroil imperial lawyers in the same way that Quebec did, but they do show how the constant threat of slave rebellion shaped everyone's rights and responsibilities as subjects, even in self-governing colonies.[29] The suffering of slaves in Jamaica's peacekeeping project is well known. A slave's status as property deprived them of all meaningful privileges of subjecthood—a deprivation that told in their daily torture and gruesome mass killing in times of threatened rebellion. However, the life and death struggle to control slaves also transformed the subjecthood of masters. Most importantly, by torturing and humiliating slaves, masters wielded delegated state power and made it arbitrary and evil. Nor was the slave peace merely the product of delegated jurisdiction: it preoccupied the Jamaican legislature more than any other subject. Jamaica's few white voters acquiesced to military expenditure at a rate unparalleled in the history of British Empire, and to martial law more cheerfully and more often than any other contemporary colony.[30] These concessions were fraught, and rested on a series of compromises between the local legislature and the crown, but they bound white masters to the imperial state in ways that would have been unfamiliar to slave owners in Boston or Montréal. The impossibility of the slave peace and the overt dependence of Jamaica's slaveholders on imperial military power not only changed their subjecthood, it helped to justify calls for crown government in Trinidad and elsewhere after 1790, fundamentally reorienting the relationship of all colonial subjects with the crown.[31]

To keep slaves at peace, Jamaica and its neighbors also refined the parameters of nonwhite subjecthood in ways that long outlasted slavery. The threat of solidarity among free Black people and slaves produced ever-increasing limits on the privileges of the former—limits justified by escalating claims about their natural perfidy and limited potential as subjects of the king.[32] The portability of this hardening racial and ethnic chauvinism is exemplified by a fierce debate about what modes of policing were justified to quell pervasive banditry in Bengal in the first decade of the nineteenth century. Parliament had passed the Regulating Act of 1773 making East India Company–appointed governors somewhat answerable to the crown. It did so in part because it worried that the Company's despotic treatment of putatively Mughal subjects would erode British liberties. They were right to worry. Thomas Ernst's well-known protests against the deployment of special magistrates and disreputable spies to round up Bengali bandits in 1809 prompted introspection by the governor-in-council about how best to balance peacekeeping and justice in India. Their debate made clear that everyone had different ideas about the rights and responsibilities of Bengalis—ideas that would have been jarringly unfamiliar to free-born Englishmen in the eighteenth century.[33] In the end, in the interests of the peace, Bengalis, whose precise relationship to the British crown remained deeply uncertain decades after the passing of the Regulating Act, would not be guaranteed freedom from police violence or arbitrary arrest in the hybrid legal order established by the East India Company.[34] But the tangled sovereignties of Bengal did not stop its technologies of governance from spreading through the British Empire. Indeed, Britain's next colonial venture, the convict colony of New South Wales, blended Quebec's 1774 constitution with a system of justice built around summary jurisdiction and preventative detention. And on it went. These small steps altered everyone's relationship with the king.

The free white inhabitants of New South Wales posed even thornier questions about order. Keeping convicts in place and at peace in the port towns and on the burgeoning pastoral frontiers of the colony in the 1830s provides one of the most fascinating examples of the instability of white subjecthood in the empire. Even as disorderly Indigenous people were being bound to the king's peace on the king's highways in New South Wales for the first time, the crisis of bushranging prompted a desperate governor-in-council to pass the Bushrangers Act of 1830—a law that allowed the summary arrest of any white person in the colony who could not prove their freedom on demand. This law was taken directly from slave colonies, where brown skin created a rebuttable presumption of enslavement. Empire had come so far since the 1760s! A military governor in consultation with a very few crown-appointed advisors, adapting an eighteenth-century law from slave colonies, could declare the peace so imperiled that free, white Protestants could be arrested for not carrying paper markers of their freedom. Like Jamaica and Quebec, New South Wales shows us that the challenges of the colonial peace altered subjecthood in ways that were deeper and broader than race.

The challenge of keeping the peace among Protestants, Catholics, slaves, Indians, free Black people, and convicts in the varied landscapes of the eighteenth- and early nineteenth-century British Empire reframed white and nonwhite colonial subjecthood in different ways. In doing so, it altered the constitution of empire. This happened, not at the level of juridical abstraction, but through the interface of crises of order, everyday ideology, and practice. If Protestant men were a problem for empire in the eighteenth century, then vulnerable colonial subjects, recrafted in time and place, became conduits of order in a disorderly world. Their winnowed claims on the king enmeshed their free, white and Protestant interlocutors in diverging iterations of colonial order. In the pages that follow, I capture some of their experience of the altered peace, even as I track their transformation into purveyors of new orders on the edges of empire.

The Waxing Crown

The transformation of empire to meet the exigencies of the colonial peace in the Age of Revolutions is, finally, a story about the growing power of the crown. The prerogative was a chameleon concept in the eighteenth century. In medieval times it described the things that the king might do on his own authority—and they were relatively few.[35] The king's prerogatives grew over time into broad responsibility for the administration of justice (through the king's courts), the keeping of the peace (appointing magistrates), and defending the realm (through powers—increasingly regulated—to raise armies, conduct foreign policy, and rule conquests). Though the English revolutions did little in law to formally bind the king's will to Parliament, in political theory and practice the ructions of the seventeenth century shifted the relationship between key institutions and offices in the metropole.[36] At the core of this muddling was the disentanglement of the king from his office. With the counsel of a ministry that became very gradually, if inconsistently, answerable to Parliament, the king slowly disappeared into the crown—a conflation that at once made it possible to trade old kings for new ones, radically empowered the king's ministers, and rendered the king subject to law.[37] So, by the end of the eighteenth century, customary "prerogatives" were subsumed by a crown decreasingly dependent on the will of the monarch. More importantly, the crown accrued enormous new powers by Acts of Parliament. Critics feared the rising prerogative in empire, but crown power grew with the collusion of imperial and colonial legislatures.

This shift was novel: in post-1763 empire, key members of the Board of Trade resolved to use the prerogative to fix America.[38] It became counterrevolutionary, as Christopher Bayly demonstrated so elegantly in *Imperial Meridian*.[39] After the American Revolution, a reactionary, mercantile elite reinforced its grip on power in Britain and used the prerogative to control what remained of the empire through autocratic colonial governance, tempered by talk of procedural fairness and the rule of law.[40] The means to these ends were riddled with contradictions. Military men-turned-bureaucrats and powerful reform networks infiltrated imperial administration during and after the Napoleonic Wars. They took autocratic temperaments, reforming zeal, and/or a strong belief in the right of the center to police the periphery with them.[41] Parliament (and the British public) aired resulting scandals, worried about prerogative tyranny and complained about costs, but, with the exception of the Hastings impeachment trial (1788–1795), played a minor role in supervising the empire's transformation.

The shift to autocracy was effected by exercises of the king's prerogative to grant new constitutions to conquered colonies, a right confirmed by *Campbell v. Hall* in 1774. After the passing of the Quebec Act that year, the crown used its power, with few exceptions, to rule empire directly. To govern "settled" New South Wales, the crown commissioned a governor who ruled without a council while Parliament legislated to create truncated, quasi-military courts, and to give the governor appellate jurisdiction. Parliament altered and reinforced this arrangement in 1823 by giving the governor an appointed legislative council and a properly constituted court. In

colonies conquered after 1783, the crown tried to avoid settling constitutions until after the Napoleonic Wars, in some cases keeping
its absolute power to govern intact for decades. When constitutions
were settled, they established governors or governors-in-council increasingly, if partially, supervised by competently staffed courts. At
the behest of influential evangelists in Parliament, the Island of
Trinidad became the poster child of this massive shift.[42]

Some colonial courts were created by Parliament, but all judges
were creatures of the crown and some became vectors of the newly
assertive prerogative. While the king had long appointed judges and
magistrates in England, the crown's right to appoint the judiciary in
empire had to be won from colonial legislatures in late seventeenth-
century America.[43] For much of the eighteenth century, even senior
judicial appointments were still local, overseen by governors in
deference to local sensibilities. In the Age of Revolutions, at the
same time as crown and Parliament were radically increasing the
powers of governors, the crown started appointing and supervising judges from London. While some of these men were colo-
nials (Chief Justice Francis Forbes of New South Wales was born
in Bermuda, and came from a posting in Newfoundland), most
were English lawyers bringing the knowledge, and sometimes the
inflexibility, of metropolitan law and courts. Almost all went to
new colonies without considerable British or European populations, where they served explicitly to enhance crown control over
colonial legal systems.[44]

However, once in office, the king's judges took it upon themselves
to flex a very different prerogative power—the king's duty to protect.
Some found themselves at loggerheads with governors or locals over
issues as diverse as the constitutionality of legislation, civil rights,
unfree labor, freedom of the press, and, of course, due process.[45]

Indeed, by the 1820s many of the most serious debates over colonial constitutions were waged between the king's colonial executives and his judicial officers. The potential for conflict among crown officers thickened when, after 1815, the Colonial Office started sending Commissions of Inquiry and Protectors of Slaves, Aborigines, and Labourers (also crown officers) to investigate or supervise both executives and the courts.[46] With varying efficacy, the crown produced and curated its own critique.

This radical shift in imperial governance reflected more than the will to power of a coalition of reactionaries and reformers in Britain after 1783. It attempted to clarify confused lines of imperial authority that percolated through repeated crises of the colonial peace. The unraveling of crown authority in the American colonies posed the important question: What could or should be done in the name of the king? In Boston, the link between the king's prerogative and the local executive's incapacity to keep everyday order was explicit in both the panicked letters home of Governor Bernard and the desperate efforts of Boston elites to recast menacing crowds as peacekeepers. The Quebec Act, the constitution of New South Wales, and, eventually, the constitution of Trinidad all reasserted crown power to avoid such empire-wrecking uncertainty.

What could or should be done to keep the peace was a question that slave colonies had confronted long ago as colonial legislatures empowered governors, magistrates, and masters with enormous powers to control slaves. However, Tacky's Rebellion prompted Jamaicans to go much further. After 1760 Jamaica's legislature frequently invested its governor with vast powers to manage slaves *and* free people by declaring martial law at the barest stirring of trouble—powers that some felt the governor abused in his prosecution of the Maroon War in 1795. Martial law went on to become a key tool in the nineteenth-century imperial arsenal.

Fourteen years later, how best to keep the peace was debated again by governors and magistrates in Bengal. All interpreted their powers to keep order much more expansively than they might have done were they acting in the name of the British king. There, a new breed of governor used extensive powers to condone widespread police corruption and the mass incarceration of innocent subjects in defense of a special kind of peace. The unsettled nature of sovereignty in Bengal amplified debates about the moral and legal boundaries of legitimate rule—the Bengali peace may not have been the king's to keep, but the unease of judicial officers like Mr. Ernst articulated the extreme difficulty of balancing order and protection in such an unaccountable gubernatorial autocracy.

In New South Wales, the competing prerogatives to protect and to keep order were in constant negotiation in the 1820s, after a local supreme court was established, in part, to keep an eye on its governor. There a succession of judges, governors, and law officers debated the constitutionality of a militarized police force; the amenability of Indigenous Australians to English law; and how to stop their convict workforce from becoming bushrangers and highwaymen. In New South Wales, the crown constantly disagreed with itself about the constitutional limits of peacekeeping.

Everywhere, the politics of the peace raised tangled questions about the privileges of subjects and the powers of the crown. But the compromises struck in the shadow of the American Revolution mostly favored crown power to keep the peace at any cost.[47] The officers who ruled Quebec from 1759 could not even impose military law when local systems of justice collapsed after conquest. The boundary between order and disorder was so confused in prerevolutionary

Boston that a menacing crowd could claim to keep peace against the king's men. Not so after 1774. While Mr. Ernst's protests from Bengal provoked deep and lasting disquiet about the powers wielded by the governor-in-council, and legal opinions penned from the mid-1820s in New South Wales debated the boundary between acceptable adaptations of British law and raw tyranny, all invoked disorder to justify peacekeeping arrangements that would have made Edmund Burke turn in his grave.

Imperial Detritus

The British Empire has left the stage but the world made by empires endures. So, in exploring the constitutional legacies of peacekeeping around the late eighteenth- and early nineteenth-century empire, I gesture at truths that are almost clichés. Empire endures in more than the vast global inequalities that undergird the wealth of Europe and Anglophone settler polities. The license of colonial peacekeeping also helped to produce Carl Schmitt's conviction that the essence of modern sovereignty is the state of exception—the sovereign's power to exceed and suspend the rule of law.[48] Colonial legal divergence grew hand in hand with liberalism, and soon after, democracy. This is a paradox that plagues modern liberal democracies as state capacities for surveillance and control multiply.

These truisms are worth exploring because Schmitt never took the complexities of empire into account.[49] As Thomas Poole noted, the state of exception resolves into an "unfruitful binary between 'norm' and 'exception'" that fails to account for constitutive and endemic debate about the legal bounds of sovereign power.[50] In the British Empire, debates about the balance between prerogative powers to order and protect were increasingly skewed, but it behooves us to take them seriously. Such debates not only refine our understanding of how imperial and colonial states worked in the past, they shape debates about the privileges, responsibilities, and rights of states and citizens that are still with us, and still contested. The king's colonial peace did not run parallel to the making of the modern state: imperial peacekeeping shaped sovereignty and crafted new powers and practices in corners of empire that would soon become states, wedging empire securely into the DNA of the modern international order.[51] So, the king's colonial peace is not just a curiosity. The moments of rupture and failure outlined here raised deep questions that did not produce clear answers. Nevertheless, they transformed the British Empire. And we live among its ruins.

I

A Peaceable Riot in Boston

A curious incident in Boston underlines the problem with the king's peace in eighteenth-century British North America. Captain Daniel Malcom had already earned himself a reputation as a smuggler and an agitator when customs officials heard that he was hiding contraband wine in his cellar in September 1766.[1] The Sugar Act of 1764 had reduced the tax on imported sugar but imposed new duties on Iberian wine: importers had to pay ten shillings per ton of Spanish or Portuguese wine, and seven pounds per ton of fortified Madeira.[2] The rate of taxation was less problematic than the fact that the act came with an intensification of policing.[3] Taxes were fine so long as no one collected them properly.

Bostonians did not riot about the Sugar Act until June 1768, when officers on HMS *Romney* helped commissioners seize John Hancock's ship, the *Liberty*. That day, a mob attacked commissioners Benjamin Hallowell and Joseph Harrison before breaking the windows of their houses, stealing Harrison's boat, and burning it on the common.[4] In the meantime, townsfolk systematically avoided paying duties. In May 1765 Governor Francis Bernard complained that "in the dead of night ... the industry of the smuglers [*sic*]" constantly thwarted the "Vigilance" of customs officers.[5] After the trouble with the Stamp Act, resistance to import duties became bolder. The Malcom affair marked the turning of the tide.

The incident occurred on September 24, 1766, at Malcom's house on Fleet Street, so close to Scarlet's Wharf that it must have smelled of the sea.[6] Hallowell and William Sheaffe arrived with Deputy Sheriff Benjamin Cudworth in tow between 8 and 9 a.m. to seize the wine.[7] Captain Malcom complained later that he was still in his bedchamber when they knocked on the door. As they had a writ of assistance, the commissioners could demand to search Malcom's house without a warrant or probable cause. All they needed was an idle report, daylight, and a constable. So Malcom showed Hallowell, Sheaffe, and Cudworth into his house, his shed, and one of his cellars, but refused access to his second cellar. This space, he claimed, was rented to Captain William Mackay, who held the only key. When Hallowell and Sheaffe fetched Mackay, he admitted to having quiet possession of the cellar, but denied all knowledge of the key. At this point Malcom armed himself with two pistols and a sword, declaring that "he looked upon his house to be his Castle" and "if any man attempted to search his house he would blow his brains out."[8] Having pleaded with him for hours, the commissioners went to consult the governor. The governor-in-council told the officers to follow the only course open to them—to get a search warrant and to raise a *posse comitatus* (a body of able-bodied civilians) to force entry to the house.[9]

By the time the sheriff and commissioners returned to his house, Malcolm had gathered some friends indoors and fastened his gate; so ensconced, he proceeded to ignore the commissioners' attempts to deliver the warrant. More importantly for our purposes, a crowd of as many as 400 people gathered nearby.[10] John Tudor, justice of the peace, said that the crowd was pleasant and quiet, but that he understood from informants that "there would be Mischief done" if anyone forced his way into Malcom's house.[11] Sheriff Stephen Greenleaf swore that the crowd would not allow entry until the name of the informer was revealed. If he forced entry, onlookers "hoped no body would hurt him."[12] As evening approached, and the validity of the writ dwindled with the sunlight, the customs officials concluded that they would breach the house at "the hazard of our lives." They gave up and went home to avert violence.[13] Malcom then treated the crowd to wine—if the gathering was indeed 400-strong, he must have had quite a lot of contraband locked in that cellar.

Malcom and his friends told a different story about the standoff. Malcom claimed that it was only after Hallowell seemed poised to break into his cellar that he had threatened violence and called Hallowell a "dirty fellow" to boot. He claimed that he "never saw any writ of assistance nor any other power or authority whatsoever to break open my house and if I had I am sure I would be the last man in the world that would stand against it."[14] William Mackay confirmed that Malcom threatened Hallowell with two guns and a sword if he persisted in breaking into the house "without Legall or Lawfull Authority."[15] He took care to note that Malcom's pistols were unloaded. Another of Malcom's visitors, Enock Rust, swore that Malcom never even touched a gun "or any Weapon of War whatsoever." All reported that they gathered with Malcom as witnesses to an illegal break-in, not as comrades in arms.[16]

They also dismissed the number and menace of the crowd. Malcom and friends numbered the crowd at forty or fifty, half of them schoolboys. The dozen or so crowd members who gave evidence were even more coy. They attested that they gathered of their own accord with "a number of people" (John Ballard said "a small number") who behaved at all times "with decency and good order and without the least appearance of a riot."[17] Nathaniel Barber was a little more generous in his estimates. He noted that the crowd (which he said "did not exceed one hundred") was composed of "worthy gentlemen and good sort of people, there was not the least appearance of disorder, much less opposition to any legal authority."[18] In their telling, the king's men, not the public, threatened the peace. To break into Malcom's house was to break his "peace." Mackay remarked that "it appeared to be War Times."[19] Riot and quiet, war and peace, the truth was in the telling.

This odd tale has long fascinated historians. This is so because it cuts across so many trends leading to the American Revolution. It shows how public resistance to imperial taxation worked in pre-revolutionary Boston. Smuggling had long fueled the Boston economy, but since the arrival of the stamps in 1765, it had become a public virtue. The Malcom affair showed the fluid alliances that underpinned that resistance—disgruntled dockside workers, boys, and respectable men could all band together spontaneously in a show of strength in defiance of the law.[20] Though things could and sometimes did spin out of control, these flash crowds could also menace officials "without the least appearance of a riot."[21]

Malcom and his friends exemplify the punctilious legalism of American resistance. In a long paper presented to the Massachusetts Historical Society in 1924, George Wolkins followed Malcom's legal arguments about writs, warrants, and processes all the way to the desk of crown solicitor William de Grey.[22] Wolkins (and later, John Reid) thought Malcom's protests about the invasion of his home without showing writ or warrant were so carefully crafted that the infamous lawyer James Otis probably choreographed the whole affair.[23] Such was the state of things in Boston courts that Malcom could threaten to murder customs officials exercising their legal authority and expect nothing worse than to be the plaintiff in a trespass action against them.

The rabble and the commissioners all demonstrate the eighteenth-century tendency to see conspiracy everywhere. Benjamin Hallowell described Malcom's attempts to "artfully tho' wickedly" misrepresent the commissioners' conduct both to excuse his own behavior and to thwart enforcement of the Sugar Act.[24] Mackay noted the commissioners' dark intimations that Malcom might be hanged and the town placed under martial law. The town argued (and John Reid has since agreed) that the governor and the commissioners deliberately exaggerated disorders like these to excuse their own ineptitude and to bolster their demands for greater executive power.[25] As soon as townsfolk heard that the king's men were swearing depositions, they rushed to demand a copy, fearing for their liberties if Bernard gathered only the crown's side of the story.[26] Events like this underpin some of the great analyses of the pathologies of late eighteenth-century public culture—pathologies highlighted by Richard Hofstader and Gordon Wood long ago. Since the 1760s, would-be rebels had looked for conspiracy in high places, for evil intention instead of incompetence, for a world eager to take what was theirs.[27]

I tell this story again here because it so carefully charts the boundary between peace and riot. In doing so, it shows the high stakes involved in controlling narratives about the peace in the lead-up to the American Revolution.[28] Order and disorder, from my reading, preoccupied British officials more than any other topic in prerevolutionary America—with the crucial exception of Indian Country, where real war was always in the offing.[29] By playing in the margins between riot, rebellion, and peace, incidents like these exposed the weakness of crown authority in the eighteenth-century

British Empire—and galvanized imperial reform. Malcom's menacing crowd magnified ambiguities surrounding the Riot Act and the king's prerogative to call for military intervention to keep the civil peace. It also underlined the untenable limits of crown power in Massachusetts both as a matter of colonial custom and under the terms of the 1691 Charter. More interesting still, Malcom and the crowd made theater of their subjecthood. The crowd did not reject its obligations to help sheriffs to keep the king's peace; instead it cast itself as a witness and guardian of the peace against the king's men. In the process the incident exemplified an emerging contest in Boston about who could keep the peace, a contest that raised early and prescient concerns about revolution.

I use the language of sport and play here, and for some, destroying a house, burning a boat on the common, or quietly threatening the commissioners assuredly constituted a fine night out. But for many Bostonians, such gatherings were a serious business with high stakes. Public action performed constitutional arguments that flirted perilously with treason. Even though they might have abhorred new taxes and distrusted colonial representatives of the crown, many still shared the governor's concerns about the ungovernability of thuggish crowds and radical leaders among them.[30] In this context, the mad scramble to report different versions of this and other conflicts to imperial officials and the British public underlined an expectation shared by "Town and Crown" that, no matter how constitutionally constrained, the king might act to defend his peace, with or without the aid of Parliament.[31] Efforts to recast the crowd's menace into solemn watchfulness guarded, in the end, against the return of the king. The king never again managed to keep his peace in Boston, but he certainly did so elsewhere after 1783. Incidents like these changed the constitution of empire.

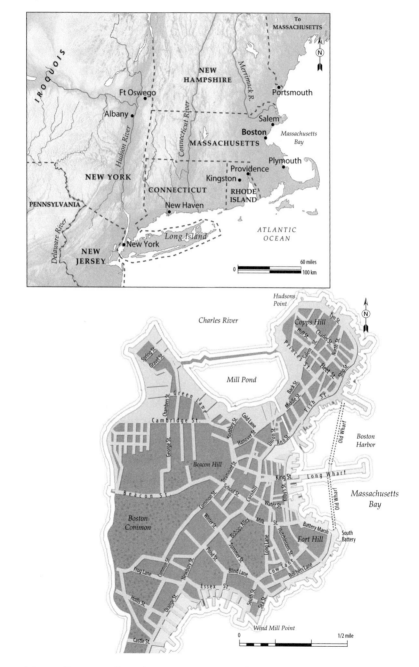

Map 1.1 Boston and northeastern American colonies, c. 1768. © Lisa Ford

Acts of Riot

Malcom and his supporters thwarted the execution of the commissioners' writ, first and foremost, by threatening violence. Whether the crowd numbered forty or 400, and whether it was chiefly composed of schoolboys or men, more people gathered outside Captain Malcom's house than could possibly be needed to bear witness to a trespass.[32] Their purpose was to intimidate.

Though both Nathaniel Barber and Captain William Wimble denied parts of the story later, customs officers and magistrates all alleged that both men went out of their way to make sure that they anticipated violence. Sheriff Greenleaf said that when he and the commissioners went to fetch a warrant and a magistrate, William Wimble followed them to warn "out of friendship" that the crowd "had formed their plan" and that any attempt to force Malcom's door "would probably cost us our lives."[33] Wimble said the crowd planned to ring the North Bell—a signal to call the town to riot. Justice of the Peace John Tudor heard about the bell from both Wimble and Barber, and noted that Wimble also warned that "a great Number of People gathered together in and about Capt. Malcoms [sic] house . . . to prevent any officers entering."[34] William Sheaffe attested not only that Malcom had threatened to "blow their brains out," but that "diverse credible People" before and after the event had assured him of the danger posed by the crowd.[35] In the end, said Greenleaf, the officers withdrew in order to "preserve the Peace."[36]

Quiet menace worked because it invoked real violence perpetrated by Boston mobs spanning the destruction of regulated markets in 1737, the impressment riots of 1747, and the Stamp Act riots just over a year before.[37] The latter were reported to be the largest public disturbances in the town's history. Stamp riots had not been limited

31

to unruly Boston: from August 1765 to May 1766, "at least sixty riots" rocked the American colonies, from Rhode Island to Nevis.[38] In Boston, several properties had been sacked on August 14 and 26, 1765. According to Bernard, Lieutenant Governor and Chief Justice Thomas Hutchinson was lucky to escape his mansion with his life.[39] Benjamin Hallowell's house was also among the properties attacked by stamp rioters—as Malcom reminded Hallowell in 1766. In Hallowell's telling, Malcom warned that he would be "served as he was before by the mob."[40] Malcom would know: some suspected that he himself had led the mob in 1765.[41]

Quiet menace also worked because the king's representatives in the colony could do very little about it. Quelling a riot was a fraught business in the 1760s on both sides of the Atlantic. The extent of prerogative power to keep the peace had been deeply uncertain for a century. Since medieval times, when the king's peace spread past his highways and his palaces to the countryside, the crown had held a vague bundle of rights to suppress disorder. Gradually magistrates and judges in England were appointed by the crown to keep the king's peace. The English public also accrued a right and duty at common law to keep the king's peace when summoned by a sheriff to do so: *posse comitatus* meant "the power of the country."[42] Because the right and duty to aid the sheriff belonged to every subject, civilian and military, from the ages of fifteen to sixty, the sheriff could also summon the military to maintain civil order.[43] Outright rebellion was another clear trigger activating the king's power to use violence in defense of the realm. The Tudors, early Stuarts, and Parliament had used those latent powers liberally since the sixteenth century. Elizabeth's infamous Provost Martials used martial law to summarily try and execute rioters and vagabonds in Britain, and, even more brutally, in Ireland.[44] By the time Parlia-

Fig 1.1 *The Bostonian's paying the excise-man, or tarring & feathering,*
print, London 1774. Five men force a tarred and feathered customs
officer to drink from a teapot; a bucket and a liberty cap lie on at
his feet. They stand beneath the "Liberty Tree," from which hangs
a rope with a noose, while in the background shadowy figures on a
ship dump tea overboard. Library of Congress, Prints and Photographs Division, LC-USZC4-14078

ment wearily invited the Stuarts back to England in 1660, crown and Parliament "had left both the . . . political élite and much of the public with a profound distaste for armies and a sharp nose for any whiff of military involvement in civil government."[45]

No sooner had William and Mary acceded to the throne after the Glorious Revolution than they were forced into a series of compromises that confined but also confirmed the king's prerogative to keep the peace. Thereafter, England's standing army was made explicitly "the servant of Parliament."[46] Yet Parliament acted quickly to hand back significant powers to quell local rebellions. It suspended the Habeas Corpus Act repeatedly after 1689, allowing the summary detention of suspected troublemakers.[47] Most importantly, after the unpopular Hanover succession, Parliament once again sought to clarify the king's power to control ubiquitous civil unrest by passing the Riot Act of 1714.[48] However, the Riot Act hampered as much as it helped the king's men to keep the peace in Britain. Its first use in 1716 was accompanied by shrill warnings of the danger of military tyranny.[49] In theory, it gave new powers to the king's magistrates to quell riots in response to "rebellious riots and tumults . . . in divers parts of this kingdom, to the disturbance of the publick peace."[50] When groups of twelve or more gathered "to the disturbance of the publick peace," the act allowed justices, sheriffs, mayors, and bailiffs to order them to disperse "in the King's name." The crowd had one hour to comply before its members were deemed to have committed the felony of riot and the magistrate could call for aid—an hour's grace to pillage.[51] After this point public officers could use all necessary force to disperse the crowd, and participants would be liable for damages, lose all their property, and be put to death.

Moreover, the act did not even mention military assistance. Instead it required any justice of the peace, sheriff or under-sheriff, mayor, bailiff, and "such other person and persons as shall be commanded" by them to assist, to "seize and apprehend . . . such persons so unlawfully, riotously and tumultuously continuing together" an hour after the Riot Act had been read.[52] Whatever the position had been at common law, it was understood that, after 1714, the military was not to intervene in any capacity without the explicit request of a magistrate.[53] As the American colonies descended into chaos after 1765, this assumption was made explicit in official instructions to commanders of the American forces.[54]

Under the terms of the act, then, there was nothing simple about the legalities of riot. In a succession of riots in eighteenth-century England, nervous magistrates refused to read the Riot Act at all.[55] Most famously, from the second to the seventh of June 1780, magistrates let anti-Catholic rioters roam the streets of London without reading the Riot Act or calling for military assistance. Their hesitation caused the ministry to focus anew on the latent powers of the king.[56] On June 7, 1780, the Privy Council called in the troops to restore the peace without the act or the magistrates. They did so on the basis of the king's prerogative, "to employ Military Force, with which We are by Law entrusted for the immediate Suppression of such Rebellious and Traiterous Attempts, now making against the Peace and Dignity of Our Crown."[57] This was a statement of prerogative power for the times.

It came too late for the American colonies, where magistrates and the governor had been even more constrained by politics and law before the Revolution. For a start, the very idea of a Riot Act had been fraught in the colonies. The first colonial Riot Act was passed in Connecticut in 1722 after a series of violent land title disputes. Massachusetts did not pass a Riot Act until 1751. All such colonial acts, except Connecticut's, were temporary. At its longest stretch, the

Massachusetts act ran for seven years.[58] When Lieutenant Governor Hutchinson urged the act's renewal in 1770, the assembly retorted that "the laws now in being, duly executed, would be fully sufficient; and, to add to the severity of the provision made by them, without an apparent and very urgent necessity, might put into the hands of the civil magistrate, a power that would be dangerous to the rights and liberties of the people." The assembly went on to assert that the powers of the magistracy were extensive enough to do the bidding of the king, and that "restraining the liberty of any individual, is a crime, which infinitely exceeds what the law intends by a riot."[59] Eventually it renewed the act, nevertheless.[60]

Perhaps the assembly renewed the act in the knowledge that no magistrate would have the temerity to use it. Being a magistrate in Massachusetts was a difficult job in the lead-up to the Revolution. Bernard's letters home noted the important role played by magistrates in the Stamp Act riots. When Bostonians assembled for a second night on August 15, Bernard lauded magistrates who "harangued" the crowd into quiescence without recourse to the act.[61] He had quite a different view of the magistracy after August 26, when the houses of customs officials and the chief justice were attacked. No one read the riot act that day either. This time, the officers charged with keeping the peace stood idly by. "The Fact was this: Between 30 or 40 of the lowest of the people worked at the demolishing of the Lieut. Governor's house for 4 or 5 hours together. At that time the Magistrates and civil officers were 3 to one, the Military Corps 30 to one, the fighting men of the town 100 to one of the Mob. And yet the whole Town acquiesced in the procedure."[62] They acquiesced for many reasons. Complicity with the mob was one. "It is said," Bernard noted on August 16, "that there were 50 gentlemen" disguised among the crowds that swamped the streets.[63] Describing the state of Boston just a week after a group of frightened British troops opened fire on a menacing crowd in 1770, Thomas Hutchinson wrote that he knew "of no Civil Magistrate who would have employed the Troops in suppressing" a riot in the Town.[64]

However, not every magistrate became a patriot. Fear of life and limb, exclusion, or prosecution restrained other men from acting. North America was full of litigators, as the commander in chief, General Thomas Gage, complained in 1765.[65] If magistrates in England were worried about falling afoul of the terms of the Riot Act, then a Boston magistrate needed to be doubly so, lest he find himself dragged before a court for abuse of office.[66] Fear of ostracism, violence, or both were even more compelling reasons to keep one's head down. Gage noted repeatedly that magistrates in Massachusetts and New York feared popular backlash if they did their duty.[67] On the eve of the first Stamp Act riot, the sheriffs of Boston reported that they could not remove an effigy of the stamp commissioner, Andrew Oliver, hanging from the Liberty Tree, "without eminent [sic] danger of their lives." Within two weeks, one very sensible sheriff and his deputies had submitted resignations to the governor.[68] By December 1765, Bernard reported systemic harassment of all officers of the crown. By 1768, after the Liberty Riot, when they had retreated to Castle William for safety, the commissioners of customs complained that "the Disorders of the Town . . . are increasing to such an enormous Pitch as to give it the Appearance more of an Insurrection than a Riot."[69] Both thought the "Magistracy have not the least authority or power in this Place that the Mob are ready to be assembled on any Occasion and that every Officer who exerts himself in the Execution of his Duty will be exposed to the Resentment of the Populace, without the least probability of receiving any Protection."[70]

Nor could the governor do much about the peace, though he was the king's representative and chief magistrate in the colony. The deep political and legislative injunctions against invoking prerogative powers to keep peace after 1688 paled in comparison to the formal limits imposed by the Massachusetts charter on the king's prerogative. Unlike a "meer royal" colony, Bernard complained in 1763, the governor of Massachusetts is "obliged to have the Concurrence of the Council in many acts, which the meer royal Governors can do alone." Worse still, in "an unfortunate error in the forming of the Government," the charter gave "the Representatives of the People" power to elect the council, subject to the governor's veto. The inevitable result was that the Council "is much too popular for them to be, as they ought to be, mediators between the Crown & people." Bernard proposed instead that Massachusetts be given a new charter in which the Council was modeled on the "house of Lords. The Dignity should be derived from the King, as the fountain of honour, & granted for life defeasible by notorious misdemeanour . . . These Councellors would naturally support the rights of the Crown, & being independent of it, would not incur the jealousy of the people. It would induce people of consequence to look up to the King for honour & Authority, instead of endeavouring to raise themselves by popular Altercations."[71] Such squabbles, he assured the Board of Trade in 1763, were not a sign of rebellion: "I know of no Colony where the compact between the King & the People is better observed. The Royal Rights are never openly invaded: the utmost that is done, is to dispute what are royal rights."[72] How differently he felt two years later!

In August 1765 the majority of the council were unwilling to support Bernard's call to raise the military or militia to protect Oliver, his house, and his family from the Stamp Act mob. The Council "lamented the impotence of the Government & said that it would be to no purpose to attempt to raise a military force; as the Militia, the only force we had, would never act against the rioters, if they would assemble at all." They would only advise the governor to issue a proclamation enjoining the town and the magistrates to "use all the Means in their power to preserve the peace of the Town."[73] If it was unhelpful in 1765, the council became much more determinedly so from early 1766. A more radical legislature used its charter powers to expel key officeholders from the council. Lieutenant Governor and Chief Justice Thomas Hutchinson and other executive officers could no longer vote, or even attend council meetings.[74] This move preoccupied government commentators in London after the fact. It became grounds for a call for urgent reform of the colony's charter.[75]

Governor Bernard blew hot and cold on the conduct of the council thereafter. On March 12, 1768, he praised councillors for their "public spirited Conduct . . . [and] great attention to the Support of the Government" notwithstanding their "constitutional imbecility."[76] Within a week they were in open conflict. A string of incidents in the lead-up to the second anniversary of the Stamp Act Repeal— including the gathering of "a large Number of Men with Clubs" outside Commissioner William Burch's house for the "great Part of the Evening," the discharging of guns, the hoisting of flags, and the hanging of commissioners in effigy—convinced Bernard that the town was again on the verge of chaos.[77] He represented the "Necessity of providing for the Defence of the Town" before the anniversary.[78] The council dismissed his concerns. These events, they assured him, were of no consequence. So Bernard spent the anniversary in his house with Commissioner Burch and family, Lieutenant Governor Hutchinson, and the sheriff of the county hiding from "the assembling a great Number of People of all Kinds Sexes and Ages, many of which shewed a great Disposition to the utmost Disorder . . . many hundred of them paraded the Streets with Yells and Outcries which were quite terrible." He could not call for troops because he did not "think it proper or prudent to make such Application upon my own Opinion only. All the Kings Governors are directed to take the Advice of Council in Military Movements" and his council was either too complicit or too afraid to move against the will of the town.[79] After the Liberty Riots, he reported to General Gage that it was "vain" to ask the council to advise him to call troops because "they did not desire to be knocked on the head." Bernard related rumors that the Sons of Liberty had threatened "that if any Person was known to apply for Troops to come here, he would certainly be put to Death."[80]

Others worried about this, too. In 1766 Gage reported, "There seems throughout the Provinces to be a Dissolution of all legal Authority, that Subordination is entirely destroyed, and that all coercive Powers in Government are annihilated."[81] Commissioner Henry Hulton's wife Ann summed up the state of mind of crown officers and their families admirably in June 1768. In a letter to Elizabeth Lightbody, she explained that "mobs here are very different from those in O[ld] England, where a few lights put into the Windows will pacify." Friends of government in Boston held themselves "in readiness" to flee the mobs at "an hours notice. . . . Government is extirpated, and it is quite a State of Anarchy."[82] According to crown delegates and their families, the king had no power to keep the peace in North America.

Boston's selectmen argued implicitly in the Malcom depositions, then explicitly in a string of newspaper articles and pamphlets published after 1766, that the governor, the commissioners and their families exaggerated disorder for nefarious ends. They have some supporters among historians: John Phillip Reid goes so far as to argue that even the Liberty Riot was, in fact, no riot at all.[83] Exaggeration is not the point here, however. The menace of Malcom's crowd did not turn on whether or not it intended violence. The scale of violence perpetrated by mobs since 1747 is not particularly important either. What matters to the history of empire is the powerlessness of the crown as a matter of law and practice to keep the peace in Massachusetts. The menace of the quiet crowd outside Malcom's house in September 1766 was a strategy that made theater of government weakness. It was just one performance of many. "Going in Bodies"[84] to intimidate government officers was *de rigueur* after 1768 whether evidenced by escorting new commissioners from their ships to their quarters;[85] standing armed and *en masse* outside a commissioner's house as he ate his dinner;[86] trampling a cherry orchard; or pointedly laying out the town's guns to be "cleaned."[87] The threat was real for the sheriff, constable, commissioners, and single JP who gathered to enforce the Sugar Act at Malcom's in 1766 because the king's power to keep the peace was so weak. It was not clear who would or could protect the commissioners, their family, or their property if they broke into Malcom's house to enforce imperial law. Law and practice combined to ensure that a peaceful gathering was as good as a riot.

The People's Peace

The powerlessness of the governor and his officers to restore order was only part of the crisis of the peace in late colonial Massachusetts. Something else was amiss in the peacefulness of Malcom's crowd. By threatening violence *in defense of the peace,* the crowd played with subjecthood itself. This gambit started with Malcom. He claimed to be a law-abiding subject, promising to kill "the first man that Offered to break Lock or Door" only if they did so "without Legall or Lawfull Authority (and he to be satisfied of that Authority)."[88] The question of authority was fraught, because the commissioners claimed to act under a writ of assistance. This was a controversial instrument, only recently reissued by the chief justice of Massachusetts. In the eighteenth century, all writs lapsed on the death of the king. So, when news of George II's death arrived at the end of 1760, the commissioners had to petition the superior court to have the writ renewed. James Otis, a radical and somewhat unhinged lawyer, gave up his post as advocate-general in the Vice Admiralty court to contest the petition. Malcom was among the men who briefed him to do so. As he was wont to do, Otis argued angrily and at length that such writs were unconstitutional.[89] On advice from home, six months later, Hutchinson and his brother judges renewed the writ.[90] The Massachusetts court was one of very few to do so in late colonial America. So the commissioners' writ bore accusations of lawlessness and the taint of tyranny.[91]

Back at Malcom's in September 1766, the validity of the writ was much less important than his claims about breaches of procedure. Malcom claimed that Hallowell had not presented him with the writ, and he had locked his house too securely for anyone to hand him a warrant. He could therefore claim before a sympathetic jury that even if the commissioners had legal authority to break into his house, they had not followed formalities. In any case, Malcom could rest assured that no grand jury in Massachusetts would indict him for refusing entry to his cellar. Instead, if a grand jury accepted evidence that Hallowell had produced neither writ nor warrant, he could be sued for trespass by Malcom.[92] In a town that had already trashed his house and refused to pay compensation, Hallowell was unlikely to win a war of words in court. The king's court in thrall to a hostile jury would not protect a customs officer in the execution of his duty. Valid or invalid, what could a writ do in such a place?

All of this legal ambiguity mattered because it cast a different light on the purpose of Malcom's audience. The friends who gathered inside Malcom's house professed to be there explicitly to "bear Witness" to the commissioners' violent entry, to support Malcom's determination to "prosecute them at the Civil Law."[93] While most of the crowd outside swore that they gathered out of idle curiosity, some also claimed to be there to bear witness. Caleb Hopkins tarried with others to see "such a thing as the breaking open a mans house which thing was not common in this Country." William Nickells "advised the sheriff not to enter Captain Malcom's house forceably . . . it was his own opinion . . . that said sheriff had no lawful authority to do so."[94] John Ballard joined "a small number of people . . . to see what was done."[95]

Whatever the crowd's account of itself, Sheriff Greenleaf claimed that it was determined to keep crown officers in check. Though John Tudor JP was much more reserved in his own deposition, Greenleaf reported that Tudor had warned "that the people were determined to withstand them in every attempt to force captain Malcoms house." The crowd assured Greenleaf "that no admission into Capt. Malcoms House would be suffered, except the Custom house Officers would go before a Justice and make Oath who their Informer was."[96] This claim was corroborated by Benjamin Goodwin, who deposed that Captain Cluston offered to join a posse to break the house open if the sheriff would "bring the informer and let him come and assist too, for that was the way in the old Countrys."[97] Greenleaf refused and asked the crowd again for help. One voice among them agreed to help, he said, but "by the manner of the pronunciation & tone of voice he took it to be Ironical & either by way of Ridicule or threatening."[98] Paul Rivere thought he heard Benjamin Goodwin say he "would assist him out of doors, but would not go into Capt. Malcom's house."[99] Nathaniel Barber claimed credit for the same statement. Both omitted any mention of irony.[100]

Two things are interesting here. First, like Malcom, the deponents claimed to meet the obligations of subjecthood. They did not deny their duty to support the king's peace by forming a posse comitatus or acceding to a writ. However, they finessed their obligations, all the while delivering menace in the guise of peace. The conditional character of their support—the suggestion that the crowd might support the crown if the crown acted lawfully, but would intervene to prevent tyranny—is key. Moments like these came to define the imminence of rebellion for Governor Bernard. As he had put it earlier in the year, the challenge here was not violence, but the public's resolve "to assist & support civil Magistrates & Officers" on their own terms *"according to the Laws & usage of this Land."*[101] Behind this suggestion lay two troubling propositions. The first was that the king's officers (and therefore the king) had no authority. The second is that peacekeeping was the obligation and prerogative of the crowd and not the king.

In short, from 1765, Bernard saw self-regulation as an attack on the dignity of the crown. He read every threat to executive officers as an attack on the king himself. When Andrew Oliver was summoned by a mob to the Liberty Tree in December, Bernard said the event "was designed as an Insult upon the Kings Authority; as a Terror to the Kings Officers . . . to show them that they were nothing in the Eyes or the Hands of the People."[102] His anxieties about the king's authority were acute in the lead-up to the repeal of the Stamp

Act, when the "despotism of the people" intimidated justices into opening lower courts without stamped paper.[103] Though the town was "quiet" in January 1766, Bernard warned that "the Government is continually given to understand that the power is the Hands of the People."[104] In such circumstances, Bernard reasoned, "the King of Massachusets [sic] Bay," as represented by the governor and judges, "must be opposed to the King of Great Britain; & his own Authority, as his Cannon may be when they are taken, is to be turned against himself."[105] By January 25 Bernard confessed to Henry Seymour Conway, "I can't help wishing they may be relieved [sic] entirely from the Act, if the Honor of the imperial Crown can by Any means be preserved."[106] At the end of 1766 Bernard reported, "I have as little prospect as ever of the [Government's] being restored to Authority & peace . . . I say the Government: for tho' [a] great part of the Attack appears to be directed against the Governor, yet it is manifestly intended against his Office & not his person."[107] His next letter claimed that resistance to all tax since 1765 "has been made a Mask for a Battery, a stalking horse, to take a better aim at the Royalty of the Government."[108] Local disorder attacked the office of the king.

Bernard was not alone. In his "Hints respecting the Civil Establishment in the American Colonies," William Knox warned of the damage done to the prerogative every time a governor conceded some of the king's functions to "gratify the People."[109] In similar vein, Edmund Burke warned in November 1768 against claiming powers that the king had no hope of exercising: "We tell the world, that his Majesty is willing to support the dignity of his Crown, and in order to show how unable he is to do that, the colonies of America are said to be going to throw off their subjection."[110]

For Bernard, the radical import of public peacekeeping was made explicit in another standoff on July 9, 1768. This incident began within a month of the Liberty Riot, while the commissioners were still holed up in Castle William for protection from the town. A schooner was seized on July 8 with "thirty hogsheads of [uncustomed] molasses." The colonial executive understood that the Liberty Riot had been caused in part by the fact that the royal navy had assisted in the seizure of Hancock's boat, raising the specter of military interference in civil government. To allay such fears, on July 9 two customhouse officers resolved to guard this new seizure themselves. It ended badly. "About thirty men" boarded the ship on the evening of the eighth and unloaded the molasses.[111] Bernard wondered what the officers expected to happen. Rescuing cargo was nothing new. According to Bernard, "every Seizure made or attempted to be made at Boston for 3 Years past . . . has been violently rescued or prevented."[112]

However, the town's response to this latest misfortune made Bernard especially nervous. "My Lord" said he, "I find myself obliged to add a Supplement to my Letter No. 10. . . . I had there informed your Lordship that 30 Hogsheads of Molasses . . . had been taken from . . . the Custody of the Custom House Officers. . . . [It] was on the next day returned & put on board the Schooner again." This return was brokered by the selectmen of the town. They "sent for the Master of the Schooner, & upon his denying that he knew anything of the Molasses, told him that would not pass; for nobody would take away his Molasses without his Privity, they thereupon ordered him to return the Molasses directly under pain of the Displeasure of the Town, which was immediately done." The problem here was not the return of the goods, *per se.* It was the fact that only the selectmen could manage it: "Neither the Custom House Officers, nor the Judge of the Admiralty, nor the Chief Justice, nor the Governor could have prevailed upon any One to run the Risk of informing where this Molasses was conveyed or to assist in recovering it, if it had been against the Humor of the People."[113]

When Bernard's letters home were published in Boston in 1769, the town was shocked at his "ill-natured Construction" of these events. "A good Magistrate," they claimed, "would have rejoiced in this Instance of the People's voluntary . . . Aid in the Recovery of the King's Due." Instead "Gov. Bernard is disturb'd that 'the Humor of the People . . .' should ever coincide with their Duty to their Sovereign—The voluntary Association of the People to promote Peace and good Order, he had before said, 'carried an Implication of Danger' to the Government."[114] Even an act of order in defense of the peace seemed disorderly to the governor of Massachusetts—why?

The public peace here was no Bakhtinian moment—no safe and temporary inversion of authority that hid within it a deep acknowledgment of hierarchy and deference. Instead it signaled the end of empire. In the details of the peace lay the question of the king's authority to govern. Bostonians might drink at the King's Arms, buy crockery bearing his image, and spend enormous amounts of money making themselves seem more English than ever before, but this did not mean they considered themselves bound to the king's peace.[115] King-worship and Anglophilia is not what Francis Bernard saw in 1765, 1766, or 1768. And what he saw mattered. In pantomimes of public peace, he saw a menace to empire, to the king's sovereignty. We must take him seriously, as recovering that logic is key to understanding the ramifications of the American Revolution for the legal history of the empire. The threat of colonial violence was palpable, but peace itself was just as troubling. The only thing worse than a riot in a town where "the authority of Government and the magistracy . . . have been continually insulted and made contemptible for near three years past" was the suggestion that the power to keep the peace did not derive from the sovereign, that the peace was not the king's to keep.[116]

The Return of the King

What is most fascinating about the Malcom affair—and indeed many major upheavals on the eve of the Revolution in Boston—is the web of lies and misrepresentations spun by everyone concerned about the keeping or breaking of the peace. Every single deponent on behalf of the town stressed the peacefulness of the crowd at Malcom's. At least until the schoolboys arrived, said Benjamin Goodwin, the crowd was better behaved than any "people that was going to a Funeral," there was no more "noise nor disturbance . . . than if Mr. Whitfield had been preaching."[117] Even Justice Tudor—the only JP to agree to support the commissioners—assured the governor that "all of them whilst I stayed with them behaved very quietly and some of them pleasantly said they came to see how Affairs was like to go . . . I left them to all appearance in good humour and quiet." Only Caleb Hopkins broke ranks, describing "a good deal of laughter and merriment."[118]

The men who warned the commissioners of impending violence backtracked furiously in their oaths after the fact. Barber and Wimble had both allegedly assured the commissioners that the crowd had resolved to prevent officers from breaking into the house and would call the rest of the town to its aid by ringing the fire bell. In his testimony after the event, Barber swore that Tudor must have misheard his warnings. He denied saying that a mob would be summoned to riot by the bell. Wimble testified that "when he told the Sheriff as set forth in his deposition before the governor and council, that the Bell would ring, and then the streets would be filled, he meant and now explains it, that it was the opinion of the people that the informer had concealed himself in the old north meeting house and that he would ring the bell in order to make his escape."[119]

This self-exculpatory testimony was gathered by the town meeting *after* it read depositions recorded by the governor's council. It was compiled explicitly to negate perceptions of the breakdown of law and order.[120] By turning Malcom into a defender of the peace and transforming a large crowd threatening violence into a small crowd seeking only to bear witness, the town disclaimed its growing reputation for defying not only Parliament, but the king's prerogative. They claimed that the king's men sought to use false allegations about disorder to endanger Boston's charter, or, worse still, put the town under martial law.

Another war of words over the peace three years later exposed the stakes more starkly. When, in 1769, some sympathetic soul in London forwarded copies of Bernard's 1768 letters home about riots and disorder in Massachusetts, the town published a whole book about its peacefulness.[121] It denounced Bernard's "artful[ness]" in connecting "an Opposition to the Commissioners with a Defiance of the Authority by which they are appointed."[122] Far from defying "the King's Authority," the town awaited his redress.[123] By reporting rumor and menace as precursors to violence, Bernard stitched fiction into fact.[124] In this tome, every huzzah outside a household is a crowd of boys playing. Fears for the peace are laughable.[125] Every frightened officer's wife is a politician and her husband a peddler of "pretended Fears."[126] Every mob is a small and peaceable gathering; every violent town resolution an exception.[127] Reports to the contrary were lies crafted to undermine colonial liberty. In the town's telling, effigies of commissioners were hung from the Liberty Tree by designing men to give credence to Bernard's allegations.[128]

The most famous war of words, however, followed the "Boston Massacre." When a crowd of boys or men surrounded a sentry on King Street in Boston on March 5, 1770, and the soldiers who came to his aid opened fire, words outstripped deeds so thoroughly that no one knows what actually happened. Everyone knew the importance of words by then—not least because Samuel Adams had been providing continuous commentary on the evils of military occupation to sympathetic audiences throughout the eastern seaboard since 1768.[129] The power of words was so well understood that Commissioner John Robinson secreted himself on a warship to take military depositions of the affair back to London before the town could have its say. His version of affairs was soon published as *A Fair Account of the Late Disturbances at Boston.* The town was trying to do the same, but JPs became too bogged down in recording the details to beat Robinson to London. James Bowdoin would later complain that the *Fair Account* "defeated every thing we aimed at by the Narrative and Depositions sent home."[130]

The ink spilled and the oaths taken to recast every act of defiance and violence into peace or rebellion, were extraordinary. And they do much more than simply expose the "paranoid style" of revolutionary political discourse. Disputes about "what actually happened" reaffirm the centrality of the king and his peace in prerevolutionary discourse. At their most basic level, accounts of the Malcom affair—the *Appeal to the World* and *A Short Narrative of the Horrid Massacre in Boston*—both claimed that the king's subjects in Boston were peaceable. The town was not out of control. In the end, the town of Boston fought its war of words against the return of the king. They did this because there was magic in the words "riot"

Fig 1.2 *The Massacre perpetrated in King Street Boston on March 5th 1770*, frontispiece, *A Short Narrative of the Horrid Massacre in Boston . . . ,* London 1770. Library of Congress, Prints and Photographs Division, LC-USZ62-45554

and "rebellion." They threatened revocation of the Massachusetts charter, a renewal of James II's efforts to impose "garrison government."[131] With or without the revocation of the charter, talk of "riot" and "rebellion" threatened deployment of emergency prerogative powers—deployment that was highly fraught in the 1760s, but would soon became the mainstay of peacekeeping in Britain and its colonies.

Fears of martial law lurked behind early local responses to the governor's requests for exceptional powers to bring order to the town. As early as August 1765 Bernard called on the Massachusetts legislature to enhance crown power to restore order. They responded, "You cannot mean, by calling the whole legislative in aid of the executive authority, that any new and extraordinary kind of power should by law be constituted, to oppose such acts of violence as your Excellency may apprehend from a people ever remarkable for their loyalty and good order." Rather, the executive government had all the power it needed and "your Excellency we are very sure need not be told, to whose department it solely belongs to appoint a suitable number of magistrates to put those laws in execution, or remove them in case of failure of their duty herein." In any case emergency power was unnecessary because there was no crisis. "We are not in particular so alarmed, as your Excellency seems to be, with the apprehension of the hand of violence being let loose. . . . There will be no danger of force of arms becoming the only governing power. Nor shall we realize what your Excellency is pleased to call a state of general outlawry."[132]

Recasting disorder as order here baldly aimed to block the power of the crown to keep the peace. If Bernard was asking this of the local legislature, what was he asking of the government at home? By 1769 the people of Massachusetts knew exactly what Bernard was asking, because his letters had been leaked back to Boston. By casting the people of Boston as "rebels" in his letters to the ministry in London, Bernard sought to "introduce a military power into this Town [a goal he achieved in 1768]—A Power which is daily trampling on our Laws, contemning our Religion, and invading the Rights both of Persons and Property."[133]

The people of Massachusetts were also right to worry about their charter. By 1766, disorder in Boston had the attention of the Parliament, the ministry, and the king and they tended toward Bernard's view of things rather than the town's. In an undated letter, "Mr. Morgan" advised the Earl of Shelburne, then Secretary of State for the Southern Department, that lawless Massachusetts "has doubtless forfeited its Charter" because obedience to law "is the necessarily implied Condition of the American Charters."[134] William Knox noted the damage done to the king's prerogative by "permitting those who settle under Charter or proprietary Governments to enjoy greater Privileges than those who settle under the Crown." The charters should be abolished, royal governments established everywhere, and "Officers of the Crown" paid from home as they "are the natural and constitutional supporters of the Prerogative."[135] Such ideas had been mooted before. A "short discourse on the present state of the Colonies in America" penned by Sir William Keith in 1740 argued that American legislatures had power only to pass "bylaws for themselves" in "no ways interfering with the legal prerogative of the crown or the true legislative power of the Mother States." It proposed reducing all councils to advisory bodies, as well as abolishing militia and keeping a standing army in every province.[136]

By 1773, Solicitor General Alexander Wedderburn was assembling a brief to justify the reconstitution of Massachusetts in defense of the peace. The king's residual prerogative power to keep the peace loomed large in this constitutional gambit. Wedderburn's archive includes carefully transcribed extracts from proclamations of kings and queens since William III, overturning colonial charters to restore order. Wedderburn was sensible enough to omit James II's dissolution of the New England charters in 1686. But he abstracted William III's winning formula in 1691 asserting his right to appoint a governor to Maryland.[137] The province, William asserted, had "fallen into disorder and confusion, by means whereof not only the publick Peace and Administration of Justice . . . is broken and violated, but also there is an utter want of Provision for the Guard and Defence of the said country against our Enemies." George I used the same words to resume government in South Carolina in 1720 (adding his concerns about the "incursions of the barbarous Indians"). Edward Northey and Simon Harcourt advised Queen Anne that she could take control of any proprietary colony in the case of "an Extraordinary Exigency, happening through the Default or Neglect of a Proprietor . . . or their Inability to protect or Defend the Province under their Government." In this case, Massachusetts, New Hampshire, and New York had complained about "disorders" and "want of good government" in Rhode Island and Connecticut. Her power stemmed, Northey and Harcourt maintained, from the "Right to Govern all your Subjects."[138]

An early draft of the necessary alterations to the Massachusetts charter reproduced in Wedderburn's archive makes it clear that the key purpose of reform would be to augment the power of the king to keep the peace.[139] "It is necessary," the document proclaimed, "for restoring order and Government, procuring a due Execution of the Law, and preserving the Peace in his Majesty's Colony of Massachuset [sic] Bay" that the governor be given extensive and independent powers to appoint judges, officers, and magistrates who would hold their offices at "the Pleasure of his Majesty." The governor, lieutenant governor, and judges, in this rendering, should "be Justices of the Peace in and for every county therein—and shall and may execute all the Powers and authoritys given to the Justices of the Peace." The governor and his lieutenant would have additional, extraordinary power to "issue Orders or Proclamations for the apprehending and bringing to Justice offenders, for the suppression of Riots and Tumults, and for the Preservation of the Peace." Indeed, whichever powers the governor could dispense "together with the Council" under the 1691 charter could henceforth be exercised without "their advice." Even town meetings (leaving aside annual elections) could not be held without the governor's consent, and the governor could control the topics to be debated there.[140] Every one of these measures aimed at making the king's representative an effective peacekeeper. In his annotations on the document, Wedderburn was concerned that this draft might even give the governor power to declare martial law out of council—a radical notion indeed in the eighteenth century.[141]

In the end, however, the crown deferred to Parliament to restore the peace in Massachusetts through the Massachusetts Government Act passed in May 1774. *Campbell v. Hall* was still before courts as the bill was drafted, but its principles were already widely accepted. By autumn the Court of King's Bench would declare that only Parliament could alter an existing colonial constitution. While that principle was supposed to limit the tyranny of the crown, the Massachusetts Government Act made nobody happy in 1774. The terms of the act differed markedly from the draft in Wedderburn's archive; indeed, the king's peace hardly rated a mention at all. Instead the act solved the problem of order by removing all formal impediments to the exercise of prerogative power in Massachusetts. The act reserved for the crown power to appoint and dismiss councillors, judges, magistrates, and juries. A compliant counsel, impartial judges, and responsible juries, it seems, were all that was deemed necessary for the king's representative to keep the colonial peace.[142]

The king's peace was everywhere in prerevolutionary Boston. Its keepers and its rituals of deference formed the core targets of malcontents. Bostonians challenged metropolitan innovations in the imperial constitution by disrupting the peace but also by closely defining and guarding it. Leaving aside the endless pontifications of the men who sought to preserve or reform the constitution of empire, the king's peace was the main game in 1760s Massachusetts. Until they picked up guns, colonists fought equally to thwart the enforcement of imperial legislation by officers of the crown and to defend their reputation as peaceable subjects. Breaches of the peace daily performed the untenable limits (legal, ideological, and practical) bounding executive authority in the colonial northeast. The powerlessness of the king to keep the peace was a constant theme in colonial correspondence. The king's men feared that it chipped away at deference and allegiance, turning peaceable subjects into rebels. Crowds challenged the peace, not only through riot, but by keeping the peace themselves. The legislature, its representatives on the governor's council, and the townsfolk insisted that the people and their representatives were the arbiters of the boundary between peace and chaos. Students of Carl Schmitt and Giorgio Agamben will see the danger here. Modern sovereignty is built, they tell us, on the sovereign's power to declare emergency, to diagnose disorder. In contests about who had power to keep the peace, to quell disorder, and to declare emergency lay the key to the Revolution.

Prerevolutionary disorder had contradictory legacies in the new United States of America, underpinning its investment in popular sovereignty, its imperial constitution, as well as its wariness of crowds. For my purposes, the disturbances of the peace in colonial America are most important for what they did to the British Empire. They chastened Parliament and shifted imperial administration decisively (if temporarily) out of Parliament's purview. No colony established after 1770 constrained the crown's prerogative to keep the peace as it had been constrained in colonial Massachusetts: the king's peace would not be the object of play in the postrevolutionary empire. America was not the only reason for this, but it was a key catalyst, along with the stirrings of industrialization and mass urbanization in Britain, and the dogged persistence of Jacobite rebels in Britain's proximate peripheries. Boston's mobs combined with the Gordon Rioters to provoke the king into reclaiming his prerogative to use military power to keep the peace in Britain. But the most dramatic legal transformations were reserved for new colonies, where prerogative power became a lynchpin of counter-revolutionary empire.[143] At the center of that story lay the waxing prerogative—the key legacy of the American Revolution in the British Empire.

2

A Military Assassination in Montréal

In 1764 on a moonlit December night in the town of Montréal, Thomas Walker JP lost his ear in a flagrant breach of the peace. He had just sat down to a family dinner when six or more disguised men burst into his house to "assassinate" him.[1] By his own account Walker put up a heroic fight, dodging several deathblows and an attempt to throw him into the fire before his attackers cut off his ear and departed. His wife fled to the "Cow house" with a number of slaves and an "Apprentice Boy."[2] She had time on the way to recognize one of the men "by his size and shape" as Ensign Hamilton of the 28th Regiment. The affair, according to Justice Thomas Lambe, was the culmination of a "combination of the Military against the civil power" that had started long before.[3]

Soldiers from the 28th and 44th Regiments did not make a particularly convincing show of their innocence. Sergeant Rogers had succeeded in alerting a whole household to his nefarious plans when he borrowed a sword from William Lewis, a tailor and grenadier from the 44th. In a painfully ridiculous cloak-and-dagger performance, Rogers tried to convince Lewis to give him his sword in secret—at one point sending a "lusty man with a blanket Coat" to arrange a clandestine interview. Rogers told Lewis he wanted to use the sword to "carry . . . off a girl," a goal that was apparently less obnoxious than attacking a magistrate. He returned it later, dressed in different clothing, and begged Lewis and his landlords not to "take my life" by testifying about his suspicious behavior that evening.[4] Though Sergeant Mea denied it, his wife swore that Rogers had borrowed Mea's "plain Soldier's coat . . . of Scarlet and Yellow Lappells but without Lace . . . one of the two days preceding the attempted Assassination of Mr. Walker."[5] The coat was found soaked in blood. Other soldiers suspected of participating in the attack swore conveniently that they were in each other's company on the night when Walker was attacked.[6] It is perhaps to their credit that the men of the 28th and 44th were all such rotten liars. After the event, military complicity did not cease. Officers made no secret of their sympathy for the perpetrators, sending jailed soldiers food and comforts to ease their suffering. Potential informants were openly bullied on the parade ground.[7] A few weeks later, a large group of soldiers attempted, and on their second go succeeded, in organizing a jailbreak.[8]

Why would two companies of soldiers collude in the attempted "assassination" of a magistrate and the daring rescue of perpetrators? Their disorder was the result of long-brewing troubles about the boundary between civil and military order in Quebec and its peripheries. Those troubles exposed gaping holes in the legal framework for regime transition in the eighteenth-century British Empire. Aside from the broad strokes of the law of conquest, what exactly happened when a colony changed hands? On General William Amherst's orders, from 1761 until 1764 Quebec had been governed by a triumvirate of military officers (General Thomas Gage among them) using largely military jurisdiction to keep the peace.[9] Applying military law to Quebec seemed perfectly sensible to Canadians.

Military leaders stationed in Quebec modeled their jurisdiction closely on French institutions and practices, so Canadians found the system largely unobjectionable.[10] They appointed French militia captains to act as trial judges, with courts-martial filling any gaps.[11] In any case, there were few alternatives. Quebec had been hard-won, a peace treaty was some years away, and most French dignitaries (judges and magistrates among them) had fled the colony at the time of conquest.

As they waged a global war, the king's ministers had better things to do than contemplate the complexities of ordering their new French-Catholic subjects, so they cheerfully left Amherst to design a legal system, and Gage, Colonel Ralph Burton, and General James Murray to keep the peace as they saw fit. The problem was that no one outside the Caribbean had thought through the theory and practice of using military law to keep civil order. So, in late 1763, a full year before civil government was introduced in the colony, the triumvirate learned that all of its exercises of military jurisdiction since 1761 had been illegal.[12] Before the American Revolution, courts-martial could not be used to keep a civilian peace after conquest.

This revelation had ramifications beyond the boundaries of Montréal. The sharp limits placed on military power in eighteenth-century imperial law also undermined efforts to order settlers in Indian Country from the porous southern and western boundaries of the American colonies to the banks of the Mississippi River. The unaccountable decision by the king in council to leave Indian Country without any sort of government in the Proclamation of 1763 amplified the problem. The realization that military law could not fill jurisdictional gaps left by the absence of civil order was devastating in fort towns like Detroit, which suddenly found themselves without the capacity to pass local ordinances or adjudicate civil disputes or criminal actions. But its consequences were worse in the "wilderness." There the impotence of the British army to keep British subjects at peace constantly threatened to provoke war with Indian Nations. The legal problem of keeping order in sites that were by choice or necessity outside government took even longer to re-solve than the problem of occupation. So much is clear from endemic jurisdictional trouble in British logging settlements at Honduras until a colony was formally established in 1871.[13]

Walker's assault was bound up with the martial peace because he and other querulous Protestant merchants had arrived from New England during the military regime, eager to muscle in on the fur trade and to take a leading role in what they assumed would soon become a robust, all-Protestant colonial legislature. These men did not take kindly to being hauled before courts-martial for every insult they offered to the military, though some demanded to have their civil affairs tried before British officers rather than French militia captains.[14] As soon as a semblance of civil order was established in 1764, Walker and his cronies made their way into the magistracy and into civilian juries. They used their new positions as peacekeepers to wreak vengeance on the redcoats by petitioning home, bringing civil suits, and thwarting the soldiers' efforts to find comfortable billets or even to commandeer firewood.[15] These incivilities turned violent as the harsh winter crept in. It was not for nothing that Walker was attacked on a clear December night.

Conflicts between merchants and soldiers highlighted more than the difficulties of keeping order in a trading hub whose edges bled into the freezing wilderness. They also underlined a transformative problem: the perceived incapacity of Protestant men to keep a just peace in the new world. The king's old "British" subjects carried a surfeit of liberty that was already threatening the peace in the American colonies. They stood in contrast to French and Catholic Canadians, whose peculiar status served as a wedge between British merchants and soldiers. The Canadians' Frenchness, their deep roots in the colony, and their legal vulnerability as conquered Catholics made them objects of suspicion and sympathy, depending on whom one asked.[16] Protestant newcomers to Quebec hoped that the empire would impose penal laws limiting the civil rights of Catholics and giving English merchants huge political and economic advantages. Luckily for the Canadians, the military had much more time for Catholic locals than for spoiled British men of commerce. General James Murray and Colonel Guy Carleton, the first two governors of Quebec, argued vociferously that Quebec should not call a legislature because British merchants would abuse self-government at the expense of Canadians. Even before the good people of Boston made such theater of their contempt for the king's peace, British merchants in Quebec showed that old subjects of the king were less governable than new ones.[17] This was a bitter lesson, but it brimmed with opportunity.

The legal vulnerability of the Canadians as Catholics and conquered subjects was a boon to empire. It became a crucible for constitutional change. Though the Proclamation of 1763 authorized the establishment of legislatures in all newly conquered colonies from Quebec to the Leeward Islands, internecine arguments among merchants and the military about who should keep the peace, how it should be kept, and what privileges should be extended to their new, Catholic neighbors turned Quebec into an experimental autocracy. This vision was formalized by the Quebec Act of 1774. The act claimed to protect Canadians by denying them an assembly. Quebec would be governed instead by a governor-in-council and partly

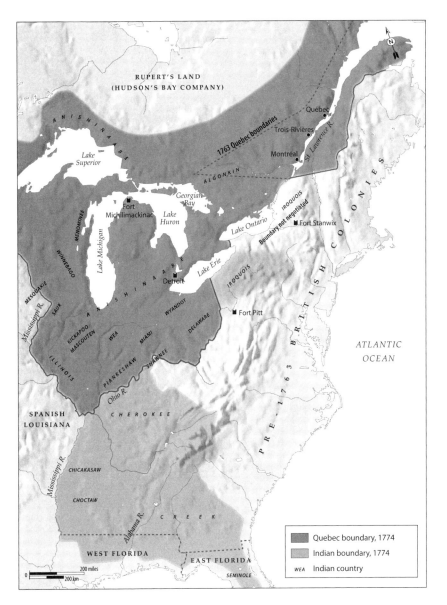

RUPERT'S LAND
(HUDSON'S BAY COMPANY)

1763 Quebec boundaries

Québec

Trois-Rivières

Montréal

St. Lawrence R.

ANISHINAABE

ALGONKIN

Lake Superior

Georgian Bay

Fort Michilimackinac

MENOMINEE

Lake Huron

Lake Michigan

WINNEBAGO

Lake Ontario

IROQUOIS

Fort Stanwix

Boundary not negotiated

ANISHINAABE

Lake Erie

Detroit

MESQUAKIE

Mississippi R.

SAUK

KICKAPOO

MASCOUTEN

WEA

MIAMI

PIANKESHAW

SHAWNEE

IROQUOIS

WYANDOT

DELAWARE

Fort Pitt

B R I T I S H   C O L O N I E S

ATLANTIC
OCEAN

ILLINOIS

Ohio R.

P R E - 1 7 6 3

SPANISH
LOUISIANA

C H E R O K E E

CHICAKASAW

Mississippi R.

CHOCTAW

Alabama R.

C R E E K

WEST FLORIDA

EAST FLORIDA

SEMINOLE

0   200 miles
0   200 km

Quebec boundary, 1774

Indian boundary, 1774

WEA   Indian country

Map 2.1 The Province of Quebec, c. 1774. © Lisa Ford

under French law. In La Paix Québécoise, the king's subjects—British settlers and French Canadians—were leveled, their "birthright" to British law truncated, and their privileges of self-government removed. Most importantly, perhaps, this new constitution was cast over a huge swath of Indian Country—bringing British traders and French habitants under the jurisdiction of a vastly expanded crown government, while Native Americans living in Quebec's expanded boundaries alternately enjoyed and suffered their status as self-governing quasi-subjects, unprotected by British law. Thus the fraught efforts of soldiers to keep the peace in Canada changed empire: Quebec's model of governance, with its legal pluralism, was rolled out throughout the British Empire after the American Revolution.

An Ungovernable Place

Montréal grew around a trading fort built in 1642 at the junction of the St. Lawrence and Ottawa Rivers, halfway between Quebec and Lake Ontario. After a severe dip in the late seventeenth century, Montréal's fur trade grew significantly in the eighteenth. By 1760 the town had a population of around 8,300 former French subjects (just over half the size of Boston).[18] That year, a further 700 workers visited the town during the fur trade season. The booming pelt trade attracted men like Walker to Quebec after the British conquest.[19]

Since 1759, when the colony was surrendered to British troops, soldiers and French militiamen had kept the peace chiefly through courts-martial (an arrangement formally approved in 1761). These courts-martial bothered Canadians much less than they did the 300-odd "Old British Subjects" who moved to Quebec after 1760. They were conducted much more like continental civil courts than

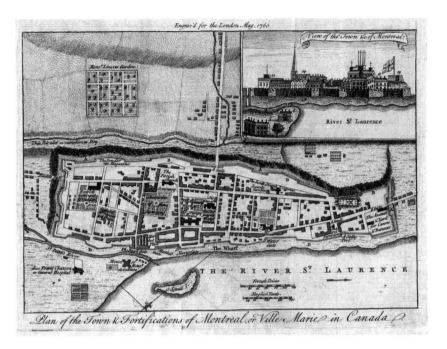

Fig 2.1 Thomas Jeffreys, *Plan of the Town and Fortification of Montreal or Ville Marie in Canada,* map 1760. Baldwin Collection, Special Collections Department, Courtesy of Toronto Public Library / 912.71428 J24 SMALL

common-law courts, and, as noted, most cases in Quebec came before French militia captains anyway. Burt argued long ago that the interim military regime not only protected Canadian interests, it improved their rudimentary preconquest system of justice and civil administration. Further, some elite Canadians formed deep bonds with the better sort of British soldiers.[20]

In contrast, British merchants rejected the soldiers' peace. Their objections were partly ideological. Since 1689, British subjects—those of the non-Francophone kind at least—were deeply mistrustful of military governance. Their objections were cultural and political. They derived from the liberal use of military power in civilian governance during and after the English civil war.[21] One of the key projects of Parliament in the aftermath of the Glorious Revolution was to formally limit the role of soldiers in peacekeeping, and, indeed, to subordinate soldiers, where appropriate, to civilian law. So, soon after his arrival in England, William III signed a Mutiny Act reaffirming the jurisdiction of civilian courts to try most military malefactions. Only mutinous soldiers would be tried by courts-martial in peacetime. A decade later, after a massive campaign by John Trenchard and others, Parliament also forced William III to sign a bill limiting the number of troops he could keep under arms in England to 7,000. Ominously for empire, the 1699 Disbandment Act gave William authority to keep 12,000 troops in Ireland, at Ireland's expense. In wartime that number increased. In 1761, for example, 24,000 troops were stationed in Ireland.[22] The act made no arrangement for troops in overseas colonies.[23] However, throughout the eighteenth-century empire, Trenchard's tracts provided a ready resource to combat efforts to keep standing armies in the American colonies. All in all, fear of military tyranny created a culture of suspicion that bound many British Americans more tightly than their allegiance to the king.[24]

There were also some very practical reasons for Protestant merchants' dissatisfaction with martial justice. Before Walker had arrived in Montréal, a string of British civilians found themselves in front of courts-martial merely for offending officers. Honor *was* order in the military, and its pursuit in Montréal sometimes tipped over into wrongful arrest, loose testimony, and malicious prosecution.[25] All were on display in the winter of 1762, when merchants

Edward Chinn, William Grant, and Richard Oakes ended up before a court-martial for assaulting and insulting officers after a drinking session ended in a brawl.[26]

The facts of the case are murky. According to Chinn, the merchants and officers had lunched together before he and "some friends" gathered at Govett's house for the evening on Friday, February 5. Afterward Chinn and Ferris proceeded to a coffeehouse where Oakes and the officers had already convened. The soldiers testified afterward that the merchants were unwelcome intruders: they arrived in a disorderly state, breaking glasses and behaving badly. In contrast, Chinn said that Ensign Nott insisted that the merchants join the party and share a drink—an invitation that, Chinn felt, promised trouble.

Things unraveled when an inebriated soldier, Mr. Jacobs, lost his purse and accused the publican of taking it. When the merchants found Jacobs's purse in his bed, the publican called Jacobs a scoundrel and the room erupted into violence. By his own admission, Quartermaster Platt pulled out his sword and threatened to dismember anyone who struck an officer. He was forcibly disarmed by the merchants. Ensign Nott joined the fray either to restore peace or defend his friends. By all accounts there was a good deal of hair pulling, and by the time the guard came to restore the peace, Edward Chinn had Nott on the ground. Chinn and Grant were arrested and taken to the guardhouse for the night. Some of the officers alleged that, the next morning, Oakes insulted Nott's honor by saying that "two hundred pounds made a Gentleman in the Army." Mr. Oakes confirmed that some words had been exchanged about the price of an officer's commission, but claimed that the discussion had ended amicably: Nott had shaken his hand and apologized for his misbehavior the night before.[27]

Accordingly, the trial was not just about drunken insults to the officers' honor, it was also involved accusations that officers perjured themselves before the military court. The merchants argued that the officers' charges were crafted to avoid a suit for wrongful arrest. Unsurprisingly, the military court sided with the officers. Though the most serious allegations made were that the merchants had joined in an affray that the soldiers had started, and said some very unkind things about His Majesty's officers, the court ordered Chinn, Grant, and Oakes to apologize and pay fines. Oakes was also sentenced to imprisonment for two weeks because he had intimated that the king's officers were not gentlemen, but General Gage thought better of that and ordered that he be released after twenty-four hours with a good-behavior bond.[28] If things were tense between the officers and these merchants before February 1762, they were worse thereafter.

Relations deteriorated further when Thomas Walker arrived in Montréal the following year with money enough to buy a "fine stone house on Rue Saint-Paul."[29] Within months of his arrival, he ended up before a military court in a civil action and was ordered to pay £16 in debt to his "Clerk or Servant" Leonard Hugo.[30] He refused, declaring "in an angry and haughty Manner...that he did not value sd Sentence," and continuing on with "many opprobrious invectives against sd Hugo, & sd Military court."[31] Walker was then arrested and forced to pay a fine for contempt. Thereafter the whole body of merchants campaigned against the legitimacy of military jurisdiction—rioting, posting pamphlets in the night about military tyranny, and petitioning British contacts for reform.[32] In the meantime, Walker's "invectives" against Hugo, and his alleged attempt to cheat him, exposed the prejudices of "old subjects" against Canadians.

It transpired that all of these proceedings were not only dubious, they were *ultra vires* the court-martial. In early 1763 the conviction of Joseph Corriveaux for the murder of his son-in-law Louis Hélène Dodier upended the whole system of justice in Quebec. A coroner had tried to cover up the crime by finding that Dodier had been "trampled to death by his horses."[33] But that plot unraveled and Corriveaux was convicted. Then, the night before his execution, Corriveaux revealed that, in fact, his daughter had murdered her husband with a blunt hatchet. She was sentenced to be hanged and gibbeted. The case was so sensational that it caught the eye of Judge Advocate Charles Gould in London. On closer examination, Gould found Quebec to be ungovernable. He wrote apologetically to Hector Cramahé, the deputy judge advocate, in 1763 to "hint to you a doubt which is entertained with regard to the Trial of Persons not Military, by Courts Martial." The situation was all the more embarrassing because the king had explicitly approved this jurisdictional arrangement and the secretary of state, Lord Egremont, had also approved of the hanging of two civilians on the sentence of military courts in Quebec three years before.[34]

The basic legalities of conquest were set by the law of nations, such as it was. On the face of it, the crown had sweeping powers to govern conquered territory. The conquering king could change laws, settle a new mode of governance, or even take the property of conquered peoples, subject only to the terms of capitulation or treaty. The first problem in Quebec was that no treaty had been signed. The second was that, until the king intervened, local law and institutions were presumed to continue.[35] However, in Quebec the local legal system ceased to function. Courts-martial exercising military law were established in their place, though with some deference to preexisting French practices.

Given that local legal institutions had collapsed, the crown might have justified its use of military jurisdiction on the ancient grounds of necessity. The twelfth-century scholar Gratian claimed that "necessity has no law," a maxim interpreted variously to mean that necessity "does not recognize any law" or "necessity creates its own law."[36] This notion had a long lineage in English jurisprudence and was about to become a ubiquitous justification for the corrosion of due process in new British colonies from Africa to Australia.[37] Just a few decades later, French revolutionaries would write the needful suspension of ordinary law into one of the first modern, written constitutions.

By 1861 the law of nations had filled this gap explicitly by expanding the conqueror's license to govern conquests before the signing of peace treaties. As Quebec had capitulated to the British and its status was yet to be determined by the outcome of the war, a mid-nineteenth-century international lawyer would argue that it was merely "occupied" between 1761 and 1763. H. W. Halleck argued in 1861 that all government in occupied territories during wartime derived from the laws of war and was, of its nature, military rule, so "it is of little consequence whether such a government be called a *military* or a *civil* government." Only the conqueror's will, constitution, and laws imposed restrictions on the governance of occupied territories.[38]

Even if these legal technologies had been available in 1761, they may not have solved the problem of the peacekeeping in Quebec. At the time of conquest, British military jurisdiction was further restricted by the Articles of War, extended to America by the Mutiny Act of 1756.[39] A simple reading of section 20, article 2, of the 1749 Articles of War seemed to validate the use of military law in Canada until the king saw fit to give Quebec a constitution. It provided that courts-martial could try "all Persons guilty of Wilfull Murder" and other capital crimes or offenses and punish offenders according "to the known Laws of the Land, or as the nature of their Crimes shall deserve" anywhere that lacked an established civil government.[40] One of very few books on courts-martial at the time suggested that, in places like "Gibraltar, Minorca &c. where there is no Form of Civil Judicature, all Persons guilty of any capital Crime or other Offences," could be tried under military law, as could aliens who invaded the realm.[41] However, as Gould told Murray, section 20 would be read strictly by the courts in the context of the act because so many "in this Kingdom . . . view the Military Arm with a jealous Eye and are ever ready to take advantage of the least mistaken excess of Power." Accordingly, *All Persons* should be understood to extend only to "All Persons Subject to those Articles [of War]" (that is, soldiers and, arguably, camp followers).[42]

After receiving Gould's cautions, Gage asked rather testily "how Canada in such Circumstances, ought to be governed," given that the French judges had fled and British emigrants refused to answer to any civil court constituted by the military under French law.[43] Gage admitted that "till the Receipt of your Letter . . . I had not the smallest Doubt of their being consistent with Law. The utility of such Proceedings you were Sensible of, when no Civil Judicature was in Force; you must therefore be sensible of the Necessity of passing Laws for the direction of Officers in such Circumstances, to prevent Anarchy & Confusion, murder, robbery, and every heinous crime being committed without Restraint or Controul."[44] When Murray heard the news, he wrote that "it was lucky we did not know, how limited our Jurisdiction has been here. . . . His Majesty's new Subjects, already prejudiced against us by every popish Art, must have conceived a Strange Opinion of their new Masters, who had no

Law to punish the most notorious Murder, that perhaps has even been committed."[45] Unsurprisingly, one of the first acts of Murray's new civil government was to confirm "the decrees of the Courts during the Military Government" in order to conduce "the peace of the colony."[46]

Gould's opinion, meanwhile, had much larger ramifications in Indian Country because the Proclamation of 1763 declared lands west of the Appalachians and south and west of the narrowly drawn boundaries of Quebec to be an Indian Reserve, outside the jurisdiction of any government.[47] Egremont and the king had worried about this formulation during the drafting of the 1763 Proclamation. They proposed including Indian Country within the Canadian government. However, the Board of Trade convinced the king that it would be both imprudent and expensive to govern Indian Country in such a way.[48] So, the proclamation required merely that traders carry licenses issued by a governor or the commander in chief, and authorized "all Officers whatever, as well Military as those Employed in the Management and Direction of Indian Affairs, within the Territories reserved as aforesaid for the use of the said Indians, to seize and apprehend all Persons whatever, who standing charged with Treason, Misprisions of Treason, Murders, or other Felonies or Misdemeanors, shall fly from Justice and take Refuge in the said Territory."[49]

This was an extraordinary pronouncement, first because the power to seize seemed only to attach to settlers who "shall fly from Justice and take Refuge" in Indian Country, rather than to settlers who committed serious crimes there. At the very least it required that those seized already be "charged" with a crime—a power conspicuously withheld from officers of the crown in Indian Country. Crimes in Indian Country, in theory, would have to be reported in properly constituted jurisdictions before anything could be done about them. So, while the Proclamation was well-received in Indian Country, hastening the dissolution of Pontiac's confederacy and the end of a destructive Indian war, it proposed a wholly unworkable jurisdictional compromise.[50] Its unworkability was enhanced markedly by Gould's interpretation of section 20 of article 2 in 1763.

A key issue was that many thousands of Francophone traders and métis lived in Indian Country. Francophone settlements littered its western reaches, "without the protection or the control of Civil Government."[51] They occupied an enormous amount of military time and imagination between 1763 and the outbreak of the American Revolution. The Illinois region southwest of Quebec took years to "subdue" after 1763. Some *habitants* insisted as late as 1764 that the British conquest was mere rumor.[52] Many maintained strong trading and political connections with French contacts on the other side of the Mississippi.[53] If the French speakers of Montréal were ideal subjects, French speakers in Indian Country were something else entirely.[54]

The problem of governing large French communities surrounding forts like Detroit was even more pressing.[55] When the British conquered Detroit in 1760, they governed it much as it had been governed before: the highest-ranking officer in the fort became its civil and military administrator. But that commandant had no jurisdiction over civilians, according to Gould. Luckily Gage does not seem to have been aware of Gould's decision, when, in January 1764, he authorized Major Gladwin to assemble a court-martial to try some French subjects who had sided with Pontiac's allies in the siege of Detroit.[56] Soon after, setting a pattern that would repeat around the empire from Honduras to Sierra Leone, this juridical gap was filled with informal power exercised by locally elected or nominated justices of the peace. In 1767 the residents of Detroit elected a judge who wielded jurisdiction enough to fine and imprison people for debt or misdemeanor. But this system was grossly inefficient in a busy lakeside port town where there were debts to be collected, conspiracies to be quelled, and crimes to be punished.[57] Canadian petitioners argued for the "re-annexation of . . . inland posts to this province" to save the Indian trade. "In the present state of things," they complained, "as there are no courts of justice whose jurisdiction extends to those distant places," merchants have no recourse when traders "prove dishonest," because they are "out of the reach of their creditors . . . which intirely ruins this colony, and turns those posts into harbours for rogues and vagabonds."[58]

Much more importantly, the proclamation was unworkable because peace between settlers and Indians in Indian Country had a double meaning. Peace between Indians and the king rested in large degree on the king's capacity to keep his subjects at peace—to stop settlers from flooding into Indian Country, to punish their violence against Indians, and to regulate their comportment in Indian trade. John Stuart's negotiations with the Choctaws and Chickasaws in 1765 are exemplary here, though they are fringed with a curious courtliness, markedly absent from the frank diplomatic exchanges with southeastern Indian Nations. In return for a promise to protect traders passing through their lands, the Choctaws and Chickasaws demanded that the king keep his subjects in order. Tomatle Mingo complained that traders "often treat our Warriors with Indecent Language, they often call them Eunuchs (Ubachaba) which is the most opprobrious term that can be used in our Language," and both he and Alibamo Mingo complained that traders sexually assaulted Choctaw women.[59] As Alibamo Mingo put it, "wherever the English went, they caused disturbances; for they lived under no Government, and Paid no Respect either to Wisdom or Station."[60] To keep peace (in its double sense), the king must police the words and deeds of British subjects on Indian land.

Such intimate governance was clearly impossible under the terms of the proclamation and the articles of war. Under a plan mooted in 1764, the Board of Trade imagined that order in Indian Country might be managed by magistrates operating in conjunction with the crown's superintendents of Indian affairs. It was never implemented, because the jurisdictional vortex established by the proclamation meant that such a plan would have to be legislated by Parliament.[61] In early 1765 Gage proposed changes to the Mutiny Act in order to bring malefactors in Indian Country under military law. He proposed: "After the 60th clause,—But if such Crime or Trespass, be committed at any of the posts, not in the inhabited parts of the Country, and where the Civil Judicature hath not taken place; Be it enacted by the authority aforesaid, that the person accused, may be there proceeded against, and tried, and convicted by a Regimental or General Court-Martial according to the degree of the Offence."[62]

This amendment was not passed. Instead the Mutiny Act of 1765 allowed "officers to apprehend criminals and send them to the colonies for civil trial."[63] The problem was, of course, that this jurisdiction was illusory too. For a start, it relied on colonial legislation criminalizing breaches of the proclamation. Many colonies were slow to legislate against squatting, for example. When settlers squatted on Indian land near Redstone Creek, all Gage could do was deploy soldiers to warn settlers that they would be exposed to Indian retaliation if they did not leave.[64] He sent Captain James Mackay to do just that in June 1766 with Indian chiefs in tow. Mackay warned that "Indians will be incouraged in this way of doing themselves Justice, and if Accidents should happen you Lawless People must look upon yourselves as the cause."[65] The 1765 amendment also assumed the extraterritorial operation of colonial law in Indian Country—an arrangement that needed to be negotiated on a case-by-case basis with Indian tribes.[66] Even when local treaties conceded colonial jurisdiction over settlers in Indian Nations, its efficacy rested on colonial judiciaries and juries. The latter did not cooperate: "No Jury wou'd condemn ... [settlers] for murdering or ill-treating an Indian." Unregulated violence and growing incursions into Indian lands showed, more generally, the "Weakness of the [colonial] Governments to enforce obedience to the Laws."[67]

In 1767 a community of settlers punctuated this last point with violence in the backcountry of Georgia. They complained to Governor Wright that their horses were being stolen by Creek Indians living across the newly drawn boundary. Before the colonial government could respond, they crossed over into Indian Country and burned a Creek town. Georgia's government showed some mettle: the settlers were prosecuted twice—first with a felony and then, when that failed, with "abuse and misdemeanour at common law against government." But Georgian juries refused to convict on either count. Other Georgian malefactors made the point even more clearly seven years later when further violence erupted on the Creek boundary. They declared that they would not "suffer themselves to be brought to punishment for injuries sustained by savages." Lord Hillsborough understood this very clearly as a threat to imperial order: "A Declaration of this nature strikes deep into the Root of all Authority, and renders it essentially necessary that the whole force of Government should be exerted to bring the ... Delinquents to that punishment, which the Law had prescribed for the Offence they have committed."[68] More than words unraveled empires, however. Disorder itself made a mockery of the king's authority. As an anonymous correspondent of Lord Dartmouth pointed out in 1774, Indian Country had become a "Theatre of disorder & Confusion leading to causes that must affect the public Tranquility and weaken the Authority of this Kingdom."[69]

The impossibility of peacekeeping in Indian Country and postconquest Quebec showed that the empire had a corrosive legal problem. Its hesitancy to embrace either necessity or to craft rules for governance during military occupations reflected the ideological detritus of the Glorious Revolution. A messy overlay of politics and statutory interpretation combined to render the king's army unable to keep the peace where no other infrastructure existed to do so. However, important workarounds quickly emerged: during the American Revolution, New York would be ruled under military jurisdiction for the better part of a decade without a formal declaration of martial law. Charles Gould complained occasionally about the illegality of the arrangement, but counseled, in the end, that the less said about it the better. He advised, "if in any case from the evident necessity of present and exemplary punishment Courts Martial have been induced to exceed the limits of their ordinary Jurisdiction, not to call attention to any of the Articles of War in the penning of their Sentence."[70] For their part, military administrators argued that there was no other way to govern during such a widespread revolt. But these compromises were made quietly. In contrast, by the time the Union Army occupied Louisiana a century later, military rule in occupied territory was utterly uncontroversial.[71] So extensive were the powers of military occupiers by the late nineteenth century that the Hague Convention of 1899 sought actively to reduce them.[72] This new certainty came too late to solve the problems of order faced by the Imperial Army in Quebec until 1764 and in Indian Country until the American Revolution. A different solution was required, and it hinged on the vulnerability of Catholics.

Ungovernable People

The crisis of military jurisdiction in Quebec abated when instructions to form a civilian government arrived in August 1764. However, tensions among soldiers, Protestants, and Catholics increased. This was so partly because the military regime stayed more or less in place. General Murray was appointed to be the first civil governor of the colony. Colonel Burton, who had governed Trois-Rivières, refused the title of Lieutenant-Governor, but was stationed at Montréal to lead a large contingent of troops. The same angry merchants opposed the regime, but now they had a share in peacekeeping. Penal laws limited the capacity of Catholics to serve as magistrates, so Murray struggled to find suitable men to serve.[73] He was forced to people the magistracy with bitter enemies—a sprinkling of soldiers, a few French Protestants, and a cadre of British merchants.[74] In their hands, peacekeeping remained a politically explosive business.

Thomas Walker was quickly inducted into the magistracy. After Murray's proclamation confirming the sentences of courts-martial, Walker and his cronies could not legally punish their officer enemies for their maladministration of justice during the transition.[75] They used other means. Quartering legislation, administered by magistrates, provided the perfect avenue for merchants to channel their grievances as it spanned the petty and profound. There had never been barracks big enough to house the king's soldiers in Montréal, so, in a process that rankled colonists up and down the eastern seaboard, the government of Quebec required civilians to host soldiers in their homes. As they would do in Boston a few years later, Old British subjects in Quebec saw quartering as the quintessence of military oppression. In Montréal theirs was not just a campaign of principle. Four cold winters had passed since the conquest of Quebec, and a fifth was closing in when Thomas Walker lost his ear in 1764. Rents were high in Montréal, and many Protestant landlords felt that quartering legislation required them to grant extravagant privileges to soldiers they hated.

In November 1764, Walker and others complained to the Board of Trade that quartering legislation required that "every officer of, or above the Degree of a Captain, shall be provided with good Bed, Chamber and Parlour, or other suitable Room in Lieu thereof and one Cellar in such private house, intirely for his own use, with the free use of the Kitchen—belonging to the same in common with the Family." The petitioners complained that these requirements were "injurious . . . oppressive, and a manifest violation and Infringement of the Rights and privileges, which they claim as British Subjects."[76] Giving officers parlors was onerous because they used them to while away cold winter evenings. Most of the men questioned in the Walker outrage attested that they had been drinking in someone's private lodgings. In a self-exculpatory letter written to Murray late in 1764, Walker complained that "the soldiers . . . sitt up all nights carousing . . . and upon the least reprimand threaten to burn them in their Houses."[77] For all its detail, however, the new ordinance made no mention of providing soldiers with wood. This mattered enormously as winter approached in 1764.

The tipping point came in November when Walker and Thomas Lambe colluded in the eviction of Captain Payne from Mr. Beaume's house. Payne had been billeted at Beaume's on the order of the magistrate and captain John Fraser. This billet was probably improper. First, Fraser had not obtained the room for Payne, he had merely signed over his own billeted rooms and given Payne a key. Second, the house was rented at the time by Mr. Knipe, a merchant and magistrate. Knipe had objected to Fraser's billet, arguing that he should have quiet possession as tenant. When Payne arrived to occupy the rooms, Knipe called on his friends Walker and Lambe for assistance. They bamboozled a fellow magistrate, John Livingstone, into co-signing a warrant demanding Payne's immediate removal or imprisonment. A Monsignor Dumas also signed the writ in ignorance; Fraser later argued that Francophone Dumas could "be made to believe every thing is English Law."[78] Payne refused to vacate, and accompanied the bailiff to the jail.

Meanwhile, Walker's coalition of magistrates started to fray. Livingstone, who was not a native English speaker either, had been deeply uneasy about signing the writ. In a letter to the colony's deputy secretary, he claimed that he had felt that it was a breach of duty to issue a writ without first speaking to Payne to hear his side of the story. But his concerns had been overruled, and, deferring to Lambe's and Walker's superior knowledge of the British legal system, he had added his name. He refused to sign a further writ authorizing the forcible removal of Payne's things from the lodgings.[79] Walker claimed that Livingstone backed out only because he had been threatened by Colonel Christie, "for when I entered his House, in order to get it Signed by him, I caught the latter with uplifted arm, Swearing at the Justice."[80]

What followed was an odd dance: Captain Payne and Lieutenant Colonel Burton wrote to Walker demanding that Payne be released from jail, and Walker replied that Payne was not in custody but had gone to jail of his own accord. By Captain Mitchelson's account,

Payne did not leave the jailhouse until being liberated by "Habeas Corpus."[81] Walker maintained that Payne "continued in Jayl as long as he thought fit, and then came out again with as little Ceremony as he went in."[82]

Payne became a symbol to both parties of undeclared war. Fraser resigned his magisterial post in high dudgeon and Livingston took over billeting, only to be repeatedly overruled by writs of ejectment signed by Walker and Lambe.[83] After Payne left the jail, Beaume and Knipe acquiesced in his billet in Beaume's house, but, instead of his former apartments, he was given "two dirty Rooms, without Fire places or Stoves, void of all sort of Furniture, such as Bed, Chairs or Tables, the Windows Broke." He was refused "Firewood and Candles saying that they are not obliged to furnish any of the aforesaid articles by the late Ordinance." "Tis impossible," complained Captain Mitchelson, that Payne "should attempt to pass this Winter in so miserable a Quarter."[84] This quickly became a pattern. Captain Johnston and several other soldiers also complained that they had been refused "Firewood and Candles" since the publication of the new ordinance.[85] Lieutenant Schalck complained that he was turned out of suitable rooms at Monsieur Rivard's house (billeted to him on Mr. Livingstone's orders). Mr. Walker had told Johnston that Schalck should instead "Quarter in . . . a small Chamber, or Closet in which was neither a Stove nor Fireplace."[86] Mitchelson complained of a "General Spirit amongst the Inhabitants of this place, stirred up it seems by some Malicious Person."[87] It was his ruthless approach to billeting that cost Thomas Walker his ear.

However, this was not Walker's only sphere of misconduct. Livingstone wrote that Walker and his confederates were usurping other powers of government by appointing civil officers and marshaling armed men to defend the streets. He described an "unlawful mutiny" of men "calling themselves Captains . . . raising these Companys of Militia under Hostile and Military Names in Bodys" to remonstrate against government ordinances and reported the refusal of his brother justices to support him in committing the organizers to jail.[88] Fraser also despaired of the peace in the hands of the merchants of Montréal: "There the Malecontents [sic] and Leaders are moved on (I suppose) from picque [sic], Resentment, turbulent and Factious Spirit ready and determined to find fault with every measure if never so well planned and calculated for the good of the Province, here trouble and Confusion arises from those formerly Notorious Leaders of Factions, but whose principals [sic] the indulgence to them shewn by raising them to a Station of Honor and trust should have entirely changed."[89] As he sat down to dinner on December 6, 1764, Thomas Walker was planning a trip to Quebec to address these and other serious allegations that he had abused his office in more ways than keeping soldiers in the cold.[90]

For the merchants, billeting formed part of a larger despotism—a combination of oppressive military power with Catholic interests. Months before the establishment of a civil government, pamphlets appeared in Montréal complaining of the "power . . . of Military officers" in Canada's "Garrison Town[s]" in breach of the "Rights & Privelges" granted British Subjects "by Magna Charta."[91] Within months of Governor Murray's accession, merchants petitioned for his removal. They claimed (not entirely truthfully) that "To Military Government, however oppressive and severely felt, we submitted without Murmur, hoping Time with a Civil Establishment would remedy this Evil" only to find that "with Peace" came none of the "Rights of British Liberty." They prayed for the king "to appoint a Governor over us acquainted with other Maxims of Government than Military only." Murray remained a soldier at heart. So much was clear from the fact that he governed in "rage and rudeness . . . as dishonourable to the trust he holds of your Majesty as painful to those who suffer from it."[92] In another petition, they accused the governor of introducing ordinances "Vexatious, Oppressive, unconstitutional, injurious to civil Liberty and the Protestant Cause," including restricting the Indian trade for longer than necessary after the Proclamation of 1763. To redress these ills, Montréal petitioners requested "a House of Representatives . . . as in other Your Majesty's Provinces; there being a number more than Sufficient of Loyal and well affected Protestants, exclusive of military Officers, to form a competent and respectable House of Assembly."[93]

The merchants cast Murray's delay in implementing the Proclamation of 1763 as another military usurpation: the proclamation had promised a legislative assembly and British law. A grand jury formed in October 1764 claimed *de facto* to represent the interest of Protestant civilians and set about challenging Murray's capacity to raise taxes or rule without the aid of a legislature. They ordered the arrest of a deputy collector of customs to underline their point. This case ended up before a jury of London merchants and resulted in a partial settlement by the crown.[94] Finally, they attacked Murray's Francophilia. By allowing Catholics to act as lawyers and rescuing them from Protestant juries, merchants alleged that Murray was perverting the administration of justice in ways that illegally empowered Catholics and discriminated against Protestants. A similar petition of grand jurors in Quebec protested that the empaneling of Catholics as jurors was an "open Violation of our most sacred Laws and Libertys."[95]

The Walker affair played into merchants' allegations that the local system of justice had been hijacked by the military governor. To ensure that the soldiers accused of maiming Thomas Walker received a fair trial, Murray passed ordinances designed to ensure that they would not be tried by Walker's cronies in Montréal. He bemoaned that there were "but Fifty two Protestant Householders at Montreal" so "it was impossible to have the Tryal there."[96] Instead he constituted a court at Trois-Rivières, also on the St. Lawrence River halfway between Montréal and Quebec. A flurry of protests and petitions followed. Walker cast this move as a breach of the imperial constitution, because it broke the nexus between the location of the crime and the place of its adjudication and subjected Walker and his witnesses to unnecessary expense and risk in attending. In any case, his witnesses alleged that the governor had no power to fine them for ignoring the crown's subpoenas. The whole business, they claimed, was "calculated to prevent . . . [Walker's attackers from] being brought to Justice."[97] So Walker refused to take part, resorting to, according to Murray, "indefatigable pains . . . to baffle every attempt the Government made to punish the perpetrators of these Outrages."[98] By late 1765 Walker was in London leveraging his injuries to castigate Murray's regime. His case was still before courts in 1767 when Lieutenant Fraser himself was arrested on the deposition of a soldier swayed by the promise of a large reward.[99] No one was convicted of the crime.[100]

In Murray's view, the soldiers behaved no better: they hated the Protestant merchants viscerally, had been "Lukewarm in discovering Delinquents," and repeatedly threatened mutiny.[101] Captain Mitchelson warned that mutiny would follow from a series of breaches in due process for the accused in Walker's case. He lamented the incarceration of Walker's attackers in dungeons "without fire at this time of the year," where they were kept "in Irons upon a verbal Order . . . by the Warrant of a single Justice antedated . . . tho the Informations against them are not upon Oath." He warned, "I can by no means answer for the Regiment I command when they see their Fellow Soldiers dragged to Goal on the slightest Pretences contrary to the Act of Parliament."[102] Murray feared that the soldiers were encouraged in their prejudices by the "Genteel" French speakers of the countryside and by Colonel Burton, who had applied for Murray's job and would not long be "contented with the command of a few Troops in a country he had so long governed without Control."[103]

Concerns about mutiny were not idle. On January 16 as many as 200 men marched on the Montréal jail to rescue Sergeants Mea and Coleman and Private McLaughlin, who had been incarcerated for their alleged role in the affair. Rogers was unreachable in a dungeon. Brave Captain Skene pursued them in a French gentleman's cariole, bringing the party to a halt. He retrieved the prisoners and brought them back, wounding someone in the process. Skene's defense of the peace did not extend to bringing the jailbreakers to justice, however. It was January, and no doubt dark and bitterly cold. Nevertheless, it beggars belief that Skene and the prisoners failed to identify a single person involved in their jailbreak. When the roll was called that evening, Skene claimed that "the whole Garrison was under Arms as usual."[104] For his part, Coleman could not say if his liberators were soldiers, if they were armed, or even if they broke open the prison door. Just a few weeks later, a much smaller group of soldiers came to the jail, and, Coleman claims, threatened the prisoners to leave or suffer violence. The party crossed the icy river and traveled on to the fortress at Chamble.[105]

Concerns about the French majority had a different cast. There were as many as 70,000 French Canadians in Quebec Province at the time of conquest, making it by far the most daunting incorporative exercise faced by the empire in postwar America. To garner any value at all from this expanse, the empire needed Canadian settlers to stay put and to become loyal British subjects. The conciliation of Canadians was made more urgent by the thousands of habitants in Indian Country, whom Gage and his officers feared colluded with France and its former Indian allies to foment war.

As Hannah Weiss Muller has pointed out, the jurisprudence of imperial subjecthood was deeply unsettled—it being unclear in 1763 (or indeed in 1830) whether, in law, a subject could shift their allegiance to a new king after conquest.[106] French people living in Canada and the conquered Caribbean colonies were given the option to swear fealty to the king of England or to leave newly British territories. Their decision to stay, however, did not resolve to anyone's satisfaction the question of their fealty. The conversation turned, instead, on how best to win hearts and minds for the crown. Protestant immigrants here (as well as Catholics unsure of their allegiance) figured as the enemies of the colonial peace.[107]

In fractious Grenada after the Proclamation of 1763, fifteen hundred white French slaveholders immediately confronted Protestant migrants who argued they could not and should not sit in the local legislature. In dreary Quebec, where fewer than 300 British Protestants moved after 1763, the conversation was quite different. French arguments there turned, not on representation in a legislature, but on law. French Canadians (particularly landed ones) sought to protect their complex seigneurial tenures by agitating for the reinstatement of French civil law. They also sought to have a say in their own governance through representation in English (or better still, French) courts, access to the magistracy, and, ultimately, a place on the governor's council.[108]

It became clear very early on that their new Protestant neighbors presented the most formidable barrier to these goals and would go to any lengths to thwart French ambitions. In an outraged address in 1764, French jurors objected to the content of a Protestant petition protesting the maintenance of French-language courts, French jurisdictions and lawyers, and Catholic juries. They also claimed that some French-speaking subjects had been inveigled into signing the petition by Protestants misrepresenting its contents. "It would be shameful" they said, "to believe that the Canadians, New Subjects, cannot serve their King either as Serjeant, or Officers, it would be . . . very discouraging to free Subjects who have been admitted to the Privileges of the Nation, and their Rights . . . our fellow citizens make us feel our Condition to be that of Slaves. Can the faithful and loyal Subjects of the King be reduced to this?"[109] In another petition sent around the same time, Canadians protested the injustice of foreign (that is, British) proceedings. Justice could not be done to them in English: "We have seen with grief our fellow citizens imprisoned without being heard . . . we have seen all the family affairs . . . obstructed by individuals wishing to make them profitable to themselves, who know neither our language nor customs." The "thirty English merchants" who would proscribe "Ten thousand Heads of Families" could only be "guided by their own Interest rather than the public good."[110]

Riven by querulous merchants, mutinous soldiers, and Canadians jealously guarding their customs and property, Quebec was in a state of disorder—disorder that was taken up by the London press in the summer of 1765. Murray was recalled to England within two years of taking office. Yet he held office long enough to lay the intellectual and institutional groundwork for a new colonial peace—a peace built on the legal vulnerability of French Catholics, on the one hand, and the ungovernability of British merchants, on the other.[111]

La Paix Québécoise

The argument went like this. The tiny minority of Protestant subjects in postconquest Quebec were unfit legislators and magistrates,
and therefore they should not monopolize the privileges that propertied British subjects enjoyed elsewhere. Anticipating arguments
that abolitionists would make against granting legislatures to slaveholders in Trinidad after 1800, Murray argued that English-speaking
merchants in Quebec were unworthy of self-government, as they
were "chiefly adventurers of mean education, either young begin-
ners, or if old Traders, such as have failed in other Countrys." These
men had demonstrated that they could not keep a just peace, so
clearly could not legislate in the interest of the French Catholic
majority. Murray warned the Board of Trade soon after taking office that English merchants sought to destroy and displace the
French as had been done in Nova Scotia: "Little, very little, will content the New Subjects but nothing will satisfy the Licentious Fan-
ticks Trading here, but the expulsion of the Canadians."[112] After his
recall, Murray described the Protestants of Quebec as "the most immoral collection of men I ever knew, of course little calculated to
make the new subjects enamoured with our laws, religion, and customs, far less adapted to enforce those laws and to govern."[113] To
keep Canadians in Quebec, to keep them loyal, and to protect them
from English merchants, a new sort of government was required—one
that would transform empire.

Murray's solution was elegant: to protect French Catholics from
ungovernable British Protestants, Quebec should be subject to prerogative rule. This was an important double move. It used the vulnerability of French Catholics—subjects deserving of the king's special
protection—to argue that a special peace should prevail throughout

Quebec. Vulnerable subjects with truncated civil rights became purveyors of a new constitutional order on the edges of empire.

The key, for Murray, was to partially exempt Catholics from penal
laws—that "rag bag" of legislation restricting the political and civil
rights of Catholics in England and Ireland. By the end of the eighteenth century, penal laws prevented English Catholics from bearing
arms, circumscribed their capacity to worship, imposed onerous
estate taxes, and, most importantly, prevented them from taking
public office. The Irish Parliament had attempted repeatedly to go
further by diminishing Catholics' rights to due process—though
they were impeded by the Privy Council.[114] Such laws were extremely
popular. As the Gordon Riots showed in 1780, it did not pay to let
the British public know that the empire was relaxing restrictions on
the civil rights of Catholics.[115]

Key law officers of the crown agreed with Murray that some restrictions on Catholic civil rights were impolitic and need not, as a
matter of law or policy, apply to new-world colonies. In a 1705 opinion
about their operation in Maryland, Edward Northey had noted that
it was doubtful that English anti-Catholic laws were inherited by
colonies acquired after the laws were passed.[116] Law officers Sir
Fletcher Norton and William de Grey agreed in 1765 that Canadians
"were not" subject to "the incapacities, disabilities and penalties, to
which *Roman* catholics in this kingdom are subject by the law
thereof."[117] This was so because of very loosely articulated rules governing the reception of English laws in the colonies. Most lawyers
agreed by 1763 that colonies could inherit only those laws that befit
their circumstances. Following this logic, penal laws should not
apply to colonies with Catholic majorities.[118]

By the 1770s leading men also argued against penal laws on
grounds of policy. Whether or not they thought the penal laws might

apply to conquered colonies, after the Seven Years' War many acknowledged that the *political* safety of Britain's conquests in North America and the Caribbean rested on the co-option of Catholic subjects. Though Edmund Burke sought the implementation of British law and a legislature in Quebec, he agreed that religious toleration should be pursued in America and "closer to home."[119] Wedderburn argued that "public safety" had been "often endangered" by "imposing any restraint upon men on account of their religious tenets."[120] Centuries of oppression in Ireland, according to William Knox, had not lessened the grip of Catholicism; instead it had hardened the "malignant hatred borne by the papists to the Protestants," and made them determined to "yield that kingdom to a foreign power whenever the opportunity presents itself."[121] To preserve Britain's new acquisitions in America from the fate of Ireland, Britain needed to give the Catholic settlers reason to shift their allegiance to the British king.

In this environment, Britain's conquests in the Seven Years' War provided an opportunity to rethink Catholic legal status in the trans-Atlantic empire, ushering in a period of qualified openness in British imperial legal practice. This openness played out very differently in different places. White French Catholics were formally allowed to participate in the Grenada legislature, albeit in limited numbers. In Quebec, however, the huge number of Catholics, combined with the seditious tendencies of the tiny British population, produced a very different compromise—a vision of Canadian subjecthood that was much less expansive and much more instrumental.[122]

In the 1760s, instead of full emancipation, Murray proposed that the stolid Canadians "would soon get the better of every national Antipathy to their Conquerors, and become the most faithfull, and most usefull, set of men in this American Empire" if they were "indulged with a few Priveleges which the Laws of England deny to Roman Catholicks at Home." The best way to comport them to British rule, he thought, was not to give them a stake in a legislature, but to leverage their tolerance for despotism. After all, they were not only Catholics, they were French—formerly subjects of that European bastion of universal monarchy. As such, they would be happier under French law and gubernatorial tyranny than under English law administered by a hateful Protestant minority.[123] This, of course, is not what French Canadians asked for. They wanted aspects of French law reinstated, but in all other respects called for "your majesty to grant us, in common with your other subjects, the rights and privileges of citizens of England."[124]

Though Murray was recalled, the lobbying efforts of his agent, Hector Theophilus de Cramahé, profoundly shaped successive ministries' thinking about Quebec. Nevertheless, it took a decade for these proposals to be translated into imperial policy. Sometimes Quebec reform stalled because of ministerial intransigence: Lord Chancellor Northington intervened in 1765 and 1767 to prevent the sending of formal instructions to Murray and Carleton authorizing them to allow French Catholics to join the magistracy and to reinstate French civil law.[125] But as trouble in North America blossomed and Protestants in Quebec seemed likely to join the fray, constitutional difference in Quebec seemed to some to be not only kinder but timely—a way to bind Canadian Catholics *and* to geographically contain disorders in the colonies. So, after another extensive round of lobbying by Carleton, the Quebec Act finally passed in 1774.[126]

The Quebec Act marked a fundamental shift in imperial governance. It had exactly one liberal strand: Catholic emancipation. It confirmed freedom to profess Catholicism in Quebec and created a new oath to allow Catholic officeholders to express allegiance without abjuring their faith. English criminal law would be applied in Quebec because it was deemed to be more just. But the act reinstated French civil law and rules of property disposition, which suited many of the French residents worried about real property and dower. These arrangements imposed material constraints on the rights of British subjects, who were accustomed, for example, to enjoying the additional freedoms granted them by holding land in free and common socage, and having a jury preside over actions determining "their Ejectment upon their mortgage Title" and their liability for trespass.[127] The act did other things too: as one "Country Gentleman" pointed out, the Canadians not only got their ancient laws, "the Laws of *France*" also deprived British subjects of the benefits of the Habeas Corpus Act.[128] Finally, the act confirmed that Quebec could be ruled by a governor with an appointed council of seventeen to twenty-three people. It would not have an elected legislature.[129]

The Quebec Act was deeply controversial. Edmund Burke, Charles Fox, and party had supported religious toleration, but not the reimposition of French law and the withholding of a legislature in Quebec. Burke pointed out that it was one thing to delay giving Canada a legislature under the terms of the proclamation, but it was another entirely to "give the people French despotic government, and Canadian law, by act of parliament." "No free country," he declared, "can keep another . . . in slavery."[130] He went on to claim that he would give English law to 360 English families, "though ten thousand Frenchmen should take it against their will."[131]

The fact that a Catholic despotism was established to their north would have been enough to exercise opponents of crown and Parliament in the thirteen colonies, but La Paix Québécoise did more.

It solved the jurisdictional crisis of a large chunk of Indian Country by incorporating it into Quebec.[132] So Catholic despotism crept into explosive backcountries from Massachusetts to Virginia, subsuming territories eyed hungrily by squatters and land speculators. While American legislatures and juries ran interference against all efforts to regulate trade, punish settler crimes, or control settler expansion in Indian Country, the governor-in-council in Quebec would face no such resistance. And he would be aided and abetted by Catholic councillors and jurors with no appreciation of liberty. In London, the *Public Advertiser* declared, "The intentions of administration with regard to America are now apparent. The bill brought in called the Quebec bill, is to enlarge that province to take in half of America, to establish it in the Roman Catholic religion, the French law, and to make the King with the governor and council the legislature of the province. . . . The King of England is to be put in the place of the King of France, and have a taste of what is deemed so delicious, arbitrary power."[133] So much seemed clear to American colonists hurtling toward revolution. As Alexander Hamilton exclaimed in his *Full Vindication of the Measures of the Congress,* in Canada,

> The English laws have been superceded by the French laws. The Romish faith is made the established religion of the land, and his Majesty is placed at the head of it. The free exercise of the Protestant faith depends upon the pleasure of the Governor and Council. The subject is divested of the right of trial by jury, and an innocent man may be imprisoned his whole life, without being able to obtain any trial at all. The parliament was not contented with introducing arbitrary power and popery in Canada, with its former limits, but they have annexed to it the vast tracts of land that surround all the colonies.

He asked, "Will they venture to justify that unparalleled stride of power, by which popery and arbitrary dominion were established in Canada" east of the Ohio?[134] As Philip Livingston of New York protested, the act established "not civil tyranny alone. . . . From the same poisonous root, arises the most horrible religious tyranny. . . . To finish the dreadful system, add all the executive powers of the State, and encircle the whole with a standing army, 'tis then compleat [sic]."[135]

Of course, no one was more incensed by the Quebec Act than Thomas Walker, who set about organizing a revolution in Quebec. He mobilized 134 merchants to petition against the act in November 1774 and ran "nocturnal Cabals" that declared their "allegiance to 'all the Friends of Liberty' in the colonies to the south."[136] Though a Jewish minor was punished for the crime, Walker's crowd almost certainly defaced the bust of the king in the spring of 1775. This act of symbolic king killing was cast by Lord Darmouth as "a daring Insult," part of an attempt to subvert "the Constitution."[137] Christie argues that Carleton may have saved Quebec from joining the Revolution by declaring martial law six weeks later.[138]

Nor did controversy recede with revolution. In 1782 Willoughby Bertie, the 4th Earl of Abingdon, claimed that the Quebec Act was the quintessence of several constitutional errors. These included the notion that colonial subjects were not the same as British subjects—that Parliament could alter the ancient constitution, and in doing so, give its legislative power to the king. This act made the king a *legal Despot . . .* greater than any Despot in Europe."[139] Around the same time, a "Country Gentleman" claimed that the act cast the Catholics as "a Kind of Check and Controul over the former [old British subjects], which must necessarily induce those People to look upon the Canadians with a jealous Eye; as a Guard kept over them

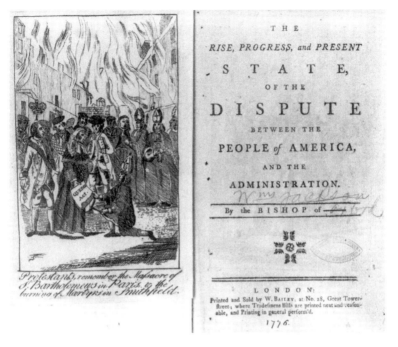

Fig 2.2 The frontispiece and title page of "The Rise, Progress, and Present State of the Dispute between the People of America and the Administration," printed in London in 1776. The illustration shows a British minister handing a copy of the Quebec Act to a kneeling bishop, with King George III standing at left, while in the background a city burns. Library of Congress, Prints and Photographs Division, LC-USZ62-45531

and ready on every Occasion to execute the Mandates of an arbitrary Administration."[140]

These reflections make an important point: the Quebec Act was one of the first British imperial statutes to territorialize limited colonial subjecthood among white subjects. The Penal Laws truncated the rights of Catholic subjects in Britain and Ireland. Slave colonies had long passed their own legislation drawing hard lines between slaves and free people and, increasingly, between free Black and white people. The Regulating Act, passed for "the better management" of the East India Company in 1773, gave parliamentary imprimatur to an existing but ill-defined variable-rights regime when it established a Supreme Court for British subjects (a category from which South Asian people were excluded). The Quebec Act did more radical work. While the act failed to resolve the status of American Indians, it flattened new Francophone Catholic subjects and old British subjects into a new kind of colonial subject—a subject who could be ruled without a legislature regardless of their place of birth, their religion, or how much property they owned. By reinstating French civil law and withholding a legislature, and by extending Quebec to subsume much of the land within the Indian boundaries drawn after the Proclamation of 1763, the act made every non-Indian within this enormous jurisdiction the object of a special peace. The Quebec Act turned Catholic Canadians into purveyors of order in a disorderly world.

Through the volumes written about Walker and the troubles he fomented in Montréal, we begin to understand how very local controversies of the peace shaped empire. The mess in Montréal suggests that solving the problem of governance was beyond the ken of the few men sent to the fringes of the wilderness to do it. Limited experience, amities, enmities, ambitions, and vastly inadequate resources all shaped their constitutional musings. They may well have read about and visited far-flung corners of the empire, and had clear ideas about what empire was and what it should be, but in the wintry wilds of Canada they struggled to solve a very few of the problems they had before them. Close constraints of time, space, and capacity made a new kind of colonial constitution not just imaginable but desirable in Quebec. For soldier-administrators, finding a way to free themselves of a Protestant monopoly in the courts and the magistracy answered one sort of tyranny with another. Catholics were protected, soldiers gratified, and merchants thwarted by giving the king's representative in council the right to rule Quebec with the aid of Catholic subjects. Murray's refusal to call a legislature in defiance of the Proclamation of 1763 responded to immediate concerns—but his refusal eventually became imperial policy. How easy was it to cast that solution over the vast ungovernable wilderness? How much better to meet the problem of settler and trader wrongdoing by giving power to a governor-in-council instead of an unruly elected legislature? So the claustrophobic tensions of midwinter Montréal shaped an empire: small steps encompassed vast distances.

It is also worth pausing here to consider the partial nature of the jurisdiction cast by the Quebec Act over Indian Country. No one seriously suggested that it would bring Native Americans within La Paix Québécoise. The moment had yet to come when Indigenous bodies throughout the Anglosphere—from the United States to the Australian colonies—would be burdened as few other humans on earth had been with the weight of the peace. By the beginning of the twentieth century, Indigenous people would carry the burden of state power so heavily that, though they were free people, their children could be taken, their movements restricted to reservations or missions, their title to land or to tribal membership redefined or dissolved at the whim of the state, and their wages garnished in trust.[141] However, in the lead-up to the American Revolution, French Canadians, not North American Indians, carried the king's peace into the wilderness. The Quebec Act covered a huge portion of North America east of the Mississippi with a jurisdiction at once more perfect in its potential to control ungovernable traders and settlers, and more porous because, like most jurisdiction in prerevolutionary North America, it tacitly acknowledged the sovereignty of Indigenous polities.

In the end, however, the import of this moment in Canadian history lies in its enormous ramifications for empire. A long time ago, the Quebec Act was read as a conspiracy against American liberty. A great historiographical correction since 1990 has read it otherwise, as a testament to a moment of constitutional openness and toleration in the Americas.[142] However, the Quebec Act looks different again when viewed through the problem of the peace. If it was not a conspiracy against Americans, the Quebec Act was nevertheless crafted to answer the problem of exorbitant Protestant British subjecthood. Walker exemplified the problem. He was an activist, a bully, and a trader. His conflict with the military suggested the need to reset the terms of transitional justice, to prevent both the civilian-military conflict that had erupted in Montréal and the accession of anti-Catholic activists into the magistracy and a local legislature. His political activism and contempt for his French neighbors highlighted the need to redress Catholic vulnerability under the Penal Acts. Small dramas in Montréal unfolded as the great men of empire were casting about for mechanisms to reassert central authority over wayward peripheries.[143] The plural subjecthood of Canadian Catholics embodied in the act was therefore always more than an act of crown benevolence. Plural subjects were also vehicles of imperial legal ambition: their status reshaped everybody's subjecthood in defense of a new sort of colonial peace.[144] By protecting Catholics against men like Walker, the Quebec Act used Catholic legal vulnerability to build a new imperial constitution. As Hannah Weiss Muller put it, such controversies helped to define "the particular privileges the British subject might expect in a transformed empire."[145]

This new constitutional moment lasted for generations. Canada was ruled by a governor and council until 1791, when the colony was divided into Upper and Lower Canada, and each was given an elected assembly. However, when these new assemblies were elected, all legislation was subject first to review by an appointed upper house and then to gubernatorial veto. These were the last assemblies established by the British Empire until after the Canadian rebellion in 1837. From 1774 to the granting of self-government to Canada in 1841, few colonies in the empire were given fully elected legislatures. Instead, the crown colony model of the Quebec Act was transplanted throughout the empire, to govern subjects of increasing diversity—racial and confessional—in colonies conquered during the Napoleonic Wars. Government by the crown became the rule in empire. The compromises crafted in early Quebec shifted the imperial constitution fundamentally—a divergence best explored through the peace.

3

War and Peace in Trelawny Town

In July 1795 a war started with a dubious exercise of jurisdiction. In Jamaica, two Trelawny Town Maroons were tried and convicted by a bench of magistrates for stealing pigs from a poor white man in Montego Bay. They were whipped thirty-nine times by an enslaved driver before an audience of derisive slaves. Thirty-nine was the maximum number of lashes a master could give a slave.

Contemporaries argued over the importance of the whipping to the war. This was no simple act of racialized justice. Maroons were free people of color in a special treaty relationship with the crown. Some were descendants of Indigenous peoples and slaves who had lived free for more than a century. They had evaded repeated attempts by English settlers to capture them for eighty years after Jamaica's conquest, until, in 1738, the colony sued for peace. Their inclusion into the Jamaican polity thereafter was partial but also essential.

In 1739—in return for land, freedom, and relative independence— Maroons agreed to help to keep the peace in Jamaica by fighting against rebels and returning runaways. As a result they underwent a jarringly incomplete metamorphosis, from a constant beacon of freedom for slaves into a fearsome (but also "wild") force in defense of slavery. They also agreed to submit to some forms of planter jurisdiction. Under the treaty, Maroons accused of committing crimes against planters outside Maroon lands could be tried as free people of color before planter courts of Quarter Sessions. This meant that the 1795 trial of two Maroons in Montego Bay for stealing pigs from a poor white planter was within the terms of the treaty. Their whipping by and before heckling slaves, however, violated "its spirit": by tethering Maroons symbolically to slaves, most commentators agreed that the court committed an error of judgment, if not an error of law.[1] According to John Stewart, the Maroons "would not have complained" if the hog thieves had been "put . . . to death . . . but to disgrace and degrade them by a punishment inflicted only on slaves, was such an injury and insult to the whole tribe as could only be atoned for by retributive vengeance."[2] The Trelawny Maroons immediately ejected the white superintendent from their town in protest. They issued terms to the Jamaican government, demanding the reinstatement of a more popular superintendent, a review of their land holdings, and some acknowledgment that the whippings were inappropriate and would not be repeated.[3] They took a stand in 1795 to defend their symbolic independence—to remind planters that they were treaty partners of the king, not racial subordinates.

Many planters from the neighborhood sympathized with the Trelawny Maroons. Maroons may have stolen the occasional pig and abused some slaves, but some also drank with their planter-neighbors, while planters relied on others to return runaway slaves.[4] Indeed, many of the imprisoned slaves who cheered as the two Maroons were whipped in Montego Bay had been returned from Jamaica's impenetrable mountains by Trelawny men. But 1795 was not a moment for such sympathies. At the height of the Haitian Revolution, reports abounded that French revolutionaries (some of whom had entered Jamaica as refugees) were plotting with Maroons to incite slave rebellion.[5] In this context, the very existence of Maroons was an affront to the peace, and their rejection of the Trelawny superintendent an intolerable threat to local order.

To protect the peace, Alexander Lindsay, Earl of Balcarres and lieutenant governor of Jamaica, confected a war. With the concurrence of the legislature, he declared martial law and diverted 1,000 imperial troops who were on their way to nearby Saint-Domingue to Montego Bay.[6] He had the captains of the town arrested as they passed through St. Ann's Bay on the way to make terms with the government. Every Maroon in Trelawny Town was ordered to submit their arms to colonial officials. The Maroons responded by setting fire to their town and taking to the hills. This, Balcarres declared, was an act of war. In truth, the war was waged by the governor, to set new terms for all Maroons in the uneasy colonial peace subsisting in the shadow of revolution. The conflict lasted five months and ended when the governor and legislature collaborated in the expulsion of the Trelawny Maroons from the island.

What can a war tell us about the king's colonial peace? This moment—and the fragile order of eighteenth-century colonial Jamaica—lays bare the exaggerated and increasing role played by the crown in keeping the peace in this quintessential slave colony. This claim may seem jarring. According to many, the king had long ago abdicated his responsibilities to protect enslaved subjects in Jamaica: he had delegated so much power to slave owners that slaves were simply not protected by law. Trevor Burnard describes Jamaica as a colony "at war" with its slaves—a place where there could be no peace.[7] In his *Historical Survey of the French Colony in the Island of Saint*

Domingue, Jamaican apologist Bryan Edwards suggested that slave orders could not be built on law at all. Rather, "in countries where slavery is established, the leading principle on which government is supported, is *fear;* or a sense that absolute coercive necessity, which, leaving no choice of action, supersedes all question of *right.*"[8]

The eighteenth-century commentator Edward Long described the situation quite differently. He thought fear underpinned all legal codes, the goal of which was to keep lesser men in order. Terror was not incommensurable with government by law.[9] Legal historians have agreed. Diane Paton and Elsa Goveia argue that law mattered enormously to peacekeeping in Jamaica.[10] This law, however, was peculiar. The garish gestures that kept slaves at peace in places like Jamaica were not so much *defined* as *permitted* by law: Jamaican slave law defined the island's peace according to what masters could not do to slaves rather than what they could. Yet, in the end, the vast license of slave owners was a delegated jurisdiction that the crown increasingly regulated yet sat in constant readiness to defend. In this context, war is not quite the right metaphor, but it is close. The king's peace in Jamaica was real, but it was uncivil.[11]

That incivility transformed everybody's subjecthood. Local legislation gave the king's constables and courts unusual and obnoxious powers to curtail the movement and civil rights of free Black subjects in an effort to keep slaves in order, creating an order (endlessly replicated) in which the privileges of free Britons depended on their skin color. Such a peace also transformed white men's relationship with the crown. Their license as masters altered their subjecthood, burdening it with evil that was too often experienced as privilege. More importantly, their constant peril made Jamaican masters uniquely dependent on deployments of imperial military power: Jamaica's was a peculiarly martial order.[12] This dependence was complicated, to be sure. As a colony conquered during the Stuart restoration, Jamaica fought long and hard against crown ambitions to keep a new kind of peace in the early eighteenth century.[13] That struggle did not recede with time. Indeed, it amplified during the American Revolution, when Jamaica's legislature fought bitterly with its governors and the imperial ministry to both protect and expand its control of internal legislation and defense. But struggles to defend Jamaica's legislature from crown ambition unfolded in the shadow of slave rebellion and Maroon indomitability. In matters of internal order and island defense, the pugnacity of Jamaica's legislature and the rights-claims of white slaveholders resolved increasingly into awkward compromise. Jamaica's legislature paid dearly to keep more imperial troops on hand and spread them throughout the island, and though the legislature won a significant advisory role in matters of defense, it did so by acquiescing more frequently than any self-governing colony in gubernatorial declarations of martial law.[14] The complicity of the legislature in martial peacekeeping reached its apotheosis during the second Maroon War.

The significance of Jamaica's vulnerability was not lost on metropolitan critics of slavery. James Stephen Sr. argued that slavery's dependence on the violence of masters and the king's army demonstrated the failure of slaveholder self-rule and the need for crown government in Trinidad.[15] More importantly, white Jamaican planters demonstrated a willingness to trade liberties for order that had not been shared by rebellious subjects in the mainland colonies. Planter malleability and brutality together showed that more than water separated the imperial center from colonial peripheries in the Caribbean and beyond. The transformations of subjecthood wrought by the uncivil slave peace—like the vulnerability of Canadians—suggested the plausibility of a new imperial order.

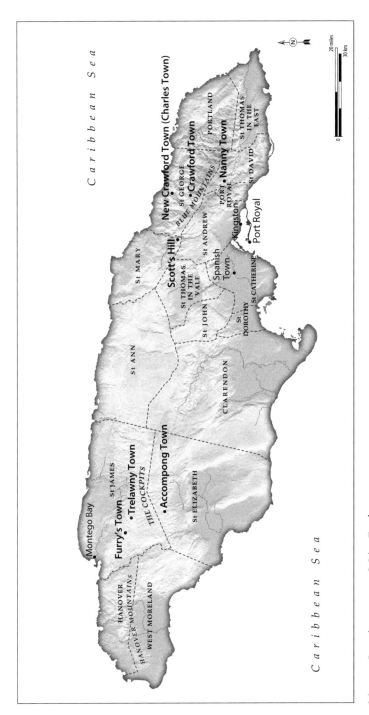

Caribbean Sea

Caribbean Sea

Montego Bay

HANOVER
MOUNTAINS

HANOVER

WEST MORELAND

Furry's Town

St JAMES

Trelawny Town

THE COCKPITS

Accompong Town

St ELIZABETH

St ANN

CLARENDON

St MARY

St THOMAS
IN THE
VALE

St JOHN

St
DOROTHY

St CATHERINE

Spanish
Town

St ANDREW

St GEORGE

Scott's Hill

New Crawford Town (Charles Town)

Crawford Town

BLUE MOUNTAINS

PORTLAND

Nanny Town

ST THOMAS
IN THE
EAST

PORT
ROYAL

St DAVID'

Kingston

Port Royal

N

20 miles

30 km

0

Map 3.1 Jamaica, c. 1790. © Lisa Ford

This was not the only lesson that Jamaica taught to empire. Martial law entered the vernacular of colonial administration throughout the British Empire after the end of the Napoleonic Wars, but the constitutional line between civil and military order had long been crossed in Britain's wealthiest eighteenth-century slave colony. That slippage is exemplified by the Maroons. Kept constantly under arms and groomed to deliver brutal justice on the orders of the crown, their fragile complicity balanced precariously on the boundary of peace and rebellion. Meanwhile, the brutality of the war against them in 1795 prompted a transatlantic debate about the balance between the king's peace and the king's honor in martial Jamaica. In treaty and defeat, Maroons served as a symbol of the impossible compromise of peacekeeping in a slave colony. The impossible slave peace, in turn, exemplified the incommensurability of colonial and metropolitan order and the hopeless dependence of extractive empire on state-sponsored violence.

An Uncivil Peace

Peace was fragile in Jamaica for many reasons. The first was geopolitics: Jamaica could have no peace because it was so often at war. Nestled between the Spanish main, Cuba, and Saint-Domingue, Jamaica had long been surrounded by imperial rivals, and Britain spent much of the eighteenth century at war with one or more of them. It had faced invasion from France and Spain as recently as 1782.[16] When the Maroon conflict erupted, however, Jamaica's most threatening neighbor was not an empire, but a would-be republic of emancipated slaves. In 1791 Saint-Domingue's free Black people and slaves began a generation-long fight for freedom. Theirs would become the first and only successful slave rebellion in the Caribbean.

Even as Balcarres declared martial law to fight the Maroons, British invaders were being picked off one by one in Haiti.[17]

Peace was also fragile in Jamaica because of its terrain. Much of the island was impenetrable. Vaulting mountains bounded plantation lands in the east. In the center and west of the island near Trelawney Town, eroded limestone ranges called "the cockpits" formed an endless maze of forested peaks and troughs, riddled with caves whose thin shells collapsed at the barest contact. From the foundation of the first Spanish slave colony in 1494, the mountains provided a refuge for Taino Indians and slaves. So until Maroons signed their peace treaties with British Jamaica in 1739, slave rebellion was not sporadic, it was perpetual. It threatened the very existence of the tiny British population for eighty years after invasion in 1655.[18] It was this eighty-year resistance—their very ungovernability—that made Maroons essential to Jamaica's peace. After the treaties of 1739, Maroons settled in towns on the perimeters of the mountains, cutting off access for escaping slaves. Only Maroons knew the mountains and cockpits well enough to police them, knowledge born of never-quelled rebellion. Their communities embodied an impasse both literal and figurative.

Peace would have been fragile in any case, because the island was a "demographic disaster" that teetered on the edge of ruin.[19] People went to Jamaica to die. The average white immigrant lived for just twelve years after landing on the island.[20] By the early nineteenth century, sickly hemmed-in masters had to keep twelve times their number in subjection.[21] The slave population peaked in 1808 at 354,000—compared to 25,000 whites and as many free Black people.[22] Slave mortality was also appalling. For every two slaves living in Jamaica in 1808, five were imported. Rebellion made more sense here than it might have on the American mainland, where slaves had always lived longer and, by the late eighteenth century, had started to have children enough to replace themselves. The result was an explosive cocktail: a tiny minority of white men tyrannized a vast slave majority who remembered freedom and knew that life in Jamaica was cheap.[23]

Every British colony dependent on slave labor went to extraordinary lengths to keep slaves at peace, but the stakes were nowhere higher than in Jamaica. So it should not be surprising that, after importing its first slave code from Barbados in 1664, Jamaica's legislature exported the law of slavery to the mainland perfected.[24] From 1684, Jamaica's key innovations were to simplify the sale, purchase, and encumbrance of slave property and to convert Barbados's distinction between "Christian" and "Negro" into a color-based taxonomy: slave, free negro, and white.[25] The real work of the Jamaican codes, however, was to prevent rebellion—work that gave extraordinary latitude to the crown-appointed judiciary and masters alike. Indeed, the 1696 slave code was passed explicitly to avert "the often Insurrections and Rebellions of the Slaves within this Island."[26] A special, slave court exercising summary jurisdiction managed serious slave offenses, although in times of rebellion slaves might also be tried by courts-martial, or be summarily executed.[27] The slave court could sentence slaves in any state of rebellion, real or imagined, to death by hanging, burning, or dismemberment (or whatever means "seem most convenient"), depending on their crime. Dismemberment by masters was outlawed in 1717, but was removed as a court sentence only by the slave code of 1781.[28] Death was mandated for any slave who struck a "white Person" and who might "compass or imagine the Death of any white Person."[29] Banishment might do for a runaway, though they would be deemed to be in rebellion if they stayed at large for too long. For obvious reasons it was deemed to be an unacceptable imposition on masters' property rights to kill or transport every slave involved in such activities. When groups were involved, the act allowed judges to single out one or more of their number for exemplary punishment. It is telling that Long defended the license bequeathed by the slave code to "judges" as being "precisely adopted from the law-martial."[30]

Paton notes that slave crimes, excepting theft and rebellion, were rarely tried in slave courts. Running away was usually privately punished, unless the slave in question was absent for more than six months. For lesser wrongs, planters opted into the court system strategically to punish other people's slaves or to bolster flagging authority on their own estates. Because the state compensated masters for loss of property, trial provided a relatively cheap mechanism for ridding oneself of difficult slaves.[31] Paton's survey of 162 cases recorded by the St. Andrew's slave court between 1746 and 1782 shows that convictions were much higher (75.7 per cent) than in other criminal courts and the court rarely acquitted slaves charged with violence against white people. When it found slaves guilty of such crimes, the court dispensed brutal justice: for killing Sir Edward Seymour in 1774, Dick was "hung up in body chains till he be dead," while Anthony was "staked down and made fast to the ground and burnt till he be dead."[32] Less gruesome deaths were also matters of stark display. Plantation manager Thomas Thistlewood noted in passing that, after his slave was executed for encouraging "two boys" to run away, he lodged the man's head on a spike "in the home pasture."[33]

The 1781 Code included additional obligations on masters and managers to prevent slave insurrection, first legislated in the aftermath of Tacky's Rebellion.[34] Their first duty was to ensure that no slave left or entered their plantation without a pass, on pain of whipping and

a hefty fine for noncompliance. Even heavier fines and "severe" corporal punishment attached to free Black people who harbored runaways or tried to smuggle slaves off the island. Masters were required to search slave premises fortnightly for arms, to allow their
own properties to be searched at will under warrant from a justice of the peace, and to join search parties when required to do so
by local magistrates. Everyone was enjoined to break up slave
gatherings and to police the beating of drums (used by Maroons and
slaves to communicate). The code stipulated that the capture and
return of runaways would be rewarded, even if the captor were a
slave, though slave catchers had to pay fines if runaways died in their
custody. Freemen or servants who killed or captured rebellious
slaves would be given forty shillings and a serge coat for their trouble.
No man would be held accountable for killing a slave found "at
night . . . out of his Owners Ground." Finally, a very few provisions
pertained to the care of slaves: masters were required to instruct
slaves in religion and to clothe, provide provision grounds for, and
feed them, subject to mild fines. Such injunctions did not prevent
masters from allowing 15,000 slaves to starve to death when four
hurricanes hit Jamaica between 1780-1786.[35]

The code had precious little to say about keeping the everyday
peace. This was so because Jamaica's peace rested on chattel property. In deference to their property rights, the legislature delegated
enormous jurisdiction to slave owners. While most modern penal
legislation prescribes punishments for carefully defined wrongs,
Jamaica's slave code mentioned only rebellion, murder, theft, violence against white people, and unauthorized mobility. Masters and
their delegates were left to decide which additional behaviors war-
ranted punishment—such wrongs might include defiance, clumsi-
ness, or cheek. As Paton points out, the 1664 act enjoined slave-

holders to manage "all small . . . misdemeanours" themselves, even if they were committed against third parties.[36] A "common Whipman" was available for hire in many parishes to help planters keep order. The codes set horrifyingly broad limits on the kinds of punishments that masters could impose without the aid of a magistrate. For example, the 1696 slave code asked, not if a master could kill his slave, but in what circumstances. It stipulated that anyone who killed a slave "willingly, wantonly, or bloody-mindedly" should be convicted of a felony on the first offense, but be given the benefit of clergy. Only a second conviction would be for murder.[37] "Willingly, wantonly, or bloody-mindedly" proved to be a narrow category; no Jamaican was executed for killing slaves in the eighteenth century, though at least one was convicted.[38]

The 1781 code added new limits to masters' license. As a concession to the sudden and enormous surge of metropolitan hostility to the slave trade and slave owners, it brought more punishment under the direct supervision of the crown.[39] After 1781, masters could only flog a slave thirty-nine times without the assistance of a magistrate, but the code did not link that punishment to any crime. Nor did the new code attempt to define or limit other brutalities. Thomas Thistlewood's diary shows in ghastly detail that masters had more means than the whip to punish a slave. Thistlewood not only whipped "nearly two thirds of the men and half of the women" on the first estate he managed in Jamaica, he routinely augmented whippings by rubbing lash wounds with lime and salt to increase the pain, or covering wounds in molasses and chaining wounded slaves outside to be attacked by insects. He would force slaves to defecate in the mouth of malefactors and tape their mouths closed for hours afterward. And, of course, he had nonconsensual sex with almost every woman on his estates, although he only occasionally described these rapes as punishment.[40] One would like to think Thistlewood was unusually cruel, but his diary suggests that his friends were worse. Indeed, it seems that brutality toward slaves only increased in the decades after the Seven Years' War.[41] The scale of punishment Thistlewood meted out suggests more than evil, however. It documents the details of order in Jamaica—showing *his* sense, at least, that it was a very difficult thing indeed to keep slaves peacefully at their work.[42]

Late eighteenth-century additions to the slave code marked a subtle shift in the balance of jurisdiction in Jamaica that escalated in the nineteenth century. Under enormous pressure from anti-slavery activists, self-governing Caribbean colonies expanded the protective function of their courts, taking more and more peace-keeping functions from masters and lodging them in the hands of magistrates and the state. But this shift was not all about metro-politan activism. An earlier marker of masters' increasing reliance on the state to discipline slaves was the building of jails on Jamaica. The island had just one site of incarceration in 1759 and nineteen by 1790. Masters sent their slaves to jail as an additional or alterna-tive mode of discipline.[43] State participation in slave discipline was also evident in a marked uptick of municipal policing laws after 1770, a proliferation that increased in pace during and after the Hai-tian Revolution.[44] Long attributed improved order in Spanish Town in 1774 to its being "partly under a civil and partly military police; a kind of *divisum imperium.*" While civilian magistrates and constables managed the town by day, "centinels . . . challenge all pas-sengers" at night "as in a regular garrison."[45]

Long's musings point to a formidable pillar of the Jamaican peace—its deep dependence on the king's army. Though they did not always do so gracefully, Jamaicans spent more money than anyone else in the empire on military peacekeeping.[46] Between 60 and 75 percent of taxes gathered by the legislature to 1802 were spent subsidizing the imperial military and internal police. As Aaron Graham has shown, these modes of expenditure cannot be clearly disaggregated. Imperial soldiers were integral to peacekeeping on the island. So much is clear from the fact that, after the Maroon Treaties of 1739 and Tacky's Rebellion in 1760, Jamaican taxpayers martialized the landscape, building barracks so that imperial troops (sponsored by the legislature) could be posted around the island. This policy was pursued at great cost to the soldiers' health and to the efficacy of the troops in imperial defense.[47] Long readily assured his London readers that "the men of property in this island pay an ample contribution" to maintain imperial troops, "in order that it may be protected, not so much from French or Spaniards, as against the machinations of the many thousand slaves."[48] Though they all argued ceaselessly and bitterly about legislative privileges and crown prerogatives, Jamaicans and Bostonians had very different understandings of the king's power to keep the colonial peace.[49]

This is nowhere clearer than in Jamaica's peculiar tolerance for martial law. As noted, martial law was the object of fierce dispute in England throughout the seventeenth century. Its abuse by Tudors and Stuarts in peacetime prompted Parliament to pass the Petition of Right in 1628, which sought to limit the crown's capacity to declare martial law to times of rebellion. This unstable settlement collapsed almost immediately during the civil war, but was revived successfully to prevent declarations of martial law on "English soil" and in most colonies for much of the eighteenth century.[50] Colonial governors continued to be given broad powers to declare martial law: from the 1660s, Jamaican governors had the power (in council) to declare martial law in war, in rebellion, or when the courts closed.[51] What stood Jamaica apart is that governors used that power often, without the cover of war or rebellion. They closed the courts and declared martial law to achieve ends as diverse as conscripting free and slave labor to build fortifications, protecting militia men from debt suits, and policing piracy.[52]

Such ploys were occasionally contested. Nevertheless, the querulous Jamaican legislature acted repeatedly and increasingly to underwrite declarations of martial law. Recognizing the peculiar jeopardy of the island, the legislature gave the governor "extensive martial law powers for the governance of the militia" from 1681.[53] This first act included a power to declare martial law "upon every apprehension and appearance of public danger or invasion," a provision that enabled the governor not only to call the militia but to oblige "Every body without distinction . . . to take up Arms."[54] As the number of slaves rapidly increased, and the state ramped up its efforts to defeat Maroons, the few elite Jamaicans who controlled local governance took a greater role in martial law's use and regulation.[55] From the 1730s the legislature took to passing acts authorizing martial law and setting its terms by devising local articles of war and securing a say in councils of war.[56]

Frederick Spurdle read this shift as a diminution of crown power in the colony.[57] This was not the case. Mirroring parliamentary involvement in suspensions of habeas corpus in the metropole (as Paul Halliday has described it), Jamaica's legislature diminished the personal discretion of the governor but empowered the crown.[58] From 1681 to 1800, seventeen acts, fifteen of them passed during or after Tacky's Rebellion in 1760, regulated declarations of martial law by the governor-in-council.[59] This is just a sample of its use in the island: we know, for example, that martial law was called casually at

Christmas for extra vigilance against slaves on holiday.[60] Martial law was called for a year during the second Maroon War, closing the civil courts to the annoyance of the agents of creditors prowling the island in the hope of collecting debts.[61] It formed an integral part of Jamaica's legal landscape that would have been unthinkable on the eighteenth-century American mainland or in Georgian Britain. By the time Jamaican attorney general Alexander Heslop came to reflect on the Morant Bay Rebellion in 1866, he could say with only a little inaccuracy that "from the time of the actual settlement of [Jamaica] as a British possession, there never has been a day during which martial law, or the power of declaring martial law, has not been a normal provision of the statute book."[62]

Maroons and rebellious slaves were not the only or even the main target of martial law in eighteenth-century Jamaica. In the late seventeenth century, it had been used to force planters to provide lodgings and resources for imperial troops needed to defend the island against invasion.[63] From the mid-eighteenth century, martial law targeted planters hesitating to support troops, and low-status white men and free people of color who shirked their obligations to muster for the militia.[64] So much was clear in 1760, when Jamaica faced its most serious slave uprising, Tacky's Rebellion. In early April sixteen planters were killed in St. Mary's Parish, but "no sooner" was that uprising "happily quelled" when another erupted in Saint Thomas, then on several estates in Westmoreland.[65] Trouble was brewing in the Leeward Parishes in early June. The assembly requested that martial law be proclaimed in the leeward potions of the island in September.[66] It was clear by then that there had been an island-wide slave conspiracy, which Tacky had botched by starting too early: it must have galled survivors that the rebellion was named for him.[67] Troops from the 49th and 74th regiments and Maroons, honoring their treaty, were quickly dispatched to meet the threat.[68] But white civilians and other free people of color were not so easily mobilized. Lieutenant Governor Moore called martial law unwillingly: "nothing but the Necessity . . . of sending the Different Corps of the Militia to the Assistance of that part of the Country, could have induced him to Declare Martial Law" in April.[69] And he did so for just a few weeks. When trouble flared again in May and June, "the Gentleman of the Leeward Parishes . . . requested that Martial Law might be proclaimed [again], that the Discipline of the Militia might be enforc'd and their hands strengthen'd."[70]

After the rebellion was quelled, martial law was used to manage a different demographic. The state set about purging "great numbers of Negroes," burning some slowly, hanging others in cages or by rope until they died, and transporting more still from the island.[71] This state-sponsored horror was easier and cheaper under courts-martial. But, again, slaves were not the only targets. Though the comparison is unseemly, in executing slaves by the thousands, the governor in chief hurt bank accounts as well as slaves. The 1696 slave code had explicitly enjoined courts to execute very few rebellious slaves after insurrection, to preserve property in the defense of a commercial peace. This norm was a strong one. In 1760 planters stood to lose a great deal of money, and some acted to thwart the vengeance of the state. Moore complained, "Many Owners and Agents of Plantations with a view of secreting their Negroes from Punishment have made false returns of their Absentees which has made it impossible to obtain a true list of all who were engaged in the Westmoreland Rebellion, but no returns to me have made their number less than Nine hundred or more than Ten hundred and fifty."[72] When the state created a spectacle of violence so exorbitant that planters themselves sought to resist it by concealing slaves, their right to resist search without warrant and their license to punish or pardon slaves became the targets of martial law.

If the property and privileges of white masters were transformed by slavery, Jamaica's slave peace had far greater impact on the subjecthood of free Black people in the colony, many of whom were the progeny of slave owners and white middlemen in the island. As this group grew, so did attempts to limit its social and economic mobility.[73] From 1711, Jamaica passed laws preventing free people of color from "voting or holding public office, irrespective of property qualifications; driving coaches, navigating boats, or holding supervisory positions on estates; [and] wearing arms, except during periods of active militia duty." It was controversial in the early eighteenth century to argue that a propertied, free Black man could not vote, as legal counsel to the Board of Trade pointed out in 1724.[74] But Jamaica went further in an *Act for the better regulating slaves, and rendering free negroes and free mulattoes more useful* (1730). This act directly linked free Black subordination to keeping the peace, mandating that they had to wear badges denoting racial status, subjecting them to special militia mobilization rules, and stipulating that they could neither trade near town nor hire white servants. The act was disallowed, but it set important precedents, picked up in the aftermath of Tacky's Rebellion, when near disaster prompted Jamaica's legislature to articulate the complicated logic of racial subordination with startling clarity.[75]

In 1762 Jamaica passed a bill cracking down on slave assemblies and plantation discipline, while requiring "all free negroes, mulattoes, or Indians, to register their names in the vestry-books of the respective parishes in this island." It also required free Black people to carry proof of their freedom at all times to ease the policing of slave movement on the island (a similar requirement was imposed on white people in New South Wales seventy years later). The very color of their skin threatened the limits placed on slave mobility, and therefore the peace. It also placed free Black people's freedom in constant jeopardy. To be found without proof of freedom was to risk being declared a slave. The act also mandated that free Black people "convicted of concealing, enticing, entertaining, or sending off the island, any fugitive, rebellious, or other slave . . . forfeit their freedom, be sold, and banished."[76] The legislature even passed controversial laws "to restrain exorbitant Grants to Negroes," fearing that the social mobility afforded to mixed-race children, freed and enriched by their by white fathers, would undermine Jamaica's peace, which "depends upon keeping up a distinction of Colour."[77]

In all, keeping the peace in Jamaica was an uncivil and encompassing business, transforming everyone's relationship with the crown. The control of African slaves by a tiny white minority imbued masters with wide jurisdiction but heavy fiscal and martial obligations. Free Black Jamaicans, many of them children of planters, also suffered special burdens. They could not trade freely, live where they chose to, vote, or travel without proof of their freedom. They were conscripted into the most onerous militia roles and subjected to terrible punishments for collusion with slaves. Everyone orbited around the vast slave majority, whose forced quiescence defined the Jamaican constitution—a peace that was not only uncivil, but also increasingly martial in character.

War and Peace

Nothing embodied the fragility and incivility of peace in Jamaica more than the Maroon treaties of 1739. This was so, first and foremost, because the treaties started with planter defeat.[78] British settlers had been trying to conquer Maroons since they invaded in 1655. Eighty years later, Maroon numbers and planter-maroon conflict had only increased, fed by a steady stream of escaped slaves. In 1730 the Jamaican governor convinced the imperial army to send two regiments to bring peace to the island by waging war. However, this campaign cost the colony £240,000 and was marked chiefly by embarrassing routs. Even when they found Maroon towns hidden in the mountains and cockpits, troops killed and captured few of their enemies. It would not do to have the king's troops humiliated by escaped slaves, so, by 1734, colony and metropole contemplated saving face by signing treaties. Still, it took years to broker peace.[79] Treaties were signed between the Maroons and the crown between April and June of 1739—a lasting symbol of planter impotence.

The Maroon treaties spoke of "peace and friendship" and promised "forever hereafter" that Maroons who had not escaped from slavery in the last two years would live in "a perfect state of freedom and liberty." This was an overstatement because the treaties brimmed with limits on Maroon freedoms. They gave Maroon leaders some powers of self-government: namely, to "inflict any punishment they think proper for crimes committed by their men among themselves." However, that jurisdiction did not extend to capital punishment.[80] As the power to legitimately kill subjects is the ultimate act of sovereignty, this last treaty term carried a marked concession, unusual in contemporary treaties signed nearby in North America.[81] The treaties also required that Maroons allow two white men to live among them, and, most importantly perhaps, that they allow the Jamaican governor to control Maroon succession (that is, to choose Maroon captains after the treaty-generation's demise).

The treaties curtailed Maroon "freedom and liberty" in other ways too. They granted Maroons lands but prescribed what they could grow. This included livestock and cash crops but not sugar, produce they could sell at market only with the license of a magistrate. The treaties stipulated that Maroons could supplement their food source by hunting, but not within three miles of settlements. They also required that Maroons make themselves physically vulnerable by cutting "open, large and convenient roads" to their towns. The key concession, for our purposes, was about peacekeeping. Maroons promised solemnly to capture runaways and defend the island against invasion or insurrection.[82]

Like many early modern treaties, these agreements meant different things to different people. For Maroons, to this day, the Treaty is a "sacred charter" that cannot be altered. In the 1790s, one Maroon described the treaty thus: "The treaty is not just any treaty . . . It was signed in human blood. To break that treaty they could not just tear up a paper; they would have to tear up human bodies. It just could not happen that the treaty could be broken."[83] In 1991, Maroon Geretius McKenzie made the same point: "De treaty mek a Peace Cave. De governor give Maroon a treaty. De white man cut fe-him blood, and give it to put ina rum, an give it to Kojo. And Kojo cut fe-him too. And de two of dem drink, drink de blood from each other. That is a blood treaty, sah. Can't broke."[84]

More importantly, the treaty did not incorporate Maroons fully into the slave peace. It established an alliance. Captain Cudjoe boasted soon after signing the treaty that "We [King George and I] are very good friends . . . his Majesty in England sends [rum and porter] to me yearly."[85] In Cudjoe's view, George II was an equal, or perhaps even a tributary. Two hundred twenty years later, Maroon colonel Ernest Dower pointed out that the treaties were signed because the Maroons "were giving so much trouble" so "were granted certain privileges." Key among these was "that they are to remain as free people."[86] From this perspective, the whippings in 1795 breached the spirit of the treaty because they denied Maroon independence from the state and, more importantly, humiliated them in front of slaves. The pact between Maroons and George II, in their view, promised freedom and autonomy in return for helping the king to keep his peace. "You are our Tattas (that is, Fathers), we are your children; our situation, and the superiority we have in this country, we derive from our connexion with you; but when we do the duty required of us for these advantages, do not subject us to insult and humiliation from the very people to whom we are set in opposition."[87] The Maroon peace here was uncivil because it did not bring Maroons into the polity, or make them "domesticated" subjects of the king. Instead the treaty turned former rebels into allied, martial peacekeepers—symbols of the tenuous peace in the empire's most prosperous colony. The Maroon peace was the suspension of war, a suspension that solemnified war's imminence.

The legislature acknowledged Maroon independence and their special relationship with the crown by placing Maroon towns under a hybrid species of martial law. *An Act for raising Companys in the Several Negro Towns,* passed in 1744, required every town to provide a company of twelve men to drill permanently under the supervision of Maroon officers but "be Commanded by a white man such as his Excellency the Governor or the Commander in Chief for the time being shall appoint." Men under arms would be disciplined by Jamaican articles of war (but were also paid as soldiers and given special rewards for catching slaves).[88] This arrangement likely built on Maroon political mores. By 1739 Maroon societies had been formed and reformed not only through eighty years of conflict with British slave owners, but also through endemic ethnic rivalries among themselves.[89] By all accounts theirs was a martial society, male dominated and constantly prepared for fight or flight.[90] However much it built on Maroon culture, the 1744 act reshaped this military society into something that looked a lot like a perennially mobilized militia.

In another act passed on the same day, the House of Assembly complained that "disorders frequently happen in the several Negro Towns . . . for want of Authority in the Chiefs or Commanding Officers of the Negroes to keep up a proper Command over the rest." This lack of authority had led to "disturbances . . . lately raised by some Turbulent and Disorderly negroes in Crawford and Nanny Towns who had received and Entertained a Negro belonging to Accompongs Town and in a Riotous manner detained and protected the said Negro in manifest Contempt of His Excellency the Governor's orders." The house demanded that "an exact discipline be observed . . . that all Disorders, Tumults, and disturbances amongst them be Suppressed on their first appearances, and the Authors and Abettors of them brought to speedy Punishment."[91] Maroon leaders' dwindling authority was exacerbated by the fact that superintendents lacked "Legal Power to Punish" refractory townsfolk. So the act subjected Maroons "who shall disobey his Excellency the Governor's Orders or excite others to do the same or shall excite cause or joyn in any disorder Tumult or Disturbance tending to break the Peace and good order" to trial and summary punishment to be "Inflicted by the White men residing in the Town . . . and four of the negroes" including the "Chief or Commanding Officer." This body commissioned by the governor or commander in chief was effectively a court-martial.[92] Hybrid martial law, here, acknowledged some rudiments of self-government, but effectively placed everyone in Maroon towns under the authority of the crown. This was a significant transformation of Maroon legal status as imagined by the treaty.

But martial law was not the most striking attempt in the act to bring Maroons closer to subjecthood. *An Act for the better Order and Government of the Negroes* gave planter justices and freeholders concurrent jurisdiction to keep the peace in and out of Maroon towns, giving them power to try Maroon peace-breakers "as free Negroes are usually Tryed and Punish[ed]." It followed up with a remarkable set of limitations on Maroon privileges, not contemplated by the treaty, but that followed, the legislature claimed, from the fact that Maroons had "surrendered." It declared that slaves purchased by Maroons would be forfeited. While the treaties merely stipulated that Maroons should not hunt within three miles of towns and plantations, this act required Maroons to have passes from their superintendent to leave their lands for more than seven days. The act suggested that Maroons "have rambled about in the several Parishes of this Island and been harboured and Concealed in divers Places" where they created "Factions and Disputes" among slaves, threatening the "Quiet and Security of the Island." Henceforth, unauthorized Maroon mobility was a crime, punishable by two justices and three freeholders, who could sentence malefactors to "such a number of Lashes on his Bare Back as to them shall seem Convenient not exceeding thirty-nine" for the first offense, and transportation and sale off the island for the second.[93]

These parts of the law were honored in breach because Jamaica's uncivil peace was not served by its enforcement. Maroons' "wildness"—their separation from the state—was key to their efficacy as symbols and agents of order. This was a matter of practicality: Windward Maroons knew the mountains and Leeward Maroons, the cockpits. Only they could police the terrain that had underwritten their own freedom for nearly a century. In this context, Maroon visibility served as a powerful reminder of their formidable capacity to police the interior for the crown. Therefore, it was in the planters' interest that Maroons remain mobile and visible agents of a martial peace, scouring the island in conspicuous finery. Thistlewood described an encounter with a Maroon in 1751, wearing "a ruffled shirt, blue broad cloth coat, scarlet cuff to his sleeves, gold buttons ... with white cap, and black hat, white linen breeches puffed at the rims."[94] Dallas described chiefs dressed in "a kind of regimentals ... some old military coat finely laced ... with ... a ruffled shirt, linen waistcoat and trousers, and a laced hat."[95] Sartorial display was as good as a billboard, conveying an important message about order on the island. Maroons' distinctive dress coupled with their mobility, reminded slaves that the mountains and cockpits were no longer a safe place to flee.

Maroon violence also mattered. Edward Long described a display of ferocity performed by Trelawny Town Maroons for Governor Lyttelton in 1764 that both honored the treaty and menaced the planter state. To the sound of a trumpet crafted from a cow horn, Trelawny Maroons

> all joined in a most hideous yell, or war-hoop, and bounded into action. With amazing agility ... They fire stooping almost to the very ground; and no sooner is their piece discharged, than they throw themselves into a thousand antic gestures, and tumble over and over, so as to be continually shifting their place; the intention of which is, to elude the shot, as well as to deceive the aim of their adversaries ... When this part of their exercise was over, they drew their swords; and, winding their horn again, they began, in wild and warlike capers, to advance towards his excellency, endeavouring to throw as much savage fury into their looks as possible ... some ... waved their rusty blades over his head, then gently laid

them upon it . . . They next brought their muskets, and piled them up in heaps at his feet, which some of them desired to kiss, and were permitted.[96]

As Kathleen Wilson noted, such a display "enacted the threat and the privilege that worked to make the Jamaican Maroons so essential a part of the plantation complex on the island."[97] This promise of ferocious violence reinforced the peace by threatening war. Barely restrained violence could keep slaves in order; however, it was an unstable tool. Maroon violence could be turned at any moment against the king. This threatening ambiguity became intolerable in the shadow of the Haitian Revolution. After all, Haiti was only 120 miles away.[98] Jamaica had taken in too many refugees from Saint-Domingue for the liking of newly appointed Lieutenant Governor Balcarres: "The Island," said he, "Swarmed with Multitudes of French People of Color . . . introduced to raise an insurrection."[99] No matter their politics, the refugee population embodied the reality of successful slave rebellion on a nearby sugar isle. Rumors swirled that French refugees had been visiting Maroon towns, preparing them to betray the king. In 1795 Balcarres was convinced that the Trelawny Maroons rebelled on French orders, because he had heard that Frenchmen released from prison hulks had joined the Maroons, Frenchmen sheltered in Nanny Town, and a free man of color had been traveling the island with French papers. Most of these reports were whispers overheard in market towns, passed on by slaves and written down by worried planters. Though one captured Frenchman did confess to recruiting free people of color and Maroons in Trelawny Town, he later recanted his testimony.[100] Through the prism of rumor, a small dispute in Trelawny Town over a whipping looked, to Balcarres, like an attack on sovereignty.

He called a council of war, and on their advice declared martial law on August 2 and issued an ultimatum to the Trelawny Maroons. When Trelawny Maroons evicted their unpopular superintendent and threatened the Montego Bay magistrates, Balcarres accused them of "unprovoked, ungrateful, and most dangerous rebellion," and of endeavoring "to massacre" their superintendent. He proclaimed "a reward for your heads" if every Maroon capable of bearing arms did not submit to "his Majesty's mercy" in Montego Bay by August 13.[101] Ignoring the promising efforts of Leeward planters to broker peace, he arrested the treaty party sent to negotiate on the town's behalf. He later complained that planters from "the Parishes of St. James's and Trelawny" refused to cooperate with the war effort, forming "an Imperium in Imperio."[102]

Trelawny Maroons responded by setting fire to their town and retreating into the cockpits, recasting their lawless mobility from a boon to planters into a powerful reminder that they had never been conquered and could not be contained. In December 1795, Balcarres warned the Duke of Portland that their knowledge of terrain gave Maroons "almost unbounded" capacity to do "mischief . . . and I do not see that an army of 20,000 men could prevent it."[103] This fear, for Balcarres, justified war by any means to restore the peace.[104] In the short term, the Maroons' retreat to the cockpits prompted Balcarres (in consultation with the legislature) to order one hundred bloodhounds and thirty Spanish handlers from Cuba to hunt them. Edwards later claimed that these dogs were trained to round up wild bullock and had the size and demeanor of English sheepdogs. The archive suggests instead that they were trained to hunt and attack humans. Lawrence told the governor that they were "large dogs accustomed to the hunting of runaways." On their arrival in Jamaica, they were allowed to attack a free Black woman, and had to be bay-

Fig 3.1 *The Maroons in Ambush on the Dromilly Estate in the Parish of Trelawney, Jamaica,* London 1801. By permission of The British Library, Maps. K. Top. 123.59

oneted to save the wife of a soldier—their savagery was thus usefully broadcast.[105] George Ricketts was sanguine in January 1796 that still defiant Maroons feared that they would be "worried by the Dogs & perhaps torn to pieces . . . the Spanish dogs will be the best ambassadors."[106]

The dogs got Balcarres into trouble, immediately prompting accusations that the governor had sullied the crown by supporting planter barbarity. In 1795, even as the war raged, General Macleod MP invoked Pufendorf and Grotius to argue that the use of attack dogs breached the laws of war, especially against "freemen, whom we are bound to protect."[107] Jamaica's supporters in England countered such claims by arguing that Maroon savagery required extraordinary means to restore the peace. Mr. Barham argued that Maroons are "not like an ordinary enemy, but were like a gang of robbers . . . who might seize upon some forest or mountain and commit depredations upon the country." Not only were dogs justified, he and Mr. Dent argued that whatever means were necessary should be deployed to restore the peace. Edwards and others described the Maroons' gory disembowelings and treacherous "ambuscades": such barbarities rendered them unfit for the usual rules of war. Reviewers in *The Gentleman's Magazine* argued that, "notwithstanding the fashionable doctrines of the *equality of man, these* men can . . . be viewed in no other light than in the most shocking state of ferocity and brutality, incapable of cultivation, or restraint from religion or law, we shall not wonder at the measures taken to remove such interruptions to the peace of society."[108] Barham wondered "whether it might not be justifiable to . . . root them out" entirely.[109]

Rooting them out is exactly what Balcarres and the legislature resolved to do. On December 24—just a week after the dogs arrived in the colony—representatives of the Trelawny Maroons sought terms with General Walpole. They were out of water and worried that they could not evade attack dogs. They promised to "on their knees, beg his majesty's pardon," settle wherever the legislature chose, and give up all runaways. A further "secret" treaty term promised that this place of settlement would be in Jamaica. The treaty was duly ratified by the governor and the assembly.[110] However, the Maroons were given only a few days to comply. Instead, it took a month for most of them to come in from the cockpits. Walpole assured all but the last that they would have the benefit of the treaty. But Balcarres had other ideas. In a carefully choreographed move, he left his council and legislature to decide the fate of the Maroons and their new treaty. On the basis of recommendations of a secret committee (which refused to hear evidence from General Walpole on the Maroons' behalf), the council and house voted that most of the Maroons had not abided by the treaty terms and should be deported from the island.[111] So Trelawny Maroons were boarded on a ship to Nova Scotia.[112] From Nova Scotia, they were shipped on to Sierra Leone, where a new martial order was hastily assembled to keep them at peace.

Balcarres argued that the Trelawny Maroons' removal followed on their failure to honor their old treaties as well as the new one.[113] It was also necessitated by the existential threat their acts of defiance posed to the slave peace in 1795: Balcarres asserted that "half of the Negroes on every [e]state were ready to revolt." Thus, the Trelawny protest risked not just the "lives of His Majesty's Subjects" but "Seventy Million Sterling of British Capital."[114] These factors combined to lose Trelawny Maroons their right to live independently within the king's Jamaican peace. But they had not entirely lost their claim to his protection. Jamaica's legislature preempted philanthropic criticism by promising to pay for the subsistence of Maroons in Nova Scotia, though they quibbled about the duration of that support. Advocates for Jamaica in Parliament went so far as to argue that this expulsion was in the Maroons' best interest: they would be better protected by a sympathetic governor in a colony without slaves.[115] These were powerful arguments drawn straight from the antislavery playbook. A similar brutal paternalism had underpinned the relocation of liberated American slaves to Sierra Leone not long before.

General Walpole—who resigned his commission and returned to England in disgust—felt differently. He argued in Parliament that, by abdicating his responsibility to honor the treaty and by not affording Maroons any manner of due process, Balcarres had impugned the honor of the crown. In an argument that also displayed deep ambiguity in the understanding of Maroon legal status, Walpole excoriated Balcarres for surrendering the real and symbolic power of the king to the colonial assembly: "It would be for His Majesty's Ministers to account why they had advised him to dispense with his prerogative only to the oppression of his subjects."[116]

> Here then . . . the matters rests; a people whom no force could have
> subdued, relying upon the sacred name of the King . . . have been
> duped into a surrender; condemned upon evidence ex parte, and
> banished without even the form of a trial. All the privileges of the
> accused; the examination and cross-examination of witnesses
> viva voce at the bar; the safeguard of justice, which consists in its
> publicity, transferred to the lock-up mystery of a private chamber;
> the officer who carried on and concluded the treaty by which they
> surrendered, not admitted, as an evidence, nor themselves
> suffered to make a defence against one single allegation.[117]

The king's failure to protect and to keep faith here became symbols of Jamaica's broken peace. Walpole demanded an inquiry, but the few MPs in attendance disagreed: his 1798 motion was defeated 5 to 35.[118]

For all this, the Jamaican peace remained tenuous. Other Maroon communities endured in Jamaica, hemmed in, closely watched, but still ferocious in their belief in their treaty with the king, and still necessary to the island's peace. Immediately following the Maroon War, Jamaica relieved all but Accompong Maroons of their role in capturing runaway slaves and assisting in the island's defense.[119] But these restrictions did not last. In 1804 two petitions were simultaneously presented to the Assembly, the first from the "magistrates, vestry, freeholders, and other inhabitants of Portland" and the second from the Moore Town Maroons.[120] In the first petition, "back settlers" of the parish of Portland called for Maroon aid in rounding up runaways settling near their plantations, and suggested that the "fate of the Trelawny maroons" was sufficient to "deter" other Maroons from "having a thought of entering into rebellion." The second petition, signed by Moore Town Maroons, requested that they be placed "on the same footing as they were before the rebellion of the Trelawny maroons," explaining their willingness to "conform to any law which the legislature shall think proper to make for their regulation and government" and to defend the island in any manner the governor thought fit. The petitions were referred to committee, and at the following session the House resolved to bring a bill to restore the Maroons as peacekeepers.[121] By April 1805 concern for the defense of Jamaica against France led Governor Nugent to call upon Maroons to defend the island.[122] Months later, in December 1805, the Maroon treaty obligations were permanently reinstated. Maroons remained essential to Jamaica throughout the nineteenth century. Indeed, Maroons assisted Governor Edward Eyre in his scandalous suppression of the Morant Bay rebellion in 1865.[123] Their treaty relationship with crown persists to this day.

Jamaica's uncivil peace holds a simple but powerful lesson about empire: the largest wedge in the eighteenth-century imperial constitution was fed by peripheries, not the center. Slavery and the cruel compromises made to sustain it in Jamaica exemplify the incommensurability of colonial and metropolitan order. This was not a simple position. Jamaican legislators fought long and hard to defend the privileges of white, British subjects. But at the same time they consistently agitated for special and especially obnoxious laws to keep slaves and free Black people in subjection. At first the center resisted this divergence, balking at the abject subjecthood carved out for slaves and free people of color by colonial legislation from the mid-seventeenth century. But London's complicity in race slavery allowed monstrous colonial constitutions to grow. Caribbean slavery taught empire that the king's peace was not universal, it was particular. It was bounded and crafted in place.

This message cut both ways. It was taken up in Somerset's Case in 1772, when Lord Mansfield declared that slavery and the system of laws that maintained it were so heinous that they could only be maintained by positive laws. Mansfield accepted the incivility of Jamaica's peace, built as it was on the license of bondage, but denied that Jamaica's order could exist on British soil. This meant that Jamaican masters could not call on the British state to control slaves when they visited the metropolis. The case fundamentally undermined slaveholder property rights. If slavery was the product of positive law, there was no natural right of property in slaves. Slave owners were therefore not property-bearing subjects in the same way as the country squires of Britain (though many were both at the same time).[124] Somerset also stressed the mutability of slave subjecthood: slaves became rights-bearing subjects in the king's metropolitan peace. This alchemy held another troubling claim. If the king's courts could transform slaves into subjects at home, the king and Parliament could alter everyone's subjecthood in the colonies. The king had long hesitated to do so, but times were changing.

Times were changing because the excessive license of slave masters transformed their subjecthood culturally as well as legally at the end of the eighteenth century. As Trevor Burnard has shown, by the time the Trelawny Maroons were deported, Jamaican slave owners had fallen from grace. The very laws that made them rich and powerful were woven by evangelical opponents into lurid tales of moral decay, spanning rape, torture, and profligacy. The expulsion of the Trelawny Maroons added treachery to the mix. Jamaican elites—even their aristocratic governor—were not men of their word; the legislature behaved "with that meanness of plan, that precipitancy of action, and that cowardly eagerness . . . which might have been expected in a parish vestry," illustrating "the absurdity of expecting much from Colonial Assemblies."[125] None of these traits comported with the emerging parameters of masculine subjecthood that held increasing sway in London. Indeed, the new nineteenth-century commercial gentleman was constructed against the characteristics of slave owners. This new gentleman profited from free labor; *he* was sober, faithful, and careful. James Stephen Jr., who basically ran the nineteenth-century empire from his cluttered corner of Whitehall, epitomized virtue by working himself into illness and refusing to use a mirror when he shaved.[126]

The irresponsibility of planters had a constitutional valence too: leading directly to the institution of crown government in Trinidad. Irresponsible subjects, argued James Stephen Sr., should not be entrusted with peacekeeping. He should know, having spent several hard-drinking years in the West Indies before his awakening. Planters could not legislate for the good of all, because their wealth and happiness was predicated on the misery of the vast majority.[127] The constant imminence of rebellion, epitomized by the impossibility of keeping peace in Jamaica, demonstrated the need for a revolution in government in the West Indies. According to Stephen, Trinidad should be the vanguard of a new imperial peace.

It took a while for the crown to get on board. In 1801 the Addington ministry appointed Colonel Thomas Picton to be Trinidad's first governor, with power to wield executive and legislative power in council—carefully noting that the arrangement was provisional, so as to avoid forfeiting the independent power of the crown to reconstitute the colony at will. However, understanding that this form of government was controversial, it appointed a commission of inquiry composed of Picton, Admiral Samuel Hood, and Colonel William Fullarton, to jointly rule and to inquire into the best system of law and governance for the island. That inquiry ended in a decade of litigation over Picton's many tyrannies. The island again defaulted to gubernatorial autocracy—a system that was finally confirmed in 1810 by secretary of state for war and the colonies and soon to be prime minister, Lord Liverpool. Liverpool declared that the constitution of Trinidad should not be decided by "reference to that State of Things which has existed for so many Years in the Old West India Islands." The predominance of free "people of colour" in the island, and the determination of the parliament to abolish the slave trade made it "essential . . . that, in a new Colony, the Crown should not divest Itself of its Power of Legislation." In doing so the crown could avoid the "Embarrassments which . . . might perhaps arise from the conflicting Views of the Imperial Parliament, and of a Subordinate Legislature."[128] Liverpool wanted the crown to keep the slave peace in Trinidad showcasing a better slavery, with a new ameliorated slave code, a registry to keep check on slave mortality, and, from 1822, the empire's first slave protector to ensure that masters, magistrates and courts heard and acted on slave grievances. That peace was bought with a reduction of free white privileges much more dramatic than any endured by the planters of Jamaica. And it long survived Parliament's emancipation of slaves throughout the empire in 1833. In the Age of Revolutions, the mutability of the colonial peace was redeployed vigorously by the center to remake the empire from the inside out.

Jamaica's legal divergence had imperial significance beyond the cataclysms of amelioration and emancipation, however. Caribbean slave societies also changed the world by producing the non-white subject—a status crafted in defense of slavery but that bequeathed a long and violent legacy to empire. If white colonial subjecthood was severely corroded by crown prerogative after 1774, the subjecthood of free people of color was adopted, expanded, and exported with the complicity of antislavery luminaries. When he argued that white slaveholders should not be allowed to govern themselves in the Caribbean, James Stephen Sr. was not proposing a democracy in which white and Black subjects would participate equally. In his view, liberated slaves were far less fit than white slaveholders for the privilege of self-government. This was a conclusion reached some years earlier by Stephen's brethren, the antislavery activists who peopled the Board of the Sierra Leone Company—a project launched after the American Revolution to provide a haven for the Black poor of London, American slaves liberated for fighting with the British in the Revolution, the deported Trelawny Maroons, and, eventually, slaves liberated during Britain's massive naval campaign to end the international slave trade. After administering the free Black colony for a year or two under a pastiche of putatively democratic Saxon institutions, the Board quickly decided that freed slaves were not equal to any real participation in governance. Rather, they were "most eminently found to fail . . . in the due regulation and command of their tempers," "remarkably rash and hasty in their judgments, and vehement in all the dispositions of their mind," and prone to irrational violence.[129] Soon after the arrival of the Maroons in Sierra Leone, the company convinced the crown to take over the colony and to move a garrison of troops there. Thereafter, the settlement became a fortress from which a war against slave trading was waged. As Scanlan puts it: "Military and civilian rule became virtually indistinguishable."[130]

In the end, Jamaica's most important divergence was arguably its dependence on the king's army, martial law, and martial order. Martial law was seldom called in Britain or its colonies between 1688 and 1800, though the power to declare martial law was given to governors by most colonial charters and governors' instructions. However, militarization and martial law thrived in the vast sugar plantations of the Caribbean. Martial law mattered in these places because of the fragility of a peace built on greed, domination, and violence. No peace was more fragile than Jamaica's. Martial law was called there every other year after 1760 to meet real or imagined crises. But Jamaica's fragility is nowhere more apparent than in its détente with Maroons. Their role in policing, so vital that not even the second Maroon War and the deportation of Trelawny Maroons could expunge it, demonstrates the collapse of boundaries between civil and military order in the king's most uncivil colony.

Sugar islands were not to be the only places in empire where cupidity and chauvinism bred martial order. Bhavani Raman's current work is showing that martial law emerged after 1800 as a key tool in the East India Company's efforts to preserve the peace in Madras and Bengal.[131] Martial law became a central (if contested) tool of imperial governance by the end of World War II in colonies with non-white majorities. It was a tool fit for racialized governance modeled by Jamaica long before. By suspending courts and authorizing the infliction of horrific, summary violence on colonial populations, the king's men waged war against his subjects in defense of the colonial peace.

4

A Treachery of Spies in Hooghly

In the first decade of the nineteenth century, the governor-general of Bengal and his council thought long and hard about keeping the peace. The countryside, it seemed to them, had dissolved into lawlessness. Forty years of economic disruption wrought by wrenching famine and the venality and incompetence of British administrators had dislodged millions from their land-holdings, local offices, and livelihoods.[1] In some provinces this disaster told in riot and rebellion. Elsewhere it resulted in widespread and often violent gang robbery, known as "dacoity."[2]

In 1808 the former magistrate of the 24 Parganas zillah complained that dacoits entered his jurisdiction from neighboring districts, particularly the zillah of Hooghly. Dr. John Leyden complained that the "decoits of Hooghly are so much in the habit of Committing depredation in the Tanna of Beidebatty, it seems fair to conclude that they derive encouragement from the lax state of the Police there, and from the fair prospect of impunity which it holds out to them."[3] Something needed to be done. The magistrate of Hooghly, Thomas Ernst, was understandably affronted by these allegations. He had heard of nothing of this crime wave, though he had been warned that dacoits might cross over from Nadia on the eastern bank of the Hooghly River after a government crackdown there. He had put the local chief constables (*darogahs*) on notice, threatening that he would "consider it as their fault, and a presumption of neglect on their part, if any Decoits, who absconded from Nuddea, should be found lurking within their Tannas by government." It had not occurred to him that such an injunction might encourage local police to understate the scale of crime, though he did "not pretend to say" that their accounts of the state of the peace in Hooghly could "be entirely depended upon."[4]

Ernst reported complacently that even though there had been a slight increase in prosecutions of dacoits in his jurisdiction in 1808, Hooghly was remarkably peaceful given the scattered geography of its towns, the lamentable state of its surrounds, and the understaffing of its police force. He went so far to wonder if "the Security, which the inhabitants of Hooghly have enjoyed from the inroads of Decoits in Comparison with those of the Mofussil, is, therefore, much more to be ascribed to the ignorance and vague apprehensions of the Decoits than to the strength of the police and to any resistance which could be opposed to their attempts."[5] If there was a problem with dacoity, he insisted that it was someone else's to solve. So satisfied was Ernst with the peace in Hooghly that he offered to take over the administration of justice of all territories on the western side of the Hooghly River. He alleged that pockets of territory like British-occupied Chandernagore (a French territory containing some 50,000 souls) and Baidyabati had both become places of resort for brigands. Such "insulated posts under a distinct Jurisdiction must be pernicious to the general police of the Country."[6]

Ernst and Leyden were not the only correspondents of the governor-general, however. The clerk of the criminal appeals court sent news of a petition from the town of Hooghly (after which the

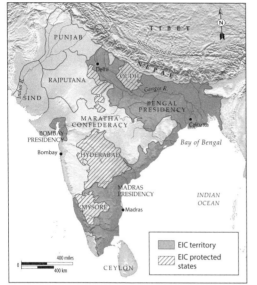

Map 4.1 Top: Territory controlled by East India Company, c. 1810. Bottom: Hooghly and environs. © Lisa Ford

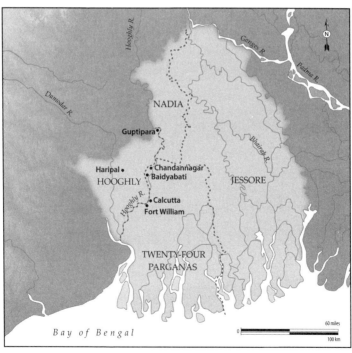

zillah was named) reporting a sensational crime in August 1808. A "Gang of 60 to 70 Men" had attempted to break into the house of Muddun Muhun Paul, a local notable who lived near the courthouse, killing a watchman in the process. When discovered, the gang escaped, robbing two houses in the course of their retreat and killing one of the owners. Local police had arrived within minutes of these crimes, but mysteriously, no one could tell them which way the robbers went. The townspeople complained that Ernst had dismissed their concerns about this crime in particular, and the security of the zillah in general. Ernst admitted that he thought local notables were culpable for any increase in crime: landholders had stopped supporting the local night watch since the establishment of the new police force in 1793, and Ernst warned that they would be vulnerable to attacks from dacoits invading from the river until they participated more actively in local peacekeeping. They should be grateful, said Ernst, that the zillah was as peaceful as it was. If they were inadequately protected it was their own fault.[7]

Town complaints and Leyden's lament were confirmed by William Blaquiere, appointed as a special magistrate to investigate dacoity in the region. He reported daily depredations in Hooghly, claiming that the district had been overrun for a year. This infestation had not resulted in recorded prosecutions because locals "connive at their Excesses from fear, or are their secret protectors."[8] Blaquiere had been responsible for "cleaning up" nearby Nadia and Jessore. His methods were both novel and apparently effective. They rested on the large-scale employment of peons supposedly drawn from criminal classes both as inferior police officers and as spies (*goindas*) charged with infiltrating dacoity gangs to discover their civilian collaborators.[9] With the aid of local magistrates, Blaquiere also liberally employed new regulations enabling preventative detention. As a result, the prisons of neighboring provinces were groaning with inmates, many of whom had been confined on the merest suspicion or, Ernst alleged, because they failed to pay bribes to Blaquiere's goindas.[10] Arbitrary arrest could result in years of detention without trial—an outcome so devastating that it appeared to overcome locals' fear of reprisals for reporting dacoits. As a result, the crime rate had dropped precipitously across the river. But, as Ernst argued passionately, this was no way for Britons to keep the peace.

Then and now, Ernst's case exemplifies the divergent and contested character of the peace in Bengal, and through it, the late eighteenth- and early nineteenth-century empire. Though Bengal's peace had been erected under the imprimatur of the Mughal emperor, this absorbing controversy matters because it so explicitly lays out both the dilemmas and the license of governance under a model of gubernatorial rule that would soon be ubiquitous. The Ernst affair was a cacophony of the peace. East India Company servants, magistrates, parliamentarians, and Bengalis all had different ideas about how to order Bengal. Ernst argued that keeping the peace through mass incarceration and the employment of poorly supervised constables and criminal spies was illegitimate, and warned that the erosion of basic rules of fairness and due process would harden Bengali elites against government. Blaquiere thought that widespread disorder justified any means, not least because the system of policing was broken anyway. The governor-in-council acknowledged that Blaquiere's methods were morally and perhaps legally questionable, but traded justice for efficacy. Indeed, this incident shows their strong investment in government by law. But it also lays out, in excruciating detail, how enlightened men turned their back on procedural fairness out of cultural chauvinism and expedience. Meanwhile, the Ernst controversy is particularly interesting because police peons and townspeople also got to have a say. Their animadversions demonstrate widespread disquiet about the everyday details of peacekeeping in East India Company territories.

This lopsided debate about peacekeeping emerged from very peculiar circumstances. Since Warren Hastings's first reforms of the administration of civil and criminal law in 1772, British administrators had told themselves that they were bringing order and justice to Bengal. No one did this more boldly than Charles Cornwallis, whose 1793 reforms untethered criminal law and social order from deep webs of social obligation, replacing what he considered to be "arbitrary" Mughal peacekeeping with a new police force and British magistrates who administered an increasingly altered Mughal criminal law.[11] But the failure of reforms to bring order or justice demonstrated repeatedly how easily autocratic imperial rule through adapted local legal structures unraveled in practice, even when it was designed to epitomize modern governance. The special policing measures Ernst railed against were more remarkable (if less horrendous) than the slave peace of Jamaica because Bengal's peculiar peace was justified by melding Mughal tradition with enlightened good government. Its authors self-consciously embraced the rhetoric and ideology of moral and legal improvement that was taking the British government by storm.[12] Though it happened under the auspices of the East India Company, this flattening of rich local hierarchies into a lesser "native subjecthood" marks a milestone in the divergence of the king's colonial peace and the coming of Victorian empire.

However, I do not tell Ernst's tale to rehash the emerging centrality of race to the British Empire. In 1809 Ernst's laments unfolded in a very different historical moment—after the histrionics of Burke and Fox about Hastings's injustices in Bengal had subsided, after Louis XVI had lost his head, and when Napoleon had conquered most of Europe. The world seemed like a very dangerous place. Bengal, here, was more than an engine of racist rule. Even though it was not directly ruled by the king, it served as a forerunner, follower, and exemplar of how governors could use prerogative and legislative powers granted by king or Parliament to craft extraordinary versions of the peace to shore up British control of people and territory in the Age of Revolutions. This debate about colonial peace would have been unrecognizable to free white men in Boston in 1760, though quite a few of them were slave owners and most knew enough of East India Company rule to fear its emerging despotisms.[13] By 1809, however, the contours of Company rule would have been less alien to free people, Black and white, in Trinidad, convicts in New South Wales, and Irish Catholics enduring an increasingly militarized Protestant rule. By 1809 the question was not whether the imperial constitution could countenance legal divergence, but how much injustice could be done in defense of the colonial peace. In this context, the Bengali peace exemplifies the shifting boundaries of colonial government in the early nineteenth century— changes that also shaped emerging nation states.[14]

Peace in the Presidency

We know from generations of excellent scholarship that East India Company rule, particularly in Calcutta and then Bengal, laid important groundwork for the conflation of cultural diversity and autocratic governance in empire. Though Quebec had been ruled *de facto* by a governor-in-council for a decade before the passing of the Quebec Act, the Regulating Act of 1773 was the first constitutional settlement outside a garrison to embrace the merging of executive, judicial, and legislative power in a governor-in-council.[15] It powerfully demonstrated the transformative potential of gubernatorial rule. For all that, the 1773 act effected no revolution in Bengal. As P. J. Marshall notes, no one considered giving Bengal a legislature when the Company won power *de facto* to administer (*nizamat*) and *de jure* to tax (*diwani*) outside its long-held urban entrepôts, and began, soon after, to think of itself as something like a sovereign. South Asian people, even more so than Catholics, had long since been deemed to be predisposed to despotism. A petition against granting Bengalis standing before the new Supreme Court created in 1773 argued that they knew "nothing of the liberty" of Britons.[16] Even Edmund Burke, who, among others, fretted about the ramifications of despotic rule in India for British liberty at home, conceded, "I never was wild enough to conceive, that one method would serve for the whole; I could never conceive that the natives of *Hindostan* and those of *Virginia* could be ordered in the same manner; or that the *Cutchery* court and the grand jury of *Salem* could be regulated on a similar plan."[17]

The Regulating Act was a significant milestone, nonetheless. Combined with Pitt's Act of 1784, it brought Bengal within the king's purview, if not his peace. The legal status of East India Company rule was complicated. Though the Company was created by royal charter, after 1757 it acquired vast new powers to govern from the Mughal Empire. Its dual status as conqueror and delegate of the Mughal emperor made it unclear what exactly the Company had won through its aggressions during the Seven Years' War. Had it conquered territory on behalf of the British king? Or had it simply won the power to negotiate with the emperor for the right to administer territory and harvest revenue?[18] The stakes were high, as the cash-strapped British crown sought access to revenue from territories conquered in its name. Yet a series of legal opinions added little clarity.[19] Meanwhile, a growing chorus of Britons worried about the fitness of venal merchants to govern these acquisitions. Without addressing the question of sovereignty, the 1773 act intervened decisively by establishing the governor-in-council and a supreme court for Bengal: the legislature acted to constitute core instruments of Company government and place them under the supervision of the crown.[20]

The new supreme court inserted the king most directly into Bengal's government. It exercised all of the powers of king's bench and was staffed with "barristers of at least five years' standing" at the English bar who "represented a new breed of the 'king's men' in India, with sources of fiat independent of the Company."[21] Key members saw themselves as crusaders against Company misrule. Chief Justice Impey's court had power to vet regulations made by the Governor-in-Council. The court also set about reading its other jurisdiction very broadly. It wielded its limited jurisdiction to hear "suits against those 'directly or indirectly, in the service of the said United Company, or the said Mayor or Aldermen, or any other of Our British Subjects'" to supervise Company employees and agents and, controversially, to bring the independent jurisdiction of Mughal courts outside Calcutta under some degree of supervision.[22] When a majority of judges read the supreme court's jurisdiction broadly enough to overturn the decision of a Company-controlled Mughal court in a high-profile inheritance dispute from Patna, even Impey's friend Hastings argued that the court "threatened to break all the Bonds of Government."[23] A barrage of complaints was sent to London.[24] As a result, at the height of the American Revolution, a sympathetic Parliament passed the Bengal Judicature Bill of 1781, radically truncating the jurisdiction of the king's court to interfere in and protect Bengalis from East India Company rule. Henceforth, the vast majority of Bengalis would not enjoy the protection of the king's courts, even as the king in Parliament slowly established itself as the sovereign foundation of Company rule.[25]

Nevertheless, the terms of Impey's usurpation in the Patna case are significant. He claimed a natural right to intervene in determinations of the adalats on the grounds that "Principles of Justice are deeper rooted in the minds of my own Countrymen, than in the corrupt Natives of this Country, and especially than such Natives as are generally attendant as Officers on Courts of Justice."[26] This logic was not compelling enough to save the supreme court's jurisdiction to meddle in Company justice. However, its chauvinism had a long afterlife in peacekeeping reforms in Bengal. Under Hastings, and even more so under Cornwallis, arguments about what could be done to keep order focused, not on the privileges and responsibilities of British subjects, but instead on what minimal protections might be given to Bengalis who could claim no real protection from the king.

The offices of governor and governor-general were equally complicated artifacts of the 1773 act. These reconstituted offices exercised enormous legislative, executive, and judicial power on behalf of the Company, but were created by Parliament.[27] From 1784 the Company could appoint governors only with crown approval—a system that quickly collapsed into ministerial appointments. The crown also acquired the power to recall any governor. Oversight of all matters to do with the making of war and the keeping of the peace was given to a secret board composed of the king's privy councillors.[28] Henceforth, government in India was "under effective control of the Crown," though Bengal was not, strictly speaking, within the king's peace.[29] Instead of providing protection to the people of Bengal, the enormous powers delegated to the governor-general meant that, from 1773, he could transform the rudiments of life in India with little ado.

In this space of productive ambiguity, government in Bengal was insistently experimental, if mostly disastrous. As Radhika Singha has argued, it involved "a constant reworking of the ambitions and perspectives of political authority and the forms in which this was to be communicated."[30] These experiments unfolded in the context of protracted crises. Scholars argue about the impact of the slow unraveling of Mughal authority on disorder in Bengal, but the more immediate causes of Ernst's crime wave lay in Company misrule.[31] The failure of successive crops in the late 1760s culminated in the death of one-third of the population. This disaster was exacerbated by artificially high food costs and taxation, which the Company failed to mitigate. Thereafter, many Bengalis were grieving, dislocated, and desperate. Many could subsist only through predation.[32]

The first governor-general, Warren Hastings, cast his interventions into the Bengali peace as a project of recovery—seeking to restore order by perfecting a Mughal "ancient constitution," a term borrowed from the hodgepodge of English constitutional law.[33] To this end, for a time, he tried to restore "authentic" Mughal and Hindu law through modest codification and by seeking to renovate the authority of adalats (civil and criminal courts) and zamindars (local landholders who acted like magistrates). By the end of his governorship, however, Hastings's commitment was waning. In 1781 he "appointed British magistrates to replace the *faujdars*" in the adalats.[34] These new men bridled under what they cast as the excesses and limits of Mughal law: its emphasis on confession, retaliatory punishment, and compensation seemed both too arbitrary and too mild to judges trained under a legal system that saw crime as an insult to the sovereign.[35]

More importantly, restorative reform could not fix what social dislocation had unraveled. Landholders had once formed "the true local unit of police administration in the countryside."[36] They had kept peace through bonds of personal obligation with their tenants, whose peaceable behavior was one of the conditions of access to land. They had also staffed the peace by supporting local watchmen. Tax collectors had also kept people in order by exercising coercive powers to collect revenue and by sponsoring the safe transition of goods through the interior. By 1770, famine—combined with British meddling with tenure, taxation, and jurisdiction—had critically impaired the capacity and motivation of both landholders and tax collectors to keep peace.

By the 1780s, reform was needed and Governor Charles Cornwallis, appointed in 1786, was no gradualist.[37] While maintaining the edifice of Mughal criminal law, he upended the system of peacekeeping radically through a series of regulations codified in 1793.[38] He removed the judicial powers of landholders. The risks involved in doing so should have been clear to Company men; the country squire magistrate, was, after all, a mainstay of the English countryside, even in the industrial age.[39] The power of tax collectors was also targeted, but, in practice, took longer to unravel.[40] In their place the 1793 regulation created police districts called *thanas* (Tannas) overseen by more paid British magistrates. In this regard, Bengal led the way in creating a compensated magistracy: the stipendiary magistrate became an expensive but indispensable sinecure throughout the empire soon after, marking an empire-wide uptick in state supervision of peacekeeping and, usually, a parallel shift toward a more coercive policing.[41] Resident magistrates were supported by a darogah (chief constable) and by lower-paid officers and constables.[42] Again, this was a novel system, clearly drawn from continental models of policing. Police forces were subsequently rolled out in other "at risk" colonies before arriving back in London in much less objectionable form.[43]

If this system sounded modern and efficient, it was not so. The new constabulary lacked local authority: a few new men effecting an enormous rupture in the order of things kept the wrong sort of peace. Many of them were Muslim and poorly supervised, and developed a reputation for coerced confessions, bribery, and torture.[44] Finally, as parsimony always trumped good government in Company Bengal, Cornwallis's police force was grossly understaffed. By 1825, Ranjan Chakrabarti estimates, some 255 policemen staffed the seventeen thanas of Hooghly, policing over 1.2 million people. Some have even suggested that unemployed town watchmen joined criminal gangs, while impoverished landholders colluded with dacoits for profit.[45] It is no wonder that crime was a problem!

Rising crime prompted a sense of crisis that lasted generations, resulting in increasingly illiberal local legislative interventions justified by "necessity." In 1772 a suite of police regulations included one requiring that the family of convicts "become the slaves of the state, and be disposed of for the general benefit and convenience of the people."[46] In 1803 the governor-in-council passed Regulation LIII, which added the capital crime of "robbery by open violence" to Bengali criminal law. Mughal law had allowed death sentences only for highway robbery "at a distance from any inhabited place." LIII also removed a set of loopholes in Mughal law that had barred the punishment of gangs that included children or lunatics; gangs who were not found with sufficient stolen property in their possession; and gangs who harmed passers-by rather than residents. It also outlawed some horrific punishments: for example, in eighteenth-century Mughal law, "robbery without murder" was punishable by the amputation of two limbs.[47] However, the regulation's chief effect was to unravel any semblance of the rule of law. It allowed discretionary punishment of suspected dacoits wherever there was "strong presumptive proof" of their guilt.[48] It also effectively allowed the detention of Bengalis deemed to be vagrant or of bad character until they could pay security for future good behavior, creating a large pool of incarcerated people who would later be mobilized in defense of the peace.[49]

Passed soon after his arrival, Governor Minto's Regulations IX and XI of 1808 went further.[50] Regulation XI excused officers or members of the public from trial for murder if they happened to kill a suspected dacoit "standing on his defence or flying."[51] Regulation IX allowed magistrates to name suspected dacoits, and if those named did not surrender within two months, they would be deemed "guilty of the crime of which he stands accused" and "imprisoned and transported for life."[52] It goes without saying that such provisions violated basic rules of British criminal law, which assumed that the accused was innocent until proven guilty, and at the very least required proof, tested at trial, before anything approaching a life sentence or transportation could be imposed.

Regulation X of 1808 established a superintendent of police. Regulation XVIII enhanced the superintendent's power by authorizing him to execute warrants within the jurisdiction of other magistrates in much of Bengal. This parallel jurisdiction underpinned Blaquiere's appointment as a special magistrate to Nadia and Jessore in 1808. In December of that year, his jurisdiction was extended to include Hooghly.[53] Under its cover, Blaquiere created of a new body of peacekeepers. He and his team recruited and trained a cadre of low-status policemen and spies—likely men drawn from the ranks of prisoners caught in the net of Regulation LIII of 1803. The use of spies had precedent in Bengal, but Blaquiere deployed them on a new scale and to new ends. Such men, he assumed, were either already part of, or would blend in well with, the local criminal element. So, a goinda in his employ might be "required to join the Gangs in order that he may be able to procure this Information." This was a risky business, making goindas the direst enemy of dacoits and putting them in constant "danger of being charged before the local Authorities with Crimes whether truly or falsely."[54] This kind of investigative policing—indeed, policing in general in the modern sense of the word—was a novel thing indeed for a government composed of Britons.

In 1809 Blaquiere's extraordinary policing network was built on subcontracts. In a letter in April, Blaquiere explained that he subsidized an establishment of goindas and constables "at the Indigo factory at Mulanaut" run by Mr. Peter Andrew. From Calcutta, Blaquiere and his associates sent orders to Andrew, who executed them "with a promptitude and secrecy by my people, which would be impossible to ensure, if the Magistrate made use of the public Establishment and Common Means."[55] These men worked independently of local magistrates and their powers were poorly understood. Blaquiere claimed that goindas were mere spies with "no Powers whatever." Their job was to infiltrate gangs so that they could identify members and learn where they hid their takings. They might then accompany Andrew's constables (who had very limited powers of arrest), so they could assist in locating particular dacoits and treasure for seizure. Whatever their formal powers, the low origins of Blaquiere's recruits and the license they assumed made them highly unpopular emissaries of order in the countryside. They not only offended British-born judges and magistrates, they also chafed against Bengali social hierarchies—tensions that bred disorders of their own.

Chatterjee's Peace

The competition among British ideas of a just peace, Bengali social order, and an emerging "jurisprudence of emergency" came to a head in the town of Guptipara in April 1809.[56] On Blaquiere's orders, Andrew's peons had entered Hooghly after reports that a notorious bandit called Calee Gwala was hiding there. A small group went to gather information, discovering, they claimed, that he "had joined a Gang of Decoyts" in the zillah. Whether because of their sympathy for dacoits, their loathing of goindas, or simply in the course of their duty, some servants of Rogonauth Chatterjee questioned (or perhaps abused) Andrew's men as they passed his house. Some sort of brawl ensued. After the affray, Andrew's peons complained to the local police, who arrested Chatterjee and put him in the stocks overnight. He was released after paying as much as 200 rupees to someone. Some of this money was alleged to have ended up in Andrew's pocket.

Accounts of the affray differed fundamentally. Chatterjee's servant, Ramkomar Ghose, claimed that Andrew's peons had behaved badly from the outset. As they passed the house, he bade his colleague, Gola Domes, to ask Andrew's men their business. The interlopers tried to seize Domes, but Ramkomar Ghose warned them that Domes was Chatterjee's servant (and thus under his protection). They released Domes but returned in force near midnight, well after the household had retired for the night. As many as thirty men attacked the house brandishing "clubs."[57] Ramkomar Ghose said they "came like Robbers, leaped the wall, and entered the Prosecutors House."[58] Chatterjee attested that they grabbed him by the hair, beating him "with Sticks, Clubs and butts of Guns," claiming that someone even "gently pierced my ear with the point of a Sword."[59] In marginal notes to his own report of the case, Ernst also noted that Chatterjee had welts on his back consistent with "stripes of a Corah." Neighbors who came to his aid were also assaulted. Village pikes arrived and assisted Andrew's peons in subduing Chatterjee, taking him and four other Brahmins to the lockup. Chatterjee and another were placed in stocks; the other three were released on security. Meanwhile, Chatterjee's house was plundered of some 1,000 rupees of treasure. A trusted neighbor was paid to have Chatterjee's womenfolk removed from the premises to protect their virtue.[60]

The next day, in the townsfolk's telling, Andrew's men shifted from plunder to extortion. "The Gomashteh of the village, Gaur Holdar and two or three more of the principal inhabitants" negotiated a sum to secure the release of Chatterjee and his companion from the stocks. The prisoners offered to pay 140 rupees, but "Chundee Churn Goeyinda" claimed that "he would piss upon such a sum as that."[61] The goindas demanded 200, a sum Chatterjee said he agreed to pay only after they had bound him and threatened to take him across the river to Nadia.[62]

Such abuses were inevitable, Ernst claimed, because the interlopers were drawn from criminal classes. He noted that Blaquiere had even recruited notorious dacoits to his service. Ernst had demanded the surrender of one such man to his custody for his crimes in Hooghly, but Blaquiere had refused.[63] These criminals, Ernest protested, could not and should not keep the peace. If ordinary magistrates had no power to check the abuses of such men, "they would be the scourges of the Country and do more Mischief in this Zillah than the Decoits have ever done. The most dangerous members of the Community would be armed with Power, in the Exercise of which they would be under not sort of Control."[64] So he ordered "a strong party of Burkeundazes" (inferior police officers) to seize seven men, including two goindas, when they returned to Hooghly to make a further arrest. However, two goindas "were set up as complainants," managed to secure their liberty, and hurried to Calcutta to tell their side of the story to Blaquiere.[65] The others were charged with false imprisonment, wounding, plundering, and extortion to make amends for what Ernst described as "one of the most grievous cases of oppression that has come before me since I have been a magistrate."[66]

Ernst objected to more than the unraveling of the proprieties of public order in Bengal; his protest was built on a very particular interaction with social hierarchies in his zillah. Ernst had dismissed the complaints of Muddun Muhun Paul at his peril in 1808. The attack on Paul's house, he noted in one of many self-exculpatory letters he wrote from 1808 to 1810, had been scandalous because Paul was a respectable man. According to Paul and his neighbors, Paul's status made the crime an "alarming outrage" that, if unchecked, might cause Hooghly to be "deserted by all men of property and respectability."[67] Paul and other townsfolk had petitioned the Nizamut Adawlut (the court of criminal justice) to protest Ernst's dismissal of their concerns about both status and order. Ernst did not make the same mistake again in April 1809. Chatterjee was also a man of status, and he was well protected. His employer, a local landowner called Gopimonhun Thaeoor, personally demanded that Ernst intervene. Chatterjee and Thaeoor sought Ernst's intervention not only to keep the peace but also to reestablish social hierarchies. Peons and pikes should not put Brahmins in stocks.

By committing such outrages, Ernst alleged, Blaquiere's police peons caused a crisis of legitimacy for the Presidency. "In Jessore, in Midnapore, in Beerbhoom, in Burdwan, in Hooghly, and in Nuddea too, when I was there on the circuit in 1804, I have seen natives of all ranks and conditions, and I have never yet met with a respectable, or a decent and intelligent man, who, in speaking of goindas in general, did not reprobate their active interference in the police as source of infinite oppression to all descriptions of people with in the sphere of their influence."[68]

That crisis was on display for all to see in an affray that occurred within days of the incident at Chatterjee's. On April 8, a crowd of residents at the Haripal factory attacked a party of "policemen" sent out by the superintendent of police, Mr. Guthrie, to make further arrests in the zillah. The policemen were handed over to Mr. Richardson, the resident at the factory, and then to the Haripal darogah.[69] Ernst responded to this new incident very carefully, as he had already sent a barrage of letters complaining of Blaquiere's concurrent jurisdiction and had been soundly chastised for his trouble.[70] He found, on inquiry, that Guthrie's men "were plainly not guilty of any provocation that could excuse the people belonging to the factory for assembling in a mob, seizing your police officers, and treating them with every sort of outrage and indignity." He could only guess at their motivations, "supposing that the people of the factory were not only as ignorant as the Magistrate of the Zillah of the appointment of these police officers, but that they likewise knew nothing of the Regulation, or authority under which they were employed." He insinuated, in the process, that the actions of Hooghly residents were caused by Guthrie's disregard for local peacekeeping institutions. Blaquiere and Guthrie had both sent men into Hooghly in 1809 without bothering to let local authorities know their business, so misunderstandings were bound to occur.[71] Other reports reaching Calcutta suggested that more was at play than a breach of courtesy. Rumor had it that violence erupted because Calcutta-employed goindas had visited the factory before Guthrie's police arrived and attempted to extort money from factory workers, threatening that they would be charged with false crimes if they did not pay.[72] In this account, corruption fed by novel methods, not local collusion, underpinned the crisis of order in Hooghly.

Blaquiere's Disorder

Andrew's men told a very different story. In their rendering, the incident began with the daring rescue of two dacoits by Chatterjee's cronies.[73] While Chatterjee's servants claimed they had challenged suspicious travelers on the road, the interlopers reported that they approached a crowd of men playing some sort of game outside Chatterjee's gate. A dacoit already in custody, called Tutolia, pointed out his accomplice among them—a man called Kalee Ghose who allegedly held a gun in his hand.[74] Mr. Andrew's servant, Randhun Gwalla, seized Kalee Ghose, but the crowd resisted. Brahmins among them ordered that he and his companions be beaten. The crowd rescued Tutolia and took some silver jewelry from the goindas to boot.[75] These details were not mentioned by another of Mr. Andrew's servants, called Chundee (Chundy) Ghose, who merely said that Tutolia called out to Chatterjee's men for aid, which was readily given. Chundee Ghose also swore that Chatterjee himself aided in Tutolia's rescue, beating Andrew's men with his cane. Unfortunately, Gwalla attested that Ghose was not even with the party during the initial affray. He swore that the injured peons "afterwards gave notice to Chundee" who brought their warrant to the village Go-mashteh and begged for assistance.[76]

Andrew's men also disputed the payment of 200 rupees. Far from accepting a bribe for Chatterjee's release, Chundee Ghose, at least, professed to have slapped the face of the offeror and left for Mr. Andrew's establishment without a cent. He conceded that others may have taken money before they left.[77] Gwalla claimed that Chundee was given only fifty Rupees, which he passed on to "Sahib."[78] Bla-quiere heard something similar from Andrew. He confirmed that "several people of the place came forward on the next day, and re-quested the Deputy Thanadar and Village Gomashtah to settle the matter; offering to make the wounded persons a compensation for the injury they had received, and accordingly lodged a sum of 200 Rupees in their hands, fifty of which were paid to my people who delivered the same to Mr. Andrew, to forward to me."[79]

The fact that Chatterjee paid compensation was, for Blaquiere, an admission of his guilt. Payments of compensation for wrong-doing had been routine in Mughal criminal law. For Blaquiere, Chatterjee's complicity in the brawl also signaled a deeper rot in Hooghly. Chatterjee might be a Brahmin, but he was also "a Man of bad Character."[80] His employer, Gopimonhun Thaeoor, had also "shewn . . . uniform disrespect to the Calcutta Magistrates."[81] In Blaquiere's telling, the incident was less an attack on social order than proof of the imbrication of Hooghly's elite in organized crime. The zillah of Hooghly had, he said, been "overrun with Gangs of Robbers and Murders" for a year—a crime spree attended with "Crimes and Depredations of the most heinous Nature."[82] The infes-tation was so bad, that "a Multitude of the Inhabitants are com-pelled by fear of their Cruelties, either to join them or connive at their Excesses."[83] Others like Chatterjee (and by implication, his employer) profited from crime, by receiving stolen property, or protecting dacoits for money. At the very least, this brawl and the violence at Haripal demonstrated deep hostility to the new order.

Ernst's hostility was equally disruptive of efforts to quell criminal activity in Hooghly. Ernst, like local elites, was an enemy of the peace. Blaquiere declared Ernst "has defeated the apprehension of several notorious offenders, and struck to the Root of my Authority in the Hooghly Zillah." He complained "The apprehension of any Gang must inevitably be rendered impossible, if instead of deriving support and Assistance from the local Authority, they are themselves liable to be apprehended in the place of the Decoyts at the Complaint of Persons who may very probably be connected with the Decoyts themselves, or the secret protectors of the Gang."[84]

Blaquiere admitted that his servants were very likely corrupt. But he argued that they must be allowed the license to do a little injustice in Hooghly in defense of the peace, "picking a slight quarrel" here and there without "immediate apprehension" of arrest and trial by the hostile magistrate.[85] The injustice was worth the gain. Said he, "If the Regular Police of Zillah Hooghly were adequate to maintain its Tranquility, of Course there would be no Object for Employing an extraordinary Police in that Zillah."[86] He and Guthrie both demanded that the Presidency clarify the relationship of special magisterial powers under Regulation X of 1808, to exempt goindas and other officers acting under their orders from the jurisdiction and interference of local magistrates.[87] In the meantime, Blaquiere ordered other goindas involved in the affair to Calcutta to lay charges against Chatterjee.[88]

Ernst felt very differently about the abrogation of his jurisdiction. He insisted that local magistrates were the only check against corrupt "peon police." As a matter of form and substance, a local mag-

THE BENGAL LEVEÉ .

Fig 4.1 James Gillray, *The Bengal Levee,* 1792. The lonely figure in the striped jacket is our Mr. Blaquiere. However enamored the governor-in-council was of his methods by 1809, Gillray suggests that Blaquiere was notoriously unpopular among Company elites in Bengal. © National Portrait Gallery, London

istrate must keep the king's peace in his zillah against government agents and local residents alike. Though Blaquiere might "prefer" to manage complaints against his own men for wrongs committed under his orders, Ernst pointed out that "the duty assigned to you in this Zillah seems to me to be quite distinct from that of taking Cognizance of offences and breaches of the peace committed within the limits of it." If Blaquiere's men were not punishable under local jurisdiction for their crimes "they would be under no Control, and they would be able to Commit all sorts of abuses and Oppressions with Impunity."[89] If complaints against his men had to be presented to Blaquiere in Calcutta, the impracticability and expense of transporting witnesses would thwart any efforts to prosecute. This would be read as an attempt to prevent justice, giving Bengalis the impression that the abuses of goindas were sanctioned by the Presidency. Ernst was supported in this demand by Mr. Harington of the Nizamat Adalat, council member Mr. John Lumsden, and ultimately, the Board of Control.[90]

In everyone's vision of order, the activities of Chundee Ghose and his colleagues congealed into complex symbols of decay, disorder, and incommensurability—a broken peace. It is likely that these particular men did not deserve this ignominy. They performed poorly in their interface with Ernst, to be sure—some among them almost certainly lied under oath. But this inconsistency may simply have resulted from the fact that they lost the advantage; they had not colluded sufficiently to match the smooth, interweaving story that Chatterjee, his neighbors, and his men had clearly rehearsed. Perhaps they felt they did not need to get their story straight because they were protected by Blaquiere's parallel jurisdiction. Andrew's men probably *had* acted improperly in some respects. Ernst reported that Chundee Ghose (variously described as a goinda and a "servant" of Andrew's) "gave out . . . that he was a Girdawur Jummadar" (with general powers to arrest).[91] He and his colleagues swore, not only that they had arrested dacoits in Hooghly under warrant, but that they had even bailed a few men (likely meaning that they released suspects after the payment of a bribe).[92] Blaquiere later confirmed that no goindas had such powers. At the same time, acting improperly was part of their job. As noted, Blaquiere's goindas were routinely ordered to join criminal gangs to identify gang members and find their treasure. To join, presumably, you also had to steal. On Bla-quiere's orders, they became criminals in service of the state. Most importantly, many if not all of these men did not choose their avocation.

Instead, it is likely that many of them had been arrested on sus-picion of dacoity and had been unable to pay a security bond. They could stay in jail or work for private masters or the state.[93] Such men were given allowances to cover the cost of their travel, but it is unclear whether and to what degree that they were otherwise remu-nerated for their work or had any choice as to the assignments they undertook, criminal or otherwise. We do not know how they were incentivized, disciplined, and instructed. However, we do know from their evidence that the men who entered Hooghly in 1809 may not have been as socially isolated as either Blaquiere or Ernst intimated. Chundee Ghose said that he and his colleagues stayed with his "wife's uncle" while in Hooghly.[94] He was no stranger to the zillah. Yet, if we accept his testimony that he witnessed the first affray, he and his companions stood out as strangers outside Chatterjee's house, conspicuous in their dress and comportment. In Ghose's case, such hypervisibility was likely feigned. The networks, aspira-tions, and value systems of the men who traveled into Hooghly at Blaquiere's request were flattened into the status of peon and pa-riah by Ernst, Blaquiere, and the Company state.

Peace, Race, and Emergency

Peons and pariahs were needed to keep the peace, reasoned Ernst's adversaries, because Bengal was in the grip of an emergency, and extraordinary measures were required to meet it. Scholars have argued about the scale of disorder in colonial Bengal.[95] But given the statistics it received from functionaries, the Bengal government could be forgiven for thinking it had a significant and growing problem. Even Ernst had started to accept that all was not well in Hooghly by June 1809. Having enquired more closely into the records of his local darogahs, he admitted that 105 "dacoities" had occurred in his zillah in the preceding year. Forty-nine of them occurred in four thannahs, with only eleven arrests. He blamed his ignorance on the misrepresentations of darogahs, who "are tempted to skreen [*sic*] themselves from censure by suppressing in their reports some of the crimes that have been committed" to make it appear that "the police has been tolerably successful in the discovery of them, and in the apprehension of the offenders."[96] Even this number appeared to be a gross underestimate. The Nizamat Adalat requested the appointment of Henry Shakespear to investigate the true state of affairs in Hooghly. He reported that 104 robberies had occurred in a single thannah in the preceding year.[97] It was one thing to have 105 gang robberies among a population of 1.2 million. It was quite another to have 104 gang robberies in a thannah containing fewer than 10,000 people.

Whatever the scale of the crisis, the language of emergency and exception infuses the records of the Presidency, excusing, as Kaye pointed out in 1853, "a sort of unscrupulous vigor."[98] This had been the case since Hastings's first attempts to socialize punishment of dacoity in 1772. As he and his council passed laws allowing the enslavement of a convict's family, Hastings acknowledged that such measures "will appear to be dictated by a spirit of rigor and violence ... as it in some respects involves the innocent with the guilty." While he did "wish a milder expedient could be suggested," he noted his fear "that this evil has acquired a great degree of its strength from the tenderness and moderation" of Company government. He noted that such measures are "in nowise . . . reconcileable to the spirit of our own constitution," but Bengal and England were not commensurable. Punishment was not motivation enough for the people of Bengal to forgo crime, so the "terrors of the law" must be enhanced. Slavery, for such a class of people (innocent or guilty) was sanitized into reform: "instead of being lost to the community," the convict's family "are made useful members of it." Slavery here facilitated others' "enjoyment of liberty."[99]

In 1801 Edward Colebrooke argued on similar grounds for the expansion of the death penalty in Bengal to stem banditry. In the context of disorder, the needs of society and the state outweighed the need for individual justice. In doing so, he appears to have quoted the utilitarian William Paley verbatim: "Crime from which Injury accrues to Society must be prevented by some means or other; and consequently whatever means should be found necessary to this End, whether they be proportionable to the Guilt of the Criminal or not are adopted rightly."[100] The severity or mildness of the crime should not determine its punishment because crimes like dacoity corroded public order and made a mockery of Company rule. "The above principles justify the Adoption of any other expedient which may be thought adequate to the object in view exclusive of the moral Turpitude of the crime."[101] By 1808 the need for extraordinary measures to restore order had outstripped the ingenuity of lawmakers. As Minto lamented in 1810, "a monstrous and disorganized state of society existed under the eye of the supreme British authorities, and almost at the very seat of that government to which the country might justly look for safety and protection; that the mischief could not wait for a slow remedy; that the people were perishing almost in our sight; that every week's delay was a doom of slaughter and torture against the defenceless inhabitants of very populous countries."[102] The Ernst controversy exposed the degree to which a perception of emergency underpinned increasing liberties taken in law enforcement under Minto's regime. Secretary to Government George Dowdeswell noted that in the present system, the state of the peace "varied materially according to the activity and ability of the local Magistrates." Ernst was clearly not the worst of them, which made his failure all the more important.

> In fact the question is not, whether a few particular Magistrates, of distinguished knowledge and talents can prevent the crime of Dacoity from expanding itself in any very great degree in their respective Districts; but whether the system is likely in the hands of such Individuals as are liable in the ordinary course to be called to the discharge of that duty to lead to the general suppression of Gang Robbery. Experience has decided the point, and at the expiration of the sixteen years that crime so pregnant with the worst evils to the community has been only very partially suppressed.[103]

New methods, including spying, undercover investigation, intimidation, and mass incarceration were needed because British magistrates and local police could not manage crime using licit means.

Blaquiere claimed that "Malpractices on the part of Police Peons require no Doubt to be guarded against with Assiduity . . . but I trust it must be evident to Government that if as in the present Case Precautions be Carried to such an extent as to deter them from ACTING AT ALL, THAT THE REMEDY IS INFINITELY WORSE THAN THE DISEASE."[104] The governor's council agreed. The success of Blaquiere's methods in Nadia, Jessore, and the 24 Parganas meant that "the only question" for Dowdeswell was how widely the new system should be rolled out.[105] Employing such "depraved instruments as the goindas might well be doubtful" but the horror of dacoity, the inefficiency and corruption of darogahs, and the manifest efficacy of spies made compromise inevitable. "The picture drawn of them by Mr Ernst is perfectly just; but the natural inference from it is that, if we must employ immoral and corrupt Instruments, if we must chuse between unprincipled Darogahs and profligate Goindas, we should at least give the preference to that class of people from whose energy, notwithstanding particular acts of depravity, some benefit may be expected with respect to the general Police of the Country."[106]

Lumsden's report is even more telling. He claimed to agree entirely with Ernst about the "general character and conduct" of goindas. He even admitted that Blaquiere's spies were not sanctioned by the regulations at all: they were extralegal. But these, he claimed, were desperate times. "Frequent attempts" since 1793 "to improve the efficiency of the Police by the adoption of various modifications of the Regulations" had been "equally inefficacious." A key problem was that magistrates were "too much fettered by fixed rules of conduct." Though it was "impracticable to prevent the perpetration of flagrant abuses by" goindas, their use was a necessary "evil." The risk, of course, was that innocent people "would be charged with heinous crimes because they refused to submit to pay the contributions which the goindas will no doubt endeavour to levy." And he had no doubt that goindas knew enough of the rules of evidence to "tutor a set of witnesses to substantiate their charges." However, "their extortions (to whatever extent they may be carried) will admit no comparison with the horrors daily practiced by the DeKoits." He argued with Dowdeswell that, not only should Mr. Blaquiere be excused for exceeding the Regulations, the discretion to do so should be rolled out to all magistrates in Bengal.[107]

The tenor of these comments matter. They talk of the risk of injustice—a remarkable elision given that, as Ernst pointed out at the end of 1809, the imprisonment of innocent people had long since become a reality. Many languished in prison for months. Quoting Ernst five years later, the Board lamented the "daring and cruel excesses" of the goindas and the fact that their "sweeping and indiscriminate operations have, to a great extent, confounded the innocent with the guilty." "Since the adoption of the new measures of police, vast numbers of the inhabitants have been apprehended on mere surmise, and have suffered a long confinement without any proof on which they could be brought to trial, and even without the charges preferred against them having been inquired into by the magistrate." Of 2,071 men apprehended as decoits in Nadia in late 1808 and early 1809, 1,828 "had been taken up as men of bad character, on vague suspicion" and only forty-four were convicted of any crime in the two court sessions following. "369 had been released by the magistrate, and sixty-eight acquitted by the court of circuit during the same period." The rest remained in confinement. Indeed, as of May 31, 1809, "there were no less than 1,477 prisoners who had not been examined." A similar pattern persisted in in the 24 Parganas; however, there men detained by magistrates, joint magistrates, and goindas "were sent down to the Presidency," contrary to regulation "and there kept in confinement."[108]

The judicial department was clearly unimpressed with goindas in particular and extraordinary policing in general, though it instructed the discontinuance of neither. In 1814 and 1815, it was of the opinion that the whole Cornwallis system was to blame. Quoting J. Stuart, it noted that "British magistrates are placed over the districts; each district is arbitrarily divided into square portions of ten coss, and these are guarded by small establishments of peons headed by native officers of our own creation, called police darogahs, in the selection of whom no attention is paid to any local fitness. . . . The arrangement is not interwoven with any institutions which previously existed in the country."[109] Such "violent measures" had ill ends.[110]

Instead, drawing on a range of opinions, including Ernst's, the committee called for efforts to reframe policing as a social responsibility. The key here was to reinvigorate policing institutions "interwoven with the frame and texture of . . . Indian society."[111] Order could never depend on a stipendiary police. The Company could not afford to employ enough of them anyway, though it had started to levy a very unpopular new tax to support watchmen in some cities. Instead, the government of Bengal must tap "and preserve . . . the social machine in a state of cohesion."[112] It was telling, the judicial department thought, that the only parts of Bengal not gripped by crime were those in which "independent . . . landed property" had taken a "common interest in the preservation of social order."[113] Landholders, thought the judicial department, might even be made darogahs. Another key proposal was to revive the town watch, which had fallen into abeyance when zamindars were stripped of jurisdiction, because watchmen's lands had been taken by town elites, and because, by and large, no one had troubled to pay them. Here the judicial department read Bengal through the English countryside. Quoting Stuart again, they noted that an efficient "police administration" must have "root in the native soil of the community." Orderly countries like England were policed by "permanent natural authorities." English police were supported by "native gentry, . . . respectable landholders, . . . corporations in towns, and . . . substantial persons of the middle classes in the villages" rather than "positive laws and artificial institutions."[114] Bengal should follow suit.

Fig 4.2 *Thugs Carrying Dead Travellers,* from *Dialogues with Thugs and Narratives of Murderers,* India, 1829–1840. This picture, likely drawn in the 1830s, illustrates how the East India Company's fears of dacoity evolved into even more lurid imaginations of South Asian criminality and violence. "Thugs" were said not only to be criminal gangs but to engage in ritual killings. They are depicted here with shaved and stripped white victims. By permission of The British Library, Add. 41300, f. 55v

While British and Bengali society might be alike in their need for hierarchy, the analogy only went so far. According to the judicial department, a key problem with the alien system of justice administered by British magistrates was the fact that Bengalis could not be trusted to cooperate with "their European superiors."[115] They were also ill-fit for British justice because "the sanctity of an oath is almost universally disregarded." The oath itself was an alien imposi-

A TREACHERY OF SPIES IN HOOGHLY

tion that, in the hands of "revengeful . . . lower orders," corroded natural social hierarchies.[116] They thought, therefore, that a different order of things was needed to keep the peace in Bengal, but that order should not be composed of hired policemen and indentured spies. In the meantime, the spy system had some effect. Dacoity declined in the decades that followed, before resurging massively in the 1840s, when it wove into the Company's obsession with the criminal practice of thuggee.[117]

The small affray at Chatterjee's folded into a torrent of argument that had a very long afterlife but reached no real resolution. These and other animadversions on the state of policing in Bengal were collated and republished for Parliament ten years later in 1819. In 1825 *Blackwood's Edinburgh Magazine* quoted retired magistrate Henry Strachey's concerns about the Bengali peace. Said he, "The good done was purchased at the expense of too much evil. Such shocking cruelty, such a monstrous perversion of justice, committed with our eyes open, and with deliberation—the imprisonment of multitudes, the harassing, the subornation of perjury, the plunder, the death of innocent men in jail—these scenes I conceive to be most discreditable to those who permitted them."[118]

So this controversy in Bengal forms a key episode in the changing colonial peace—one of many reasons historians of crown colonies need to pay more attention to East India Company governance. It played a very important role in modeling how expanded gubernatorial powers could drive legal divergence in empire—a role often lost in the administrative oddity of Company rule. The fact that the governor of Bengal did not answer directly to the king (though he could be removed by the crown) gave the regime's relationship with imperial law reform in the early nineteenth century a peculiar cast. The complex infrastructure of reporting to the Company, the Privy Council, and Parliament, combined with orientalism and the intergenerational involvement of some leading families in Company governance, means that a veil of expertise obscures the relevance of Bengal to empire. India was different.

We need to look more closely, notwithstanding. This is so because, in the process of keeping Bengal's peace, its governors explored new terrain. Bengal became an engine of experimentation in many spheres. Government and magistrates in Bengal used legislative powers to create and executive powers to implement new modes of everyday peacekeeping. Bengal invested in stipendiary magistrates and a paid police force at the same time as Ireland. Both became mainstays of empire from New South Wales to Canada, where they deployed considerable brutality against Indigenous people. Bhavani Raman is currently demonstrating that Bengal both followed and exceeded slave colonies in the militarization of the peace, repurposing the Caribbean's corrosion of fragile eighteenth-century boundaries between civil and military power for more general use.[119] Not only was the East India Company army the largest in the empire; from 1800, martial law was declared there with increasing frequency, underlining the growing racialization of suspensions of civil law. Bengal helped to repackage professional police, martial law, and military peacekeeping as key tools for Victorian empire.

But this story shows other things, too. The Ernst controversy is significant for its explicit engagement with the stakes of extraordinary policing. Torture, bribery, spying, and arbitrary imprisonment were all acknowledged parts of this system. Only the first two were unauthorized, but all were openly tolerated, their cost weighed and dismissed in the defense of the peace. Having read across many archives in this period, I have never seen such a bold articulation of exception outside the slave colonies of the Caribbean.

Injustice was tolerated in Bengal, as Singha pointed out many years ago, because a key product of the crisis of the peace was the ungovernable native subject ruled by the Company, first on behalf of the Mughal emperor, and then under the patchy supervision of the crown and Parliament. This native subject would articulate, after 1857, into a lesser subject of the crown. According to the generations of Company men sent to Bengal, everyone from landowners to darogahs thwarted Company order. Antoinette Burton and Priyamvada Gopal have reminded us recently that Bengalis had very good reason to do so, and that perhaps the real history of empire lies in colonized peoples' trenchant, constant, and crippling refusal to cooperate in extractive imperialism.[120] The early governors of Bengal saw the problem, but understood it differently. Hastings cast gang robbery as an intergenerational vocation in which whole communities colluded. Leading men were charged either with conniving with dacoits or with failing to fulfill their social obligation to keep the peace after their formal jurisdiction was rescinded. The prevalence of dacoity was even blamed on victims of crime. The rate of complaint, surmised Dowdeswell, dropped in inverse proportion to the frequency of crime because victims feared reprisal in districts where law and order had collapsed.[121] Finally, policemen themselves colluded in disorder, by underreporting crime to save their jobs, and by corroding authority by using inappropriate means of punishment.[122] At the root of the problem, in their telling, lay Bengali culture. Not all Bengalis were criminals, but according to almost every British man involved in the Ernst affair, all lacked the law-abiding sensibility of British subjects, rendering them ineligible for the protections and responsibilities bequeathed by anything approximating due process.

There can be no doubt that this argument was transforming the empire at the end of the eighteenth century. Race and status had long limited subjecthood in slave societies. As eighteenth-century slaveholders argued against weak pushback from the center, legal divergence was required to accomplish what everyone acknowledged to be a great wrong—working African men and women to death against their will. Though some commentators like Edward Long made an early start by comparing Africans to animals, it took a good while longer for most slaveholders to seek moral ease by ar-guing that it was the fault of slaves that slavery was so cruel.[123] In Bengal, and in other parts of the empire, colonial administrators got there sooner. Their conversations were leavened by decades of revolution and war in America, France, and Haiti. By 1810, Britain faced the challenge of administering a much more diverse empire that included several Caribbean colonies with free Black majorities, Catholics, and formerly French, Spanish, and Dutch subjects. In this context the rules of the game changed with startling rapidity. Con-versations like the one described here would have been unthinkable outside a slave colony just a few decades earlier. Indeed, not so long before, Hastings had been impeached for his departures from fun-damental maxims of law and judicial process in Bengal.

The Ernst controversy shows us that after 1773, Company and royal governors used their vastly expanded powers to rewrite the rules of peacekeeping. This is not to say that empire had not always been violent, but before 1800 its violence fell largely within the realms of inter-state aggression, treaty disputes, lawlessness, or slavery. After 1773 the colonial peace itself changed, opening new space for colonial administrators and lawyers to distinguish among the rights and privileges of free subjects of the crown. By the end of the eighteenth century, what it meant to be a British subject varied enormously from place to place, and, increasingly, according to one's status and color.

Race was not an exclusive driver here. Just as French Canadians were deemed better suited to autocracy, so an array of free people of color and unfree or culturally divergent subjects were deemed ill-suited not just to self-government but to the fundaments of due process. For example, at the same time as Ernst was arguing with his betters in Bengal, military, naval, and civil administrators in the island fortress of Malta were under attack from Maltese elites for their tyranny. Nobles in Malta demanded a share in local government, after Britain had helped them liberate their island from Napoleon. However, they, like Bengali elites, found themselves cast as culturally inferior subjects, unfit to enjoy the full privileges and protections of subjecthood.[124]

There were still limits. Ernst's protest gained some traction. He and other critics were quoted in endless musings about British tyranny in Bengal. Ernst's drama coincided with other noisy efforts to control the new colonial despotism. While Ernst wrote angry letters, Thomas Picton was tried, first for the extrajudicial killing of twenty-five British subjects (including slaves) in Trinidad, and then for torturing the young, free Black woman Luisa Calderon. Trinidad had a free Black majority, many of whom spoke French and some of whom had fled to Trinidad after the failure of Fedon's rebellion in British Grenada. Picton's efforts to control the island by killing slaves involved in obeah, arbitrarily arresting advocates for free Black rights, and torturing information out of a young female thief scandalized the British public even at the height of the Napoleonic Wars and the Haitian Revolution. Ernst's protests and Picton's trial remind us that peacekeeping was contested in the empire, even as the rules of the game changed.[125]

Such controversies also demonstrate widespread support for the changing peace. Disquiet about the unraveling of protections for the native subjects of India was dismissed by antislavery advocate Lord Wilberforce. In 1813 he explained the "moral degradation" of Bengalis for the benefit of Parliament. Who were they to second-guess the prescriptions of men on the ground? "I cannot conceive that there can be any set of men better qualified in all respects to form a correct opinion of the general character and conduct of the natives, than such of the Company's servants as are resident magistrates."[126] His remedy was not British justice, but Christian conversion—a remedy that might one day befit Bengalis for the benefits of British law. Though Picton stood trial in the shadow of huge public controversy about his actions in Trinidad, his use of virtually unbounded prerogative power in defiance of British ideas of justice seemed worthy to a peculiar cast of people. The great antislavery advocate James Stephen Sr. defended Picton on appeal on the grounds that the power of the king's governor to keep order in a conquered colony extended even to torture. Such defenders show that the stakes of the Ernst controversy are bigger than subjecthood or race (though both inflect deeply in abolitionism). Wilberforce and Stephen Sr. made arguments for the times, radical in their expansive vision of crown and Company power, advocating for diminished colonial subjecthood, and newly insistent on the need to use any means to keep the peace. The marked contrast between these, and arguments about the character of the imperial constitution waged in Boston in the 1760s, show just how far the imperial constitution had traveled since the late eighteenth century and the significance of its transformation.

In the end, then, the conversation about the Bengali peace is important because of its emphasis on good government. Everyone had long understood that the brutality of slavery required enormous legal compromises. Though the Bengali government knew it was floundering, the logic underpinning the extraordinary policing it deployed there was more sophisticated, more self-assured, and, paradoxically, grounded in the twin logics of rational improvement and the common good. It justified exception in defense of society and the state. These arguments were both counterrevolutionary (crafted in the wreckage of the American Revolution) and enduring in their modernity. It is with good reason that Nasser Hussain and others have focused on India in their expositions of the emergence of modern state power, and with it, the "state of exception."[127] In all of its verbosity, this spat about the efficacy of a magistrate in Hooghly lays bare a logic that had enormous ramifications for modern governance.

5

Bush, Town, and Crown in New South Wales

In late 1830 the government of New South Wales was nervous. In September between 70 and 200 convicts, depending on whom one asked, rose against their masters in Bathurst and in the Hunter Valley.[1] They had plundered farms, and one group defeated "parties of Troops . . . of the Mounted Police." Settlers had "quitted their farms" in alarm, and Governor Ralph Darling prepared for the worst, sending "reinforcements of Troops" to various stations and deploying a detachment to guard men in chain gangs—some 1,500 convicts. "Should these people rise," he mused, "the Consequences might prove of the most serious nature."[2]

The most prolonged incident—the Ribbon Gang uprising—began with an execution in the central west of New South Wales, near Fitzgerald's Mount. A group of Irish convicts assigned to work on Mr. Liscombe's estate robbed their master and left, first to gather some sympathetic countrymen to take revenge on bad masters, and then to free themselves from labor without reward. Chief among their targets was a police magistrate, Lieutenant Thomas Evernden. In late 1829 Evernden had ordered the whipping of Ralph Entwistle and Patrick Byrne, then canceled time served toward their tickets of leave (a dispensation given to convicts allowing them to work for money on their own time during good behavior). They had committed no crime. They merely had the misfortune of bathing naked in plain view of Governor Darling's entourage. This act of injustice was transformative: Entwistle, who had been a faithful servant, became a leader of the Ribbon Gang, though he hailed from Lancashire.[3]

Lucky for him, Evernden was not at home on September 23. His overseer, James Greenwood, was not so fortunate. He refused to leave with the gang, so they shot him. This might have been their plan anyway, as Greenwood was known to be a police informant. When Greenwood died, one gang member allegedly declared, "There was an end of one villain, that had brought many a one to the gallows, but he would bring no more."[4] Afterward they proceeded from property to property, gathering more men and 300 pounds of ammunition. Their violence was not indiscriminate. One station owner reported that they took only blankets and provisions from his property, because he "was not a bad master."[5] Pillage was necessary to their survival.

Things started to unravel early. "One man, who had been entrusted with the greater part of their ammunition, absconded with his trust; and . . . gave it up to the proper authorities."[6] He likely reasoned that handing over such a prize would earn him early freedom. From then on, the gang leaders took to locking up their entourage at every station, until, eventually and sensibly, they let unwilling conscripts go. Three weeks later, though the group had been reduced to ten, they were still evading capture. Only when a contingent of 130 solders marched from Sydney to join with the Bathurst mounted police were the stragglers captured, Entwistle among them. They were tried and executed within weeks—their handiwork prompted the first Supreme Court hearing outside Sydney, followed by a mass execution on November 3, 1830.

Convicts were not the only people menacing the peripheries. In the same letter, Governor Darling reported that "the natives have also Manifested a disposition of late to be troublesome," killing cattle and menacing "the borders of Argyle and St. Vincent." He worried that "the almost boundless extent of this Country" would make it impossible to defend settlements against Aboriginal depredations. Darling met this new challenge by withholding the 57th Regiment, which was due to depart for India.[7] His concerns were not idle. New South Wales's northern and western frontiers had experienced violence since the onset of settlement in the Hunter Valley, north of Sydney, in 1822. As millions of sheep and a few convict shepherds poured down the sparse waterways of the colony's arid hinterland, things were about to get much worse.

New South Wales was a tinderbox. Its disorders were endemic: convict escape and Indigenous resistance had plagued the settlement since its beginnings in 1788. But by 1830, disorder was spinning out of control. In 1821, ninety-four percent of the settler population lived within seventy kilometers of Sydney.[8] In 1822 an imperial commission of inquiry recommended that the colony expand its boundaries, using convicts to work farms on the frontiers of settlement. This would be a rich man's game; land grants and the assignment of convict labor were linked to capital. Controlled expansion would serve the moral purpose of reforming convicts through wholesome rural labor. And by tightening up the system of convict pardons and punishments, New South Wales would more fully serve its original purpose—becoming an "Object of real Terror" to potential malefactors in Britain.[9] To this end, from 1822 some large farms were sold to well-to-do emigrants in the Hunter Valley. These farms were staffed by large numbers of convicts. More-established families took new grants (and convicts) west across the Blue Mountains to Bathurst. However, farming was hard on the arid western plains, so they did not plant crops for long.

Plans for the controlled expansion of crop farming began to fail when the imperial government reduced tariffs on colonial wool in 1823. They collapsed entirely in 1828 when a parliamentary select committee in London declared that Australian wool was good enough for cloth manufacture. In 1823 New South Wales and Van Diemen's Land exported 175,400 pounds of wool. By 1831 they exported 2.5 million pounds. This wool was not grown on a few land grants on the fringes of the colony. In Van Diemen's Land, the wool boom precipitated the sudden occupation of almost all viable land in the island—a landgrab that precipitated the infamous "Black War."[10] On the mainland, new districts became conduits for livestock and shepherds who followed river systems north, south and west of Sydney, without government permission. Low-status vagabonds with (stolen) cattle started the exodus, but moneyed and respectable men followed, some with convict servants in tow. All of them occupied land illegally. Yet by the end of the 1850s, most of the eastern third of the continent was held as pastoral runs under some species of tenure.[11]

Convicts liked Sydney. They were unhappy farmers and mutinous stockmen, leaving their posts in droves. Many left temporarily. So long as a convict turned up for government musters, he was unlikely to be punished for taking a short break from shepherding a flock. However, in the 1820s a rising number of convicts absconded for good. In 1824 the *Sydney Gazette* advertised 112 runaways from Bathurst alone—most of them from government, rather than private, employ. At least a dozen more runaways not advertised in the

Gazette were sentenced to flogging for unexcused absence by the Bathurst bench.[12] Running away worsened over the decade. The very thought of managing convict mobility on such a vast geographical scale cowed imperial bureaucrats. As Viscount Goderich noted in 1831, "The great extent of Country, over which the Settlers are now scattered, must put almost insuperable difficulties in the way of an effective superintendence of the Convicts, while it renders it almost equally impossible to prevent those, who succeed in escaping, from procuring an easy subsistence by plunder."[13]

And, of course, farmers, pastoralists, and convicts were all unwelcome intruders. Every single bit of land that could hold a farm or contained water enough for livestock was already someone's country. Every theater of expansion north, west, and south became a war zone. Aboriginal resistance at Bathurst prompted the colony's first declaration of martial law in 1824. Aboriginal resistance in the Hunter Valley settlements came to a head in 1826 when rumors of violent collusion between the mounted police and local settlers prompted the very rare trial of a mounted police officer for killing an Aboriginal man.[14] Even as Darling wrote in 1830, the government and settlers of Van Diemen's Land were fighting a genocidal war against the island's Indigenous population. Indeed, nowhere exemplifies the impossibility of orchestrating the orderly dispossession of Indigenous people from their homelands more viscerally than Van Diemen's Land, which was under martial law for four years from 1828. Violence was also endemic on the mainland. By the mid-1830s, sustained conflicts had erupted in Brisbane Waters to the north, the Liverpool plains to the northwest, and Port Philip to the south of the vast colony.[15] They culminated in series of high-profile massacres—some committed by soldiers and some by convict workers—that the colonial government scrambled variously to cover up or to punish.[16]

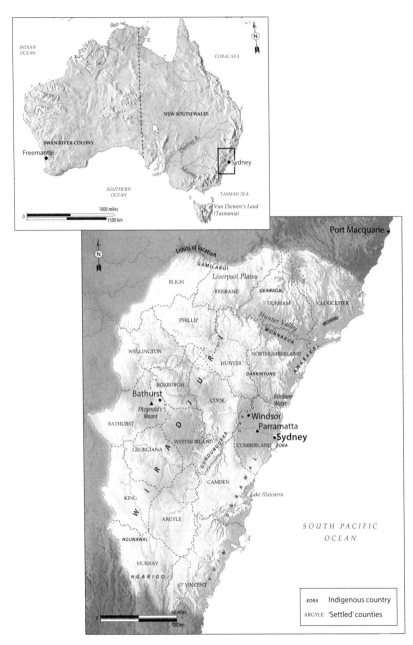

Map 5.1 The Nineteen Counties of New South Wales, Australia, c. 1830.
© Lisa Ford

Here we will explore the riven peace in the colony of New South Wales in the 1830s through the rapidly changing interface of convicts and Indigenous people with the colonial state. Peacekeeping in this strangest of colonies, established as an open-air prison in 1788, was a problem both intellectual and practical. As in Jamaica and India, keeping the peace in New South Wales required distortions of metropolitan law and a frank acknowledgment of the constitutional peculiarities of colonial order. What makes New South Wales so interesting is that many of its most troublesome subjects were unfree and white. So emergency peacekeeping measures in New South Wales remind us that status vied with race well into the nineteenth century as a hard limit of British subjecthood. We could learn a similar lesson from Ireland in this period.

But race mattered enough. When the New South Wales Legislative Council adopted and adapted techniques from slave colonies to keep the convict peace, it did so carefully and explicitly, laying bare the constitutional parameters of colonial divergence. When it established a mounted, military police force to capture convicts and Aboriginal people, and deployed soldiers throughout the countryside to hunt escapees, the colonial government acknowledged that such moves would be unthinkable in the metropolis. When it passed the Bushrangers Acts, which required all white men to carry proof of their freedom or suffer imprisonment, it used the language of emergency and of colonial difference perfected in Bengal. This move was not self-evident: debates about the legality of the act show deep division among lawyers and bureaucrats in the colony about the relationship between colonial and metropolitan order. In these discussions, place mattered enormously. "Scattered" settlers and the "great extent" made "convict superintendence" impossible without special measures.[17] The problem of convict robberies close to major settlements was imagined from the outside in: it was especially threatening because convicts might disappear into the wilderness. In contrast, Indigenous violence was imagined from the inside out.

This was so because, in 1830, Black bodies in New South Wales were radically free from state regulation. Aboriginal people unsettled the king's peace with their ambiguous legal status and cultural autonomy as well as their trenchant resistance to the spread of settlement. But this freedom from law had an ugly underbelly. Only very occasionally subject to criminal trial for killing settlers since 1823, Aboriginal people resisting pastoral expansion faced terrible risk of unregulated violence at the hands of settlers, soldiers, and mounted police. That risk was written into colonial law: Governor Darling instituted the limits of location in 1826 and declared all pastoral and agricultural endeavors outside that line to be beyond the protection of the state, a zone of lawlessness or war. In the unmanageable vastness of New South Wales's hinterlands, the government recused itself from managing frontier violence.

The vulnerability of Aboriginal people to violent dispossession at the beginnings of the great settler economic boom became a scandal of empire. Humanitarians who had just won the battle against slavery turned their attention to Indigenous people in settler colonies, but no simple imperial act could slow their violent dispossession.[18] British wealth was far too mired in booming settler economies to shut down pastoral expansion.[19] So humanitarian protest folded into conversations about how best to use law to keep the peace between settlers and Indigenous people. The result, after 1836, was the conflation of protection and increasingly genocidal policing.[20]

It is a fitting symbol of the impotence of the colonial state that the most important step toward incorporating Aboriginal people into the king's peace did not pertain to the frontiers at all. It focused on managing Indigenous violence in towns. Aboriginal people met and fought in settler towns and on the roads that connected them, and their immunity from prosecution underlined their prior occupation, their self-government, and their unjust dispossession—all of which unsettled the king's claims to New South Wales.[21] To tell this story, I revisit Justice William Burton's unpublished notes on the epochal case *R v. Murrell* (1836), which argued that Indigenous tribal law could not compete with the king's peace in the centers of settlement or anywhere in New South Wales. In this case, the murder of an Indigenous man on a road near the town of Windsor served to project a peculiar and truncated colonial order over half a continent. The terms of that peace were grossly unequal. Even in Burton's humanitarian-inflected telling, Aboriginal incorporation into the king's peace was predicated on subjection rather than equal subjecthood for Aboriginal people. That assignation was entirely symbolic. Aboriginal people became a symbol of British sovereignty only when they visited towns or traversed roads. Elsewhere they continued to be victims of violence whose encounters with settlers, soldiers, and policemen looked much more like war than peace.

Perhaps more clearly than anywhere else, 1830s New South Wales made explicit the constitutional problem of peacekeeping in the empire. Solving the problem of the peace became one of the most absorbing tasks of the New South Wales government. The state's ideological and practical struggle to order convicts and to dispossess Indigenous people demonstrates the centrality of ordering people in place to evolving understandings of the imperial constitution. The result, in 1830s New South Wales, was an extraordinary inversion of the terms of colonial subjecthood. White bodies became bearers of exorbitant state power, carrying with them extraordinary vulnerability to arbitrary arrest in the defense of the king's colonial peace. Only later did Aboriginal bodies come to carry the hopes of settler sovereignty—as selective acts of jurisdiction pushed Aboriginal violence out of the sight of townsfolk while military aggression, disguised as policing, aided the theft of Aboriginal land and lives.

The Convict Peace

New South Wales was an extraordinary colonial project with an appropriately extraordinary constitution. After Bengal and Quebec this was the third great experiment in crown colonial governance. Enormous executive and judicial power was reposed in its governor from first settlement in 1788. Until 1823 he was not even required to consult a council. He was authorized by commission to "do and execute all things in due manner that shall belong to your said command and trust Wee have reposed in you according to the several powers and directions granted or appointed you by this present Commission and the instructions and authorities herewith given to you." These included the right to appoint magistrates, coroners, constables, and other officers as required, to pardon and/or arm the populace, to constitute courts-martial, and to declare martial law when it was lawful to do so (a very unhelpful caveat, as the jurisprudence of martial law was a mess).[22] Sadly none of the founding documents mentioned a right to legislate—an oversight that Jeremy Bentham and a few querulous settlers used to question the constitutionality of the government of New South Wales.[23] However, the governor legislated anyway, raising taxes, banishing refractory convicts, and regulating every aspect of colonial life.

The colony had a makeshift court system, comprised of a court of criminal jurisdiction and a court of civil judicature (reconstituted as a Supreme Court with limited jurisdiction in 1814). These were staffed largely by untrained officers for the first twenty years or so. At the head of the Criminal Court was a judge advocate—a title that made clear its close analogy to a court-martial.[24] The military character of the court was underlined by the fact that all criminal cases were heard by military juries. Indeed, aside from a brief hiatus in the 1820s, military juries continued to hear all criminal cases until 1833, and were not abolished until 1839.[25] More importantly, until 1824 no court or judge in New South Wales had jurisdiction to check the power of the governor or government. Though governors held chancellery and some appellate jurisdiction in most British colonies by the end of the eighteenth century, New South Wales's quasi-military court structure amplified the power of the governor uniquely: as ranking officer, he had significant power over the judge advocate, and he held appellate jurisdiction in civil and criminal matters. Moreover, until the new Supreme Court was established in 1824, no court held the power to issue prerogative writs, habeas corpus included.[26] So for many years, a succession of military and naval governors kept a martial peace, checked only by settlers' complaints to London.

Until the passing of the New South Wales Act in 1823, which created an appointed Legislative Council and a properly constituted Supreme Court, Chief Justice Francis Forbes surmised that colonial life centered on the will of the governor: "The police, the roads, the markets, the importation of supplies, the cultivation of provisions, and even the prices of every article of daily consumption, were regulated by orders of the Governor." The place was run like "a gaol [jail] upon a large area." But this mode of governance ill-fitted a society "increasing with emigrants from England, India, and other parts of the world, who brought with them the light of latter times."

Such people were glad enough to have convict servants, but would not accept that "they likewise were liable to prison-discipline."[27] Forbes's observations were mostly true, though settlers (many of them soldiers) had held a peculiar sort of power from the outset—demonstrated by the fact that New South Wales burned through governors like few other colonies before 1810, and one governor was deposed at gunpoint by the New South Wales Corps.

The New South Wales Act gave the colony a constitution closer to 1774 Quebec than to 1773 Bengal. From 1824, the colony was still governed by an extraordinarily powerful governor who was only required to hear, not to follow, the advice of his Executive and Legislative Councils. However, if he failed to do so, he was required to submit a "full explanation" to the colonial office.[28] Chief Justice Forbes, raised in Bermuda and fresh from a posting in Newfoundland, was appointed to lead a Supreme Court wielding original and appellate jurisdiction and was given a seat on the governor's council, where it was his duty to advise the governor if local legislation was repugnant to English law. Forbes, as head of the king's court and a special member of council, was mired in controversy. He clashed repeatedly with the autocratic Ralph Darling (who had served in the West Indies from 1793-1802 and governed Mauritius from 1817-1820) over everything from freedom of the press to convict assignment. He was only occasionally backed up by the Colonial Office, which was formed in 1801 to manage the empire for the crown. Robert Hay and James Stephen Jr. (the permanent undersecretaries who ran the portfolio under a rapid succession of ministers after Bathurst's retirement in 1827) came to see Forbes as an overzealous protector of convicts and radicals in a fragile periphery.[29] Forbes and his court made explicit the enormous constitutional compromises required by the convict peace.

One of the flashpoints of the colonial peace in the Forbes period was the enormous license given to civilian magistrates. As in other British colonies, magistrates not only constituted local civilian government, they acted as informal diplomats in frontier conflicts. They adjudicated wage and contract disputes between free servants and employers, enforced government orders, collected census data, and took depositions and information for trials in the truncated Criminal Court. To keep the fragile peace in a colony populated chiefly by convicts and emancipists, magistrates also supervised the administration of the convict labor system and recommended convicts for tickets of leave and pardons.[30] Most importantly, they exercised extensive jurisdiction to summarily punish convicts for all noncapital offenses from insolence to theft. They sentenced convicts to penal stations, chain gangs, government prisons, and, most notoriously, flogging. Whereas from the 1790s a single magistrate in Barbados or Jamaica was empowered to sentence an indecorous slave to no more than thirty-nine lashes, some magistrates in New South Wales had been in the habit of sentencing insubordinate convicts to upward of 500 lashes.

Magisterial license remained so broad in part because it had no formal sanction or limits in law: the New South Wales Courts Act 1787 (27 Geo 3, cap 2) and the subsequent Charter of Justice of 1814 made no effort to define magisterial jurisdiction. The 1823 act tried disastrously to form magistrates into benches—a step that paralyzed frontier peacekeeping until emergency legislation was passed to allow magistrates to act alone again. Then the Supreme Court gave magistrates pause by entertaining a number of cases about their malfeasance and wrongful arrests.[31] However, the first comprehensive effort to define and limit magisterial jurisdiction (including limiting the number of lashes a single magistrate could prescribe to fifty) was the enormously controversial Summary Jurisdiction Act of 1832.[32]

Until then, the power of magistrates was a legal mire. Questions about the legality of magistrates' power and their proclivities for cruelty tipped into scandal in the early 1820s when members of the Parramatta bench started accusing one another of seducing and torturing convicts. It got worse when the new attorney general decided that the internal transportation regime was based on illegal sentences, most of them passed by magistrates.[33] For all this, magistrates were not cowed into meekness, as Ralph Entwistle discovered in late 1829. The magistrates' reaction to Governor Richard Bourke's Summary Jurisdiction Act of 1832 was particularly telling.[34] So attached were magistrates to their broad customary right to punish, that one wrote a whole book in protest. In *The Felonry of New South Wales,* Major James Mudie blamed a "rebellion" on his estate on the corrosion of magistrates' authority by the Bourke regime. New South Wales, he argued, was a site of special jeopardy. Unlike slaves, who "had violated no British law to which they were amenable," convicts had been "divested of their natural and legal rights" and were sent to New South Wales for punishment.[35] The proper role of the colonial government in this disorderly place was to empower the local magistracy to protect remote settlers "in their industry by proper laws."[36] Proper laws would not limit the violence of magistrates.

The role of military power in the colony was also significant and peculiar. Soldiers and their military order pervaded local institutions. All governors until Bourke held naval or military office at the time of their appointment, and until 1861 all had held a military post at some point in their career. Arguably, none wore his military rank more haughtily than Governor and Major Ralph Darling

(1824–1831), although, of course, the foul-mouthed Governor and Vice-Admiral William Bligh (1806–1808) would have given him stiff competition. In addition to their pivotal role in criminal juries, officers also had a jump start as capitalists in early New South Wales. Because they wielded special powers in a tiny, largely unfree society, they enjoyed elevated status, which they used alternately to cheat, exploit, and invest to get ahead in the fledgling economy. As a result, men like John Macarthur catapulted from obscurity to great wealth and metropolitan influence. For all this, until the 1820s, soldiers played a scant role in everyday peacekeeping. When the first fleet arrived, military personnel refused point blank to keep the ordinary peace. Their role, they insisted, was merely to defend the colony against external invasion and internal rebellion. This refusal to assist in everyday policing put the colony in the awkward position of having to appoint convicts as constables—a practice that persisted throughout the colony until the end of transportation. The military did defend the colony when Irish political exiles led the Castle Hill Rebellion in 1804, and it waged war against Aboriginal people in 1790, 1795, 1799, 1801, 1804, 1805, and 1816. These actions often occurred in concert with settlers, who in times of trouble were formally or informally authorized to shoot Aboriginal people on sight.[37]

These arrangements were not fit for purpose after the Bigge Report of 1822. Bigge recommended bolstering the colonial economy and better punishing convicts by allowing agricultural and pastoral expansion. The chief innovations here were to increase land grants and send thousands of bitter convicts from the comforts of town to clear land, grow crops and tend sheep in the wilderness. Convicts left their rural posts in droves, so new methods of peacekeeping were required. Most interesting of all was the creation of the mounted

BUSH, TOWN, AND CROWN IN NEW SOUTH WALES

police, designed in 1825 to maintain order in New South Wales's law-less countryside. This force was first mooted by Governor Brisbane in June 1824. After seven settlers were murdered by Aboriginal people in the hills outside Bathurst, Brisbane thought it "indispensably req-uisite to obtain Your Lordship's sanction to raise a Troop of Colo-nial Cavalry . . . not only with the view of keeping the Aborigines in check . . . but also for the general Police of the Country."[38] Worried about cost, Secretary of State Earl Bathurst refused to countenance the creation of a force without a much fuller explication of the crisis. Accordingly, Brisbane was much more explicit when he announced that he had established the force anyway in November 1825. By then convicts were the most immediate problem. A cavalry was needed, Brisbane claimed, because of the vastness of the interior: "In a country like this, where a thin population is scattered over a large tract of Country, the temptations to plunder are increased by the fa-cilities of escape." He had acted without permission because "once Bushranging has become sufficiently concocted to have its ramifica-tions and connexions in different parts of the Colony, nothing short of regular Military Movements will be sufficient to put it down."[39]

Brisbane's case for the mounted police had rich imperial tendrils. The problem of dispossessing Indigenous people and controlling subject populations dominated most early-modern colonial enter-prises (with the partial exception of trading outposts in the Indian Ocean and South China Sea—although, of course, by the mid-eighteenth century the East India Company had assembled the largest army in the world). It is for this reason that colonies came to lead experiments in policing. Managing unfree labor was always an intractable problem in Caribbean slave colonies. Jamaica's dé-tente with the Maroons is only the most extreme example of their improvisations. Sally Hadden noted the long-standing difficulty of organizing civilians into militia units and slave patrols in eighteenth-century British North America. Her work demonstrates, nevertheless, that paramilitary patrols emerged as a mainstay of policing in the postrevolutionary South. In their conception, if not always in reality, colonial militias did increasingly important state-building work. My own research has noted the role of militia units in effecting extralegal violence on the southeastern frontiers of the early United States. In early nineteenth-century Georgia, having served as an Indian-fighting militiaman was a passport to high office. Indian fighting was often cast as war, but the endemic low-level conflicts that kept militiamen in arms had a hybrid character: they blurred the boundaries of war and peacekeeping.[40] In New South Wales, transferring military men into the mounted police merged war and peacekeeping much more efficiently.

Forces like Brisbane's mounted police became a mainstay of colonial expansion. Brisbane followed experiments in Ireland, which had been trialing various models of armed peacekeeping since 1786.[41] Most recent and relevant was Robert Peel's "Peace Preservation Force," an armed and mounted constabulary created in 1814 to patrol "disturbed" districts without the inconvenience of justifying a declaration of martial law.[42] Canada's famous mounted police force came later but lasted much longer, acting as an important agent of Indigenous dispossession.[43] Mounted police marked an important divergence between center and periphery precisely because they were overtly paramilitary. As Illan rua Wall noted, such forces "mimicked the magistrate / constable structure but were actually the beginnings of a very different form of power" crafted in response to the special precarity of the colonial peace.[44] Contrast Peel's London Metropolitan Police Force, which was rendered acceptable to a suspicious public only by being disguised as a disarmed, civilian constabulary.[45] Mounted and armed police would have been unthinkable in England at the end of the eighteenth century, even though the military were deployed frequently against the seething population under the Riot Act.

Armed "police" were unacceptable in England because they offended the close limits placed on military peacekeeping in the aftermath of the Glorious Revolution. Such limits had plagued Gage's efforts to bring order to North America in the lead-up to the Revolution. This constitutional peril was noted apologetically by the Legislative Council in New South Wales in 1825. "Repugnant as the Council feel to recommend a resort to the use of a Military force to repress civil outrages, Yet, they are convinced that, under the peculiar circumstances of the colony at present, it offers the only . . . remedy." In addition to proposing the mounted cavalry, they also requested that "small parties, composed of three of four soldiers, and one or two natives under the direction of one Constable" be deployed to guard major roads "between Sydney, Liverpool and Windsor, and other roads of frequent resort."[46] Brisbane noted his preference for a more tried and tested colonial divergence—arming subjects under the mantle of the militia. However, he noted that "in the present state of the Population of the Colony," arms should not be delivered indiscriminately "into the hands of the people." In a generation, the colony's free youth might be inducted into compulsory military training and then into militia units. Meanwhile, "Mounted Soldiers" would form a cavalry conducted under military discipline.[47]

This would not be the last time a council pleaded for repugnant laws to meet the "special circumstances" of New South Wales. This was so because a few detachments of mounted police were unequal to the scale of proximate and distant violence in New South Wales

Fig 5.1 Augustus Earle, *Skirmish between bush-rangers and constables*, 1827.
National Library of Australia, nla.obj-134500811

after 1825. They could not keep order because they were always too
few in the face of ceaseless metropolitan demands for retrenchment.[48] Mounted police were scattered around the Bathurst region
in early 1830, but even after the Ribbon Gang had reduced in number
from the rumored 200 to thirteen, they could not muster in sufficient numbers to find and detain the band. Indeed, in 1830, the
mounted police and ordinary constabulary had grave difficulties
keeping the peace closer to Sydney. Beginning in April the government had scattered an additional 188 soldiers in the Cumberland
district and adjoining areas to "scour the country" in "small par-

ties" looking for convicts.[49] The executive also instructed magistrates to cooperate with the military to round up suspects—even those "not known to the Police."[50]

Even as it was sending soldiers and trackers everywhere to help the mounted police find absconding convicts, the Legislative Council endorsed another, dramatic innovation in peacekeeping to meet the growing bushranging crisis. In 1830 it passed *An Act to Suppress Robbery and Housebreaking and the Harbouring of Robbers and House Breakers.* Citing the need to enact extraordinary measures to meet "the emergency" caused by widespread robbery and break-ins, the Legislative Council authorized "any persons whatsoever having reasonable cause to suspect . . . any other person to be a transported felon unlawfully at large [or a robber]" to "without a warrant apprehend" the suspect and bring him before a justice of the peace. The suspect would "be obliged to prove to the reasonable satisfaction of such Justice that he is not a felon under sentence of transportation." If he failed to do so, he could be detained until his status was clarified. The act also provided that any person found with "fire-arms or other instruments of a violent nature" could be arrested and, whether they be prisoner or free, could be imprisoned if they could not show that their arms "were not intended for an illegal purpose." The act gave broad powers to magistrates to issue general warrants allowing constables to search houses at will in disturbed neighborhoods. Finally, it required that anyone convicted of "robbery or of entering and plundering any dwelling-house with arms and violence" and sentenced to death should be executed "on the day next but two after sentence passed." This was not a mandatory death sentence, but it certainly limited the capacity of the governor-in-council to grant mercy. Entwistle and his crew were one of the first gangs to be tried and executed under this law.[51] Such was the first "Bushrangers Act" in New South Wales.[52]

The act passed without fanfare, though one oblique letter to the editor on April 21 suggested that feeding convicts well rather than passing repugnant laws would solve the convict crisis. Another, published three days after the law was passed, commended the Legislative Council for its wisdom and creativity.[53] When the first bushrangers were hanged under the act in June, the *Sydney Gazette* noted that "crimes of rapine and of violence had arrived at a fearful extent; property, nay life itself, was not safe even in the streets of Sydney, and to strike terror—the extreme of terror—was the only chance left by which security could be anticipated."[54] The tenor of these reports did not mean everyone in New South Wales was happy with the legislation. When the colony's first civilian governor, Richard Bourke, was called upon to renew the act in 1832, he hesitated. The crisis, he noted in a letter to Lord Goderich, had passed. The roads were every bit as safe (or unsafe) as those of the English countryside. "It was therefore with extreme reluctance," said he, "that I yielded to the Unanimous Application of the Council" to renew the act for two years.[55] He yielded in 1832 and again in 1834, not to *restore* the peace, but to keep it.

The issue with the act, of course, was the burden it placed on free white men who held the most exorbitant privileges in empire. As Judge William Burton pointed out at length in 1834, the act breached fundamental principles of English law: it assumed guilt rather than innocence. Whereas English law allowed for citizens arrests to prevent a felony or treason, this act allowed arrest merely for failing to carry proof of one's freedom. It also allowed long periods of incarceration in the absence of proof of any wrongdoing. A free man with a gun who could not convince a magistrate that he meant no harm could be imprisoned for up to three years without trial. Burton pointed out that in extreme cases where a citizen-arrestor killed an innocent suspect, the effect of the act would be to transform their murder into manslaughter. He felt strongly that English vagrancy laws (themselves breathtakingly invasive of civil rights) would do nicely to restrain the peculiar population of New South Wales.[56]

In his defense of the act, Chief Justice Forbes almost agreed. He noted that the most recent British vagrancy legislation (thought not to be in force in New South Wales) required people with no visible means of support to give "a satisfactory" or "a good account of themselves" to "any person whatsoever" who may apprehend them. In this respect, it was not so different from the Bushrangers Act. However, the vagrancy law allowed exemplary costs to be awarded to those wrongly apprehended: while it placed the poor at risk of arbitrary arrest, it provided significant legal safeguards.[57] Forbes argued that more scope for abuse was essential to order in New South Wales. The need for the act was clear to "every man, who has local experience of the great number of Convicts who are always at large, and have no other mode of subsistence than such as may be acquired by plunder, of the facilities to escape and concealment, which are supplied by the uncleared forests and trackless retreats of the Colony, of the previous habits and reckless characters of the Convicts, and above all, of the frequency and malignancy of the Crimes."[58]

Justice Burton had argued that the Bushrangers Act was repugnant to British law. Forbes countered that it was necessary to the "peace, welfare, and good Government of the Colony" in its present state and was, therefore, within the power of the Legislative Council to pass. Forbes drew the council's attention to "the numerous laws which have been passed in the American colonies, particularly such as relate to Slavery, and the discipline of Slaves."[59] The imperial government had expressly or impliedly approved such laws from the seventeenth century even though none could exist in England. Forbes did not mention it by name, but the Somerset decision that in 1772 had declared that slavery could not exist on English soil also acknowledged the fact that colonial law could diverge fundamentally from core English constitutional principles. Slave codes were allowed because they were deemed to be essential to the king's colonial peace, ergo the Bushranging Act was necessary to the peace in New South Wales.

Remarkably, Forbes did not mention race, but it was on others' minds. The chief problem with convicts, according to one loquacious magistrate, was that "the prison population can be met on the highways, undistinguishable from the general mass of the free inhabitants."[60] In short, the trouble with convicts was that the vast majority of them were white.[61] They did not wear status in their skin, and it was altogether too expensive to buy them distinctive uniforms (which they could slough off at a moment's notice, in any case). As a result, every white person in the colony—or rather, every non-Indigenous person—had to carry the burden of the convict peace. Ironically, whiteness itself placed free men in special jeopardy of arrest as they traveled the colony and of arbitrary search and seizure in their homes.

White men, however, did not carry the burdens of this act equally. Class mattered enormously in 1830s New South Wales. It mattered because the taint of crime was ubiquitous. Convicts outnumbered free people in the colony by fewer than 5,000 according to participants in the 1834 debate, but only one magistrate hinted at the real problem: that "the *material* of the population" more generally endangered the peace.[62] The free population itself included an overwhelming majority of ex-convicts (emancipists) and their children, who, magistrates imagined, were likely to sympathize with prisoners. These people shared much more with convicts than with colonial elites: many had been Irish dissidents or machine breakers; most had been petty criminals from the streets of London. And by 1830 their prospects were much more limited than they had been in the first decades of colonization. They were less likely to prosper after emancipation, less likely be befriended by respectable people, and highly likely to be unfairly treated in their encounters with the state.[63]

After April 1830, signs of low status meant fear of arbitrary arrest. Alexander Harris's *Recollections* devoted a chapter to outlining the arrest of non-elite free emigrants searching for work in the colony.[64] He begins with an encounter "beyond Windsor" with a new emigrant, "who evidently by his English dress had not been long in the colony," surrounded by armed constables. Though "there was not the slightest indication . . . of his being a bushranger," he was hauled back to Sydney "for identification." After being shuffled around Sydney in various states of incarceration, the emigrant was freed but refused papers that might have saved him from being arrested again. This fate was shared by others—incarcerated on suspicion, interrupted in their pursuit of work, then "discharged" sometimes months later "without anything to protect him against the repetition of a similar outrage by some other constable the very next day."[65] That said, poor immigrants, emancipists, and convicts were not the only people at risk of harassment under the law. Even Chief Justice Forbes and Justice Dowling were rumored to have been stopped and asked for papers.[66] Harris himself was detained overnight in a damp cell "of a few feet square" then "marched" to Wallis Plains because he was found at large, after dark, in his working clothes.[67] He reported that such arbitrary arrests grew much more egregious when graziers employed convict "farm-constables" and built lockups on their property.[68]

Even before the passing of the Bushranging Act, status had cost Entwistle and Byrne a hiding and the prospect of a ticket of leave. They had bathed near the bullocks they were driving to market—suggesting that they were more likely than not to be convicts, ticket-of-leave men, or (far less likely) emancipists. Lieutenant Evernden, an erstwhile soldier and police magistrate, like Governor Darling, embodied the overlay of military and civilian governance in the colony. He had been a lieutenant, so would have ordered plenty of floggings for breaches of military comportment. While in the company of an imperious governor, skinny-dipping men likely symbolized the disorder of the countryside. So Evernden had them flogged and blighted their futures. As there was no wrong, there could have been no charge. This injustice was enough to drive Entwistle to join Irish convicts in a much larger performance of disorder.

In the Ribbon Gang's plot against masters and magistrates and in the generality of convict complaint, we catch a glimpse of how convicts—particularly Irish Catholics—saw the colonial peace. Entwistle joined the Ribbon Gang uprising to avenge a clear injustice. By all indications (including their name) the Irish ringleaders were motivated both by the oppression of Irish Catholics at home and by the arbitrary injustice and poor conditions that defined convict life around Bathurst. We can only glimpse their motivations through brief anecdotes: as noted, they did not kill a neighboring landlord because he was not a "bad master."[69] Another notorious uprising against bad masters and magistrates in the Hunter Valley in 1833 gives more insight into convicts' idea of a tolerable colonial peace. In the infamous "Castle Forbes" uprising in the Hunter Valley in November 1833, six convicts tried to shoot their master on one of the region's largest farms. Unlike cursory reports of the trial of the Ribbon Gang, the newspapers explored the grievances of these rebels in such satisfying detail that Governor Bourke ordered an inquiry into the administration of convict labor in the region. At their trial, the rebels claimed that they were "driven to desperation" and "brought to this unhappy end" by "the bad treatment, flogging, and bad provisions they had to endure" from their masters. In court and before the commission, convicts testified to having received maggoty meat and blackened wheat (which were duly produced and inspected). They claimed also to have been unjustly deprived of "indulgences" like milk, tea, and sugar. Insults and humiliations by their overseer ranked high among their complaints.[70] Most importantly, they complained that the local bench of magistrates afforded them no protection. Instead, magistrates ignored convict grievances and ordered floggings to uphold the tyranny of their friends and neighbors.[71] James Harvey swore to the commission of inquiry at Castle Forbes that he "never made any complaint to the Magistrates; it was a dangerous thing to do." James Browne swore that "when any man was about to complain, he was brought up on another charge."[72] Peter Ponsonby said he had overheard the rebels saying that "the magistrates were so friendly to each other, no justice could be done them."[73] This was enough to drive some convicts to arms.

Convicts' expectations of the peace underline how very different their lot was from that of slaves, though by 1830 masters and magistrates in the Caribbean had to look over their shoulders as they tortured and cowed their human property. Grace Karskens has shown the enormous and unexpected privileges enjoyed by convicts in the early colony.[74] Nevertheless, in 1830 convict social mobility was more restricted than ever before. New rules imposed after the Bigge

Inquiry limited their access to tickets of leave, pegging it to min-imum terms of servitude or to collaboration with the state against other convicts. The latter explains why a trusted conspirator ab-sconded with most of the Ribbon Gang's ammunition. Harris also reported that promises of diminished sentences incentivized "some fellows" to make a vocation out of "peering after every labouring man they can get sight of, and demanding his name, business, and pass."[75] In contrast, the new Supreme Court and new executive offices, like the attorney general and solicitor general, gave convicts new ave-nues for complaint, and opened the collusion of masters and magis-trates to scrutiny by the executive and judiciary. As a result, the king's peace was a much more complicated and divided affair in the second quarter of the nineteenth century.[76] Though the system was stacked against convicts, the growing colonial state provided an in-creasingly visible check on the everyday keeping of the convict peace.

The very structure of the colony of New South Wales fostered legal divergence, by investing vast powers in the governor, by estab-lishing a curiously martial and summary legal system, and, by omission, giving magistrates enormous discretion in convict disci-pline. The Bushranging Act was only one of many novel laws passed to keep convicts at peace in New South Wales in the aftermath of the transformations wrought by the Bigge Report. As early as 1825 the "Runaway Convicts Harbouring Act" tried to curtail convict mobility by means of a range of measures, including enjoining employers to check the status of apparently free laborers and fining pubs that served alcohol to convicts drinking without their master's permission.[77] An 1828 act set penalties for purchasing or receiving goods from convicts.[78] A harsh labor law of the same year limited the mobility of free workers and ticket-of-leave holders by giving magistrates the power to jail them for infringements of contract.[79] With the creation of the mounted police in 1825, these laws all demonstrated a pervasive sense of crisis about convict mobility and status that showed, again, just how far the colonial peace had traveled since the American Revolution. As apologists for the Bush-rangers Act argued year after year, New South Wales was not like England—its convict majority transformed white subjecthood, adding another layer to an emerging jurisprudence of emergency triggered, not by riot or rebellion, but by the vast scale of settlement and its reliance on unfree, white labor.

Settler Sovereignty and the King's Peace

Convicts were not the only problem of order in New South Wales. Indigenous people made a constant mockery of the efforts of the fledgling state to govern bodies in colonial towns, rural districts, and the wilderness. The dual specter of their disorder—attacking livestock on the colony's peripheries and breaching the peace in colonial towns—constituted an existential legal problem for the colony by the late 1830s. An incident in January 1835 combined the menace of both. Patrick Sheridan met a "party" of Aboriginal men on the king's highway in Brisbane Water—a site of endemic settler-Indigenous conflict. Sheridan knew the group's leader, Lego'me, well. It appears that before the troubles, Lego'me and Sheridan were friends. Sheridan had shared his hut with Lego'me and seen him "once or twice a week" for several years. But times had changed and Sheridan was nervous. He had heard that local men were out to get him. He feared for his life as the group approached. The group first asked him for tobacco, which he happily shared. Then Lego'me "poised his spear in the direction of the prosecutor and darted it forward, but the point went into the ground," before taking Sheridan's pipe and knife. This ambiguous transaction was enough to land Lego'me a conviction of transportation for seven years.

It was a relatively novel trial. Until 1816 no Aboriginal person had been tried and convicted by a settler court for committing any crime, though a handful had been banished. Some were even sent to Tasmania.[80] The reasons given for exempting Aboriginal people from trial were inconsistent. Some, like Richard Atkins, thought it absurd to try savages in court when they could not possibly understand the process. This is why the first Aboriginal man tried in New South Wales in 1816 was an adoptee, raised in the settlement and therefore presumed to both understand and be especially amenable to British law.[81] Others argued that Indigenous people had their own laws, as we will see.

Aboriginal resistance against settler expansion took longer to come to court. Hatherly and Jackie were tried for murdering a frontier settler near Bathurst in 1823, thirty-five years after the arrival of the first fleet.[82] Soon after their arrest Governor Brisbane declared martial law in Bathurst in 1824 to legalize the "indiscriminate slaughter" of Indigenous people as pastoralism exploded and their resistance grew. It was a one-off.[83] No Indigenous people were hanged for murder until 1827. Then, a large crowd of Aboriginal people gathered to witness this bold transition from retaliatory violence to solemn execution.[84] The court did not try an Indigenous person for theft until 1832.[85] In that very same year, Major Sullivan wrote from Port Macquarie that the prospect of arresting Indigenous people for trial was ludicrous and conviction all but impossible.[86] This led to an exchange among the colonial executive about whether it might be possible to pass legislation allowing groups of Aboriginal people to be tried for the crimes of individuals—more troubling innovations in defense of the peace.[87]

The novelty of Lego'me's trial was not lost on his counsel. Mr. Therry asked Sheridan "if he was not aware that he had been a squatter for some time on Legome's ground, and had frequently committed great depredations on his kangaroos." Sheridan countered that he "believed the ground belonged to Government, and, as for kangaroos, he had something else to do than look for them."[88] It was an important exchange. First, it demonstrates the growing certainty that Aboriginal land (if not Aboriginal people) belonged to the king. The trial and Sheridan's retort signaled a not-so-subtle shift in the relationship between Aboriginal Australians, the colonial peace, and the empire. So did the fact that Lego'me was one of twenty-one Aboriginal men arrested for frontier violence in 1835. But the case itself was modest in its jurisdictional arrogations. It is important that the event happened on a road. Lego'me was charged, not with simple theft, but with highway robbery. The significance of his menacing actions was amplified by their location on an ancient symbol of the king's peace. In that place, Lego'me transformed from a savage at war into a highwayman or bushranger—not just any subject, but one who was an object of special jurisdiction because the location of his crime posed a special threat to the peace.

Place was more than a symbol in Lego'me's case. In 1835, had this transaction occurred farther north or west, it might not have come to court at all. Since 1826 the New South Wales government had declared that it would not protect settlers in conflict with Indigenous people if they resided outside the "limits of location." This was part policy; the government used Aboriginal resistance as a disincentive to try to slow the seizure of land by "squatters" (illegal occupiers of land beyond the boundaries). But it was also part realism; the tiny colonial government simply could not protect distant pastoral runs. In this respect, these boundaries expressed ambivalence about the king's authority in New South Wales. What did it mean to claim a vast continent, parts of which would not be visited by settlers for more than a century? The problem was too large, and the mechanisms required to solve it were unclear.

So, it should come as no surprise that the questions raised in Lego'me's trial about the legal capacity of the colonial government to keep Aboriginal people at peace were not answered in a case about frontier violence. They were answered in a case about Aboriginal violence in town. Unlike convict disorder, which was imagined from the outside in, Aboriginal disorder was redefined from the inside out, through brawls between Indigenous men on roads in towns. Indigenous people had met and fought in Sydney since its founding. These payback ceremonies were frequently recorded in the *Sydney Gazette*. As the disruptions of colonialism spread, Sydney drew more and more Aboriginal people. The town became a meeting place for strangers as well as a place of ancient recourse.[89] These meetings did not always go smoothly. Aboriginal carousing, meeting, camping, and violence were part of the experience of town life in New South Wales. This violence had deeply disturbing implications for the king's peace.

Those implications were canvased long before Lego'me's trial in 1835. They were written into a proclamation issued by Lachlan Macquarie in 1816 declaring war on the frontiers of New South Wales. Macquarie's Proclamation allowed farmers to shoot Aboriginal people who "lurk or loiter about any Farm in the interior." More importantly for our purposes, the proclamation declared:

> That the practice hitherto observed amongst the Native Tribes of Assembling in large bodies or parties armed, and of fighting and attacking each other on the plea of Inflicting punishments on Transgressors of their own customs and manners at or near

Fig 5.2 Augustus Earle, *Natives of N.S. Wales as seen in the Streets of Sydney,*
1830. Earle's picture does more than depict the "disruptive" presence of
Aboriginal people in Sydney. As Grace Karskens has noted of another Earle
painting, he illustrates Aboriginal firstness and belonging. His Indigenous
characters are solid and visible, while settlers and their townscape are
faded and ephemeral. National Library of Australia, nla.obj-135290431

Sydney, and other principal Towns and settlements in the Colony
shall be hence forth wholly abolished as a barbarous Custom
repugnant to the British Laws . . . any armed body of natives
therefore who shall assemble for the foregoing purposes either at
Sydney or any other settlements of this Colony after the said forth
date of June next, shall be considered as Disturbers of the Public
Peace and shall be apprehended and punished in a Summary
Manner Accordingly.[90]

The spatial division between lurking in "the interior" and fighting "at or near Sydney, and other principal towns" is striking, again reflecting the special significance of streets and towns to the colonial peace.

But the juridical stakes involved in this unprecedented jurisdictional assertion only became clear thirteen years later, when, in 1829, an Aboriginal man named Ballard was arrested for killing Dirty Dick at the Governor's Domain in the center of Sydney. The stakes changed because the attorney general asked the chief justice if Ballard could be tried for murder. Chief Justice Forbes said no. He declared Ballard and his victim to be "wild savage[s] . . . wandering about the country, and living in the uncontrolled freedom of nature." The colony of New South Wales, like the North American colonies before it, had never "interfere[d] with or enter[ed] into the quarrels that have taken place between or amongst the natives themselves." This was so because "the savage is governed by the laws of his tribe."[91] While "there is reason & good sense in the principle that in all transactions between the natives & British subjects, the laws of the latter shall prevail," there was no reason in "municipal or natural law, which shall subject the inhabitants of a newly found country, to the operation of the laws of the finders, in matters of dispute, injury, or aggression between themselves." Justice Dowling was even more adamant about Ballard's capacity to stand aloof from the king's peace: "Amongst civilized nations this is the universal principle, that the lex loci shall determine the disputes arising between the native & the foreigner. But all analogy fails when it is attempted to enforce the laws of a foreign country amongst a race of people, who owe no fealty to us, and over whom we have no natural claim of acknowledgment or supremacy."[92]

Dowling and Forbes did more than apply maxims of the law of nations here. By absolving Indigenous people of any obligation to keep the peace in the center of Sydney, they created a fundamental problem for British claims to sovereignty and for New South Wales's colonial government. Even in the fulcrum of settlement, forty years after the colony's founding, Aboriginal people could kill each other with impunity. The logic here was not merely that they were "harmless inoffensive savages"; it was also that they had "laws for themselves, which are preserved inviolate, & are rigidly acted upon."[93] The notion of *lex loci* itself was uncertain. In this rendering, the king himself was foreign in New South Wales. His peace was not grounded, it had no territorial bearing.

This position could not hold in a period when the relationship of states with territories and peoples was being revisited and realigned, not only in the British Empire, but on the borders of many European and diasporic states. It could not hold in Sydney where a free elite had struggled since the Macquarie period to gentrify the town, by straightening its streets, remaking its public buildings, and excluding convicts from office and society. This project must have seemed more urgent after 1830 when the Bushranging Act made free white men liable to search and seizure throughout the colony.

The issue came up again in 1833, just two years before Lego'me came to court. When two men, Quart Pot and Numbo, were arrested for killing another Indigenous man, once again in the Governor's Domain, Attorney General John Kinchela asked the chief justice what he should do. Despite strong support for prosecution from the new governor, Richard Bourke, the court again dissuaded him from bringing the case to trial "as the decision of the court must be against me."[94] But this was not the end of the matter. In December 1835, Jack Congo Murrell and George Bummaree killed two of their countrymen on the "king's highway" between Richmond and Windsor in the colony of New South Wales. They were arrested and a coronial inquiry suggested that they be tried for murder. This time the attorney general resolved to bring the matter to formal adjudication—had the court not just participated in a new drive to punish Aboriginal-settler violence with law? So, in February 1836, Jack Congo Murrell stood before the Supreme Court of New South Wales, tried with the murder of another Aboriginal man.

Murrell's counsel, Sydney Stephen, demurred that Aboriginal people were not subjects of the crown or aliens bound by British law because they were *ante nati,* first peoples, with their own laws. Great Britain had neither conquered nor treated with Murrell's tribe. British authority in New South Wales meanwhile was premised on the subjecthood and allegiance of British settlers, rather than the exclusive territorial sovereignty of the British crown. Murrell and his victim were not protected by British law. Nor could they be tried under it. They were not part of the king's peace, such as it was, in New South Wales.

The court had heard—indeed, key members of the court had *made*—this argument before. However, in 1836 the executive and judicial negotiations of the 1830s combined with the changing nature of imperial legal orthodoxy to alter the court's position. 1836 was the final year of Francis Forbes's tenure as chief justice. From 1832 his health and his influence had been in decline. New imperial orthodoxies had crept into the court with the arrival of Puisne Judge William Burton. Burton was an Englishman trained at the Temple Bar. Like so many officers of the New South Wales establishment, he arrived as a man of the world, having served for several years as a puisne judge at the Cape.[95] Burton's brief tenure at the Cape had coincided with momentous legal reform, including the establishment of the first Supreme Court and fierce local debate about the status of Africans in the colony. Burton had played a central role in the drafting of "Ordinance 50 for the Improvement of 'the Conditions of Hottentots and Other Free Persons of Colour' and Giving Them Civil and Political Equality with the Settlers." Indigenous rights, in his frame of reference, were best protected by their incorporation into the legal system.[96]

In 1836 Burton penned the court's response. His opinion exists in a number of forms. Its briefest version pronounced that "1st . . . the aboriginal natives of New Holland are entitled to be regarded by Civilized nations as a free and independent people" but that "the various tribes had not attained at the first settlement of the English people amongst them to such a position in point of numbers and civilization, and to such a form of Government and laws, as to be entitled to be recognized as so many sovereign states governed by laws of their own."[97] He argued "2ndly," that the British state had taken into "actual possession" half of the continent of New Holland, between Cape York and the South Coast, between 10°37's to 39°12's "and embracing all the country inland to the Westward as far as 129° East longitude"—this despite the fact that a large portion of the colony remained uncharted and government itself was limited to a number of officially settled counties within a few hundred miles of the east coast. "3rdly," Burton contended "that the English nation has obtained and exercised for many years the rights of Domain and Empire over the country"; this despite the fact that the first Aboriginal person was tried by a settler court in 1816 and the second and third were tried (and acquitted) in 1823. "4thly," Burton argued, the crime fell within the territorial jurisdiction of the court as laid down by statute—a jurisdiction that the court could not renounce. Finally he noted, "This Court has repeatedly

tried and even executed aboriginal natives of this Colony, for offenses committed by them upon subjects of the King"; accordingly, "there is no distinction in law in respect to the protection
due to his person between a subject living in this Colony under
the Kings Peace and an alien living therein under the Kings
Peace."[98] Aboriginal people were henceforth subject to British law,
while their own law, if it involved violence, became crime.[99]

A heavily annotated draft of the decision in Burton's hand gives
much more insight into his understanding of the colonial peace.
This draft notes that Aboriginal people were "only just removed
from the most simple state of nature" and as such their "loose &
vague practices" were not "entitled to be respected as . . . 'in the
nature of laws by a Christian Community.'" Burton denied that
they had a "settled form of Government:" "The several tribes have
never owned any common superiority or any common bond of
union, but have ever lived in a state of enmity with one another—
their practices are only such as are consistent with a state of the
grossest darkness & irrational superstition." Their rituals of tribal
punishment, were merely a "mode of vindication for personal
wrongs" grounded "upon the wildest most indiscriminatory [sic]
notions of revenge."[100]

Following Locke and Emer de Vattel, Burton argued that Aboriginal people had no property or dominion in land because they had
not appropriated it to themselves through cultivation.[101] He acknowledged, in his draft judgment, that Aboriginal people were a
category of persons *sui generis* living under the king's protection
within the king's peace. In the process, he resolved a decade's uncertainty about whether Indigenous people were aliens or subjects
of Great Britain by arguing that they were neither. Burton catego-
rized them instead (again using de Vattel) as *"perpetual inhabitants . . .*

who have received the rights of perpetual residence. These are certain of citizens of an inferior order, & are united & subject to the Society without participating in all its advantages."[102] Should they choose to live under the protection of the law as subjects, they could certainly do so.[103] But even if they did not, they were subject to the king's peace and the king's laws. This settlement was temporary. By 1841 Burton claimed that Aboriginal Australians "had been naturalized by a general Act of Parliament, under which they were entitled to all the rights and privileges, and subject to all the liabilities, of British subjects."[104]

In his demurrer, Stephen had argued that British law was determined by subjecthood and allegiance rather than territory:

> The Subjects of Great Britain have come to reside amongst the Natives having laws & usages of their own—& rather subject to the laws customs of the Blacks in being, than the Natives to our laws.
>
> But the laws of England are binding on the subjects of G. B. That is in respect of that allegiance they owe to their sovereign—of necessity—in Nature. . . .[105]

Burton argued instead that in New South Wales, as in Britain, the king's peace could not coexist in place with distinct Aboriginal social and legal orders: "The King's Majesty . . . is by his office & dignity royal then principal conservator of the peace within all his dominions; & may give authority to any other to see it kept & to punish such as break it." Thus, "all offences committed within his realm are & must be laid to be committed against the king." Subjects and aliens alike can thus be kept at peace in the realm. "From this it is evident that not only all those who are subjects but all who live within any country of the realm are under the King's peace or protection, & that any offence committed against any local person is committed against the King's Peace—all offences are local & triable at common law."[106]

Burton premised this discussion on ancient sources of British law and the law of nations, but the novelty of his argument lay in his application of British law without qualification to a settler periphery. He cast the king's peace over half a continent, over places that settlers had never been. In doing so he declared that the colony of New South Wales was more than a periphery of empire, it was part and parcel of a modern territorial state—a state in which Indigenous jurisdiction was an unacceptable anomaly.

Viewed from Sydney, this claim seemed like a basic principle of orderly urban life. Expunging Indigenous law throughout the colony was necessary, because if Indigenous Australians were not governed by settler law, they could carry savage law into the very heart of settlement. Summarizing the attorney general's pleadings, Burton wrote that "barbarities the most revolting & cruelties the most shocking may be transacted by them in the midst of a . . . Perfectly Christian Country ~~governed by Christian laws founded upon Christian principles~~ even in populous streets ~~& in the eyes of Christian people~~ without restraint—provided they be only committed upon one another . . . it were a scandal."[107] His "cross-outs" are significant. In this view, Indigenous disruptions of the king's peace in Sydney or on the king's highway near Windsor were far more disruptive than bushranging because they unsettled British claims to sovereignty in New South Wales "in populous streets & in the eyes of Christian people." If violence could not be contained in the very center of settlement, "Christian laws founded on Christian principles" were unsettled, made contingent.

But even at this moment when colonial territorial sovereignty was first declared in defense of the peace, the colonial state and the settler population bracketed the *Murrell* decision in absurdity. Murrell was acquitted by a settler jury and Bummaree was released without trial. In any case, the colony's first Vagrancy Act, passed just a year before in 1835, exempted "black natives" and their children from its provisions, ensuring that they could continue to move freely (if more peacefully) through colonial towns.[108] Finally, viewed from the periphery, Burton's claims about the king's peace were nonsense—as growing frontier violence demonstrated even as Murrell came to court.

Increasingly, the colony dealt with this disjuncture by clothing violence in law. After 1824 the government of New South Wales did not declare martial law to license unrestrained colonial violence, as Van Diemen's Land did when it tried to remove its entire Aboriginal population between 1828 and 1832. Instead it responded to violence by expanding its experiments in military policing. In 1838 the government augmented the mounted police force with a border police comprised chiefly of convicts whose job was to assist a commissioner of crown lands in policing people beyond the limits of location.[109] From 1848, on the violent frontiers to the north, a police force composed of Indigenous men from the south was deployed to wage genocidal war against Aboriginal people.[110]

I find it difficult not to return to New South Wales. It is an absorbing colonial experiment that both exemplifies and challenges our understanding of empire in general and of the evolution of the king's peace in particular. As in Massachusetts, Quebec, and Bengal, officials in the colony of New South Wales grappled with the relationships among sovereignty, subjecthood, and order so explicitly that we cannot but learn about empire from their efforts. In New

South Wales that conversation was particularly illuminating, first because the colonial government acknowledged that the methods it adopted to keep the peace were grossly unconstitutional, and second because (as in Quebec) the objects of the most illiberal measures were white men. In Quebec, French Catholics' imagined penchant for despotism made it possible to withhold a local legislature from all white subjects, altering the course of imperial history for nearly a century. Seventy years later, the convicts' fall from grace (but also their ungovernability) recast the rights and privileges of every white subject in the colony even more fundamentally, depriving them of security of person, in the defense of the peace.

A massive gulf separated these legal milestones, demonstrating the enormous changes in the king's peace made possible by the shift to crown rule after 1773. That shift allowed colonial states everywhere to draw deeply on the reservoirs of tyranny modeled by Jamaica. New South Wales was not the first to create a mounted military police force to capture escapees and to pacify rebellious peripheries. Like Bengal and Ireland before it, the convict colony adapted practices from the militarized Caribbean peace in its efforts to manage convict and Indigenous resistance after 1823. Likewise, the increasingly contested legal status of free Black people in the Caribbean provided a model for variable subjecthood that pushed far beyond the special status carved out for French Canadians after 1763. Hardening discourses of race aided the flattening of Bengali subjects into native subjects unfit for the privileges and responsibilities of full British subjecthood after the advent of East India Company rule. In 1830, New South Wales went much further. By turning whiteness into a rebuttable marker of servitude, the Bushrangers Act effected a delicious inversion. Black skin combined with markers of "savagery" signaled freedom in this strange place at the ends of the earth. Of course, that freedom was of dubious benefit: freedom from law too often meant freedom to suffer violent dispossession.

In this respect New South Wales, like 1760s Quebec, shows us the doubleness of conversations about the peace in Anglophone settler projects. While white bodies carried a special kind of peace into the North American and Australian wilderness, Indigenous bodies revealed the partial nature of the king's peace even in the very centers of settlement. The difference is that this pluralism was difficult to stomach by 1830 in the growing towns of New South Wales. While war raged on the colony's peripheries, the colonial courts started to perform a different sort of peace on the king's highways and in the king's colonial towns. The struggle to define Indigenous peoples' relationship with the colonial state between 1816 and 1836 reminds us that the king's peace was a symbol of sovereignty that constantly frayed at the edges of empire.

Conclusion: Small Stories and the Transformation of Empire

The ruptures of the peace described in this book span vast distances, revolutions, and generations. Each plots small steps toward colonial legal divergence, steps that were cumulative, if not always sequential. All begin, and some end, with a story about the eighteenth-century British Empire that folds into an epochal transformation of British imperial order. That transformation has occupied scholars for generations. My purpose has been to better explain its causes and consequences through a series of controversies linking London with disorders from the riverbanks, roads, parlors, and mountain passes of the colonies.

The first and most important arc of this story shows how quotidian disputes hastened the unraveling of the recent and unstable constitutional settlement that followed the Glorious Revolution. That unraveling is a core strand in the transformation of empire under a resurgent crown, the constitutional groundwork of which had been imagined in Quebec in the winter of 1764 and laid before the first shots of the American Revolution were fired. This vast constitutional transformation grew out of breaches of the king's peace, because disorder always embroiled the king's prerogative, the nature of imperial sovereignty, and the rights and privileges of different kinds of colonial subjects.

My tale began in the interwoven disorders of Boston and Montréal, where ungovernable Protestant men showed governors the perilous state of the post-1688 prerogative. As he watched the king's authority collapse in Boston, Governor Bernard lamented the limitations imposed by the Massachusetts charter, which had been renewed by William III in 1691. By tethering the governor's power to call the military to the consent of a counsel appointed by the legislative assembly, the charter gutted the king's authority to bring order to Boston's streets. As Boston descended into riot—or, even worse, when its townsfolk kept the peace in defiance of the king—the interwoven character of sovereignty and urban order were made clear to all. By 1768 no one in Boston doubted the relationship between prerogative power and everyday order, or the deleterious impact of disorder on empire. To imperial luminaries, this rowdy town on the other side of the Atlantic signaled the need for a fundamental shift in modes of imperial governance, binding subjects more tightly into empire, managing their expectations of liberty, and, most of all, reserving power enough in the crown to keep the colonial peace.

This was a lesson cascading to the center from many different corners of the expanded empire at the end of the Seven Years' War. The most important of these sites was not so far from Boston, in the wintry township of Montréal. There the demands of Protestant subjects for self-government, and with it a monopoly on the everyday mechanisms of peacekeeping, had a very different legal valence. First, their campaign against military rule showed the gaping legal lacuna left by the political and legal truncation of military power and martial law in the aftermath of the Glorious Revolution. The Mutiny, Disbandment and Riot Acts preserved Britons' liberty by limiting the role of the king's soldiers in keeping the peace. But no one had considered the ramifications of such strictures in transitional regimes or places where no other jurisdiction existed. Without some species of martial jurisdiction, the problem of keeping soldiers and civilians at peace in the aftermath of the conquest of Quebec proved intractable—as did keeping greedy traders in order in Indian Country. The bleating of Protestant merchants about military tyranny shone a bright light on a constitutional absurdity that would soon be fixed by quiet resort to martial law.

That bleating did other work too. When Protestant merchants in Quebec called for an end to military tyranny after 1763, they sought to monopolize both the magistracy and the legislature promised by the Proclamation of 1763 to the grave disadvantage of the Catholic majority. Their vision of liberty rested, not only on subordinating soldiers to civilian law, but also on the application of the Penal Acts to Quebec, depriving some 70,000 Francophone Catholic residents of the new province of the right to hold office. Before 1763 this had not been so controversial—were not the Catholic multitudes of Ireland deprived of a stake in their own governance? Yet in Montréal in 1764 such claims threatened the future of the empire. For soldier-administrators, imposing penal laws on Quebec seemed unworkable. They much preferred pliable Québécois to seditious British merchants, and argued that stable government in the colony must rest on the protection of Catholic interests. To men in the center reading volumes of tedious correspondence about Walker's severed ear and the ungovernability of colonists from backcountry Georgia to Michilimackinac, this call for Catholic emancipation provided an opportunity.

The result was a new sort of colonial constitution that radically truncated British subjects' pretensions to liberty by emancipating

Catholics, but not entirely. Under the Quebec Act of 1774, Catholics could hold office but could not govern themselves. Instead the act established an autocratic governor with an appointed council that Catholics could join. It also allowed them to join the magistracy, and it reestablished French civil law in Quebec. In the same breath, it cast this new order over a large part of Indian Country, pushing gubernatorial autocracy into the violent backcountries of the thirteen colonies even as the latter mobilized for revolutionary war. This solution was as elegant as it was controversial—giving French Catholics reason to embrace the British monarchy, and obviating the outlandish claims of Protestant merchants, squatters, and traders by investing the crown with vast power to govern the North American interior. This innovation had small origins—and, indeed, it did not long outlast the influx of loyalists after the American Revolution—yet it set the course for imperial rule for the better part of a century. Governors ruled every new colony without a legislature until the shift to responsible government in a few non-Caribbean settler polities after 1840. In other British colonies, crown government persisted until decolonization in the twentieth century.

Jamaica had burst the boundaries of the postrevolutionary settlement long before the Quebec Act of 1774. Its first slave code was passed just a few years into the Stuart restoration. While the island's planters argued harder than most for their share of liberties, working slaves to death required a very different sort of peace. So, slave societies like Jamaica became engines of legal innovation in the seventeenth and eighteenth centuries. Long before the Somerset Case, it was well understood that slavery itself violated fundamental tenets of British law. A simple survey of laws first disallowed in the center, then let slip through with minor amendments, demonstrates the myriad constitutional compromises made in London to facilitate

Caribbean slavery. Some of these laws allowed masters to torture and murder their human property, others deprived free people of color of rights of free movement and association, and still others radically limited the franchise, excluding free people of color and most white property holders in the island from a say in its government. Such laws were crafted in the vast discretionary cavern created by the most important constitutional maxim in early modern empire: that colonial law could vary from British law to the extent required by local circumstances. According to some, local circumstances in Jamaica occasionally required the slow burning of slaves merely for entertaining the thought of rebellion, and the training of dogs to tear Maroons "to pieces."[1] Even after the great nineteenth-century humanitarian gestures of amelioration and emancipation, the legacies of those compromises—and the deep scars of racial differentiation they had carved into political discourse, jurisprudence, and policing practice—remained, shaping peacekeeping in empire until its demise. Similar scars mar policing practice in the United States of America to this day.

The impossibility of keeping peace in Jamaica bequeathed still more to empire than the enduring injustice of racism. The policing of racial slavery changed everyone's subjecthood. Just as the constitutional "protection" of Catholics in Quebec subordinated new and old subjects to an expanded crown prerogative, so too the pyrrhic struggle to terrorize a vast slave majority into submission chipped away at the subjecthood of slave masters. The chief instruments here were military power and martial law. One hundred years before Edward Eyre called martial law in southeastern Jamaica, martial law did more complicated work in the empire's richest island. Its ubiquitous use was one of several important innovations in peacekeeping introduced after Tacky's Rebellion in 1760. To keep slaves at peace, masters garrisoned their island, paying the imperial army to guard against slave rebellion, even at the expense of regional security. The tiny governing elite worked with the governor to call martial law at least every other year after 1760. Their purpose in doing so was assuredly to keep slaves in order, but the targets of martial law were free whites and, to a lesser extent, free Black people who could not be counted on to mobilize to keep the island's tenuous peace. So, the near disaster of 1760 showcased the malleability of even the most pugnacious white men's subjecthood. It also helped to usher in the shift to crown government: the moral and legal disorder of self-governing slave colonies formed a core argument for withholding a legislature from Trinidad after its conquest in 1797.

Race, martial culture, and the impossibility of the slave peace in the difficult landscape of Jamaica's interior combined in the fragile détente between slaveholders and Maroons. As never-conquered rebels, Maroons made uncomfortable collaborators in keeping Jamaica's peace. Their imperfect incorporation into Jamaican jurisdiction, their insistent mobility in defiance of law, and their self-conscious displays of ferocity that warned slaves and their masters of impending violence, all exemplify the incivility of peace in Jamaica. Meanwhile, the Maroons' constant mobilization and their governance under martial law demonstrated the degree to which that uncivil peace threatened constantly to collapse into pan-Caribbean rebellion. That intolerable compromise imploded in Trelawny Town in 1795 under the weight of the French and Haitian Revolutions. But martial order survived, following Trelawny Maroons into exile in Sierra Leone, and rippling through colonies with nonwhite majorities long after the demise of slavery. The terrible elasticity of the slave peace provided a repertoire of technologies that could be repackaged and rolled out around the empire by newly empowered emissaries of the crown.

With Ernst's troubles in Hooghly in 1808, the story shifts to another register—exploring both cause and consequence of the empire-wide shift away from representative government. Bengal's governor was installed even before the Quebec Act was passed. It was the first autocratic colonial regime to be legislated by Parliament. By 1808, East India Company governors ruled vast territories, and from 1784 their peacekeeping operations were supervised with varying degrees of attention by a secret council appointed by the king. In Bengal, regulation after regulation not only altered Mughal criminal law but unraveled many of the safeguards of due process. The Ernst controversy is offered as a case study of how absolutely untethered Bengal became from the core principles that had governed the British Empire. In 1760s Boston, the governor sat by, impotent, while local magistrates refused to arrest arsonists, looters, and rioters. In contrast, the governors of Bengal used their virtually unfettered legislative power to authorize the arbitrary arrest of innocents, and to resort much more readily to civil and military violence to keep the peace—sometimes over the objections of more scrupulous (if racist and incompetent) magistrates. This was nowhere more apparent than in the novel methods of policing trialed in early nineteenth-century Bengal. In 1793 Cornwallis created a new police force and magistracy, overthrowing established modes of peacekeeping. Laws from 1800 allowed not only the arrest but the peonage of vagrants, while a succession of laws allowed the incarceration of men and women on the mere suspicion that they might be in cahoots with gangs of robbers. The governor-in-council repeatedly encouraged new stipendiary magistrates to employ a cadre of peon spies to infiltrate robber gangs. All involved acknowledged that this system not only wrought grave injustice, it also corroded Bengali social hierarchies.

This move is fascinating because of the deep misgivings almost every British administrator expressed about its imposition. Ernst and others excoriated the governor-in-council for breaking fundamental rules of due process. Councillors agreed that the spies deployed by their special magistrates were corrupt; one even thought that their use was extralegal. Their misgivings are most interesting because they led nowhere. Ernst's adversaries argued that the benefits to order were worth the evils of injustice. Given that the regular police (imposed by Cornwallis in 1793) were also corrupt, using criminals was not so much worse if it reduced the incidence of crime. Meanwhile, Bengalis caught in the net of preventative imprisonment languished in jail for months without release. The law that allowed their incarceration without trial was expanded by Regulation III of 1818.[2]

These laws and practices were justified by the purported ungovernability of Bengalis—their unfitness for the full protections of anything approximating due process. This was an argument drawn straight from the lawbooks of Jamaica in its efforts to strip legal privileges from free people of color. In India such arguments combined with the enduring belief that "Oriental" people were peculiarly tolerant of (and suited to) despotic government. These logics stuck in Victorian empire, defining the rights and responsibilities of the vast majority of British subjects for more than a century. Innovations in peacekeeping in Bengal traveled farther than Africa and Southeast Asia. Extraordinary policing also became a mainstay of colonial rule in colonies with white majorities, from New South Wales to Ireland. The most important lesson we learn from Bengal, then, is that gubernatorial rule had enormous ramifications for everyday peacekeeping, which in turn radically truncated the rights and privileges of colonial subjects everywhere, at least for a while.

It is to underline this point that I return to the highways and byways of New South Wales. New South Wales was the third nongarrison, after Quebec and Bengal, to be ruled without a local legislature. Here, as elsewhere, a series of military governors used their expansive powers to transform the king's colonial peace. When the colony was beset by bushrangers in the 1820s, its governor-in-council drew from the playbooks of Jamaica, India, and Ireland to meet the crisis. In 1825 the colony established a mounted police force, staffed by military men, to hunt down escaped convicts and marauding Aboriginal warriors. In 1830 it passed the first of a series of laws requiring, *inter alia,* that every non-Indigenous person carry proof of their freedom or to be arrested as absconding convicts. The latter was drawn directly from slave societies, but its use to unsteady the status of free white subjects was an extraordinary departure in imperial constitutional law that troubled the colony's first civilian governor and its newest Supreme Court judge. Again, their disquiet could not displace "necessity." It was beyond the state's capacity to stop convicts from disappearing into the endless wilderness, so extraordinary means were required. The character of free white colonial subjecthood was so altered by decades of counter-revolution that it was only mildly controversial to detain a judge on his morning stroll in defense of the king's peace.

In contrast, as in prerevolutionary North American Indian Country, Indigenous people wore jurisdiction far more lightly than white men in early New South Wales—an immunity that was as much a burden as a boon. That immunity came under scrutiny in the 1820s as the frontiers were overrun with sheep and shepherds and as an influx of free immigrants evened the numbers between convicts and free settlers. The colonial state started to arrest and try Indigenous men for a string of offenses, starting with settler murders and extending to settler thefts. These efforts culminated in 1836 in the trial of an Aboriginal man for killing another Aboriginal man on a road near Windsor—an event I have described elsewhere as a milestone in the articulation of settler sovereignty. Here I pull a different thread of the *Murrell* decision, focusing instead on its careful elucidation of the colonial peace. Whereas the Bushrangers Act imagined droves of convicts disappearing into the wilderness, the *Murrell* case focused squarely on keeping the peace on roads and in towns. The trial in 1836 resolved two decades of rising disquiet about Aboriginal violence in and about Sydney— violence that denied the king's authority to govern the continent. Justice William Burton's unpublished notes on the judgment place the problem of the peace at the center of this story. The king's sovereignty, said Burton, rested on the king's exclusive power to keep the peace. Therefore, Aboriginal people in Sydney could be punished for killing one another in exercises of tribal law. Indeed, according to Burton, the king's peace in New South Wales required the reclassification of acts of Aboriginal jurisdiction as crime, even in parts of the continent that Europeans would not visit for the better part of a century. This judgment would later justify the imposition of stultifying and intimate controls on Aboriginal people from Broome to Melbourne. But it began with a quest to tidy a few plausible sites of crown authority in the colony's center.

The stories I tell here wend their way back to much larger issues— the power of the king's men to govern; the applicability of the Bill of Rights to colonial subjects, white and nonwhite; the privileges of propertied Britons to participate in colonial peacekeeping; and the character of British sovereignty over other peoples' countries.

A million different stories from the colonies explicate the frayed edges of the imperial constitution. They are all worth telling, because without them we cannot understand how empire worked and how its workings changed over time. In the end, *The King's Peace* insists that the making of the imperial constitution was global and local. Huge decisions about the empire—the move away from colonial charters, the shift to crown and company autocracy, the normalization of martial law, the erosion of legal safeguards against arbitrary arrest, the abnegation of Indigenous law, and the legal presumption that British subjects were unfree, all turned on the collision of very local problems of ordering people in place with the fundaments of imperial law.

Those collisions had devastating consequences. They laid the groundwork for the great violence of Victorian empire. Nothing exemplifies the violence of the peace more clearly than the proliferation of martial law as a tool of colonial governance after the Napoleonic Wars. There were earlier stirrings. Some 30,000 Irishmen died when martial law was called to put down the Irish rebellion of 1798, one of vanishingly few such declarations in the eighteenth-century British Isles.[3] Martial law continued to underpin the peace in self-governing slave colonies in the Caribbean after the turn of the century. Thousands died during periods of martial law in nineteenth-century slave uprisings in the Caribbean, including Barbados (1805 and 1816), Demerara (1823), and Jamaica (1831). Martial law was also deployed ruthlessly elsewhere. Untold thousands (some have argued, millions) died at the hands of imperial and colonial troops during periods of martial law declared to quell rebellions in Ceylon (1817 and 1848), Canada (1838), Jamaica (1865), and especially India (1857).[4]

But martial law played a larger and more diffuse role in colonial governance in the nineteenth-century empire than these oft-cited incidents suggest.[5] After 1820 it was deployed with sudden ubiquity in difficult terrains as disparate as Honduras, the Cape, and New Zealand. New work is showing its central role in the governance of early nineteenth-century Bengal and Madras.[6] This shift reflected the militarization of civilian bureaucracies after the Napoleonic Wars, but it was also facilitated by the altered parameters of the colonial peace.[7] There is much more work to do before we understand the true scale of its deployment against colonial subjects, almost all of whom, by the mid-nineteenth century, were not white. But this is a tale for another day.

One of the reasons Victorian violence fell so heavily on nonwhite subjects was that the vast constitutional license of the counter-revolutionary moment was suddenly truncated in settler polities at midcentury. When Canadians rebelled in 1838, their reward (after a rash of deportations under military jurisdiction) was not the withdrawal of the partial self-rule granted to them in 1791; it was the granting of more fulsome self-government. A decade later, "responsible government" took select parts of the empire by storm. As Britain slowly liberalized its own voting system, it began to let white settlers do the same.[8] This move was driven, in part, by a combination of racism and resignation. After the end of slavery, metropolitan attempts to make settler colonies less violent and to stem their uncontrolled dispossession of Indigenous people failed. Settler polities were generating far too much wealth for the metropolis to seriously intervene. This retrenchment of effort was aided by the waning of humanitarian intervention in the colonies. In the aftermath of slave emancipation, humanitarian reformers started to lose faith that Indigenous people and ex-slaves could reach suitable heights of self-denial, parsimony, and virtue to become full rights-bearing subjects. The humanitarian impulse that had fed the growth of crown rule in empire slowly dissolved into something like racist indifference.[9] Their concerns about the welfare of colonial subjects were drowned out after 1857, in any case. Though the Indian Rebellion was met with astounding retaliatory violence by British governors and company troops, somehow it was cast as a great betrayal by Indian subjects. It further "proved" the incommensurable subjecthood, not just of South Asians, but of every nonwhite person in the empire. Thus began a pan-imperial "rule of colonial difference."[10]

In southern Africa, Australia, and Canada, white subjects were left to oppress traditional landowners, and imported laborers more or less as they liked, short of enslavement.[11] Indeed, in the Australia colonies for generations after self-government some iteration of the armed and mounted police created in the 1820s used their weapons to protect settlers far more often than Indigenous people. Canadian mounted police did the same.[12] By the end of the century, most Australian colonies and Canadian provinces clothed their increasingly intimate violence against Indigenous people in the language of protection.

In most of the rest of the empire, crown rule remained. After 1857, however, it tilted toward "indirect rule." Instead of trying to reform colonial subjects into Britons, British administrators settled for using "native" infrastructures to help keep a very partial version of the peace. Though the growth in declarations of martial law began well before midcentury, the system of indirect rule placed even greater emphasis on imperial violence, whether administered by the imperial army or by its delegates. As Antoinette Burton has pointed out, one of the reasons Victorian empire was so deeply mired in violence was that colonized people resisted empire's graft, corruption, and cruelty at every turn.[13]

Understood as a series of coercive practices, as performances of authority, and as a key marker of sovereignty, the king's colonial peace was a porous and confusing construct. After the American, French, and Haitian Revolutions the imperial peace was expanded to meet the existential threat posed to empire by revolutionary disorder. In Company India and the new crown colonies, civilian law could be bent and stretched as never before to order colonial subjects, though subjects bore the consequences of that shift quite differently depending on their status, creed, or race. In the era of counter-revolution, colonial order was a good that trumped liberty, justice, and equality before the law.

This lesson from empire is also a founding principle of modern statehood. Writing of the boundless ordering ambitions of states after September 11, 2001, Giorgio Agamben observed that we now live in a permanent state of exception in which governance always exceeds law. I do not think this is true, and it is certainly not helpful. Though a million contingencies separate the late eighteenth-century British Empire from twenty-first-century Great Britain or the United States, there is value to be gleaned from the countless arguments about what the empire should or should not do to keep the colonial peace in the Age of Revolutions. Executive power grew enormously in the twentieth century and has grown further in anglophone liberal democracies since 2001. The prerogative is real and it is growing. Its sphere of action has been expanded dramatically by extraordinary legislation that gives police and ministers wide discretion to decide the boundary between acceptable action, breaches of the peace, and terrorism. The majesty of nineteenth-century empire was grounded in increasingly illiberal rules and practices of order performed by largely unaccountable servants of the crown. In contemporary states, the majesty of government is maintained by vast executive discretion and SWAT teams who menace tiny protests with lethal force. Crises of colonial order spawned endless debates about how to keep the peace in distant places, the privileges owed to new and vulnerable subjects, and the king's responsibility to protect, to do justice, and to keep order—all echo eerily in the present.

Who says we've learned nothing from history?

NOTES

ACKNOWLEDGMENTS

INDEX

NOTES

INTRODUCTION

1. Ali Parchami, *Hegemonic Peace and Empire: The Pax Romana, Britannica and Americana* (Abingdon: Routledge, 2009), 1–8.

2. Thalia Anthony and Harry Blagg, "Hyperincarceration and Indigeneity," in *Oxford Research Encyclopedia: Criminology and Criminal Justice* (2020), https://oxfordre.com/criminology/view/10.1093/acrefore/9780190264079.001.0001/acrefore-9780190264079-e-656.

3. Frederick Pollock and Frederic William Maitland, *The History of English Law before the Time of Edward I*, vol. 1 (Cambridge: Cambridge University Press, 1895), 22. What follows is taken from one of my first reflections on "the Peace": Lisa Ford, "The Pig and the Peace: Transposing Order in Early Sydney," in *Law and Politics in British Colonial Thought: Transpositions of Empire,* ed. Shaunnagh Dorsett and Ian Hunter (New York: Palgrave Macmillan, 2010), 170–171.

4. Michael Ross Fowler and Julie Marie Bunck call this "the basket approach to sovereignty" in Fowler and Bunck, *Law, Power and the Sovereign State: The Evolution and Application of the Concept of Sovereignty* (University Park: Pennsylvania State University Press, 1995), 70–80.

5. Margaret Kelly, "King and Crown: An Examination of the Legal Foundation of the British King" (PhD diss., Macquarie University, 1998), 55–63; Shaunnagh Dorsett, "Thinking Jurisdictionally:

A Genealogy of Native Title" (PhD diss., University of New South Wales, 2005), 47–94.

6. The Age of Revolutions is enjoying an enormous revival in the scholarship of the British Empire of late, particularly in work of pan- or trans- imperial perspective. Even as this book goes to press, a wealth of scholarship is being published. Sivasundaram invites us to reconsider the fallout of the revolutionary period on the forgotten third of the globe. Sujit Sivasundaram, *Waves Across the South: A New History of Revolution and Empire* (London: Harper-Collins, 2020). Cohen explores pan-imperial *mentalités,* linking Massachusetts, Jamaica, and Bengal. Ashley L. Cohen, *The Global Indies: British Imperial Culture and the Reshaping of the World, 1756–1815* (New Haven: Yale University Press, 2021). Mulich explores the peculiar fate of the Caribbean as an inter-imperial micro-region in this period. Jeppe Mulich, *In a Sea of Empires: Networks and Crossings in the Revolutionary Caribbean* (Cambridge: Cambridge University Press, 2020). Muller's 2017 book has already reshaped thinking about subjecthood in this period. Hannah Weiss Muller, *Subjects and Sovereign: Bonds of Belonging in the Eighteenth-Century British Empire* (New York: Oxford University Press, 2017). I engage with recent work focusing on relevant jurisdictions throughout the book.

7. This shift was exemplified by Trinidad, conquered in 1797. In general, see Lauren Benton and Lisa Ford, "Island Despotism: Trinidad, the British Imperial Constitution and Global Legal Order," *Journal of Imperial and Commonwealth History* 46, no. 1 (2018): 21–46; Christopher Leslie Brown, *Moral Capital: Foundations of British Abolitionism* (Chapel Hill: University of North Carolina Press, 2006). The best account of this shift remains D. J. Murray, *The West Indies and the Development of Colonial Government, 1801–1834* (Oxford: Clarendon Press, 1965).

8. In 1773 the Virgin Islands and Prince Edward Island were given legislatures. New Brunswick, a new loyalist settlement, received a

legislature in 1782. Note, however, that weak quasi-legislative bodies were retained in Demerara and Berbice by the terms of capitulation, and the Demerara Court of Policy claimed exclusive rights to legislate internally in the 1820s. These were claims that the crown disputed, but, at various times, did not actively challenge. Murray, *The West Indies,* 61, 135.

9. Rajat Kanta Ray, "Indian Society and the Establishment of British Supremacy, 1765-1818," in *The Oxford History of the British Empire,* vol. 2: *The Eighteenth Century,* ed. P. J. Marshall (Oxford: Oxford University Press, 1998), 513.

10. Quebec received a partially elected legislature in 1791, in response to loyalist agitation after the American Revolution. For a discussion of this move and its impact on French Canadians, see Helen Taft Manning, *The Revolt of French Canada, 1800–1835: A Chapter in the History of the British Commonwealth* (New York: St. Martin's Press, 1962).

11. Stephen Saunders Webb, *1676: The End of American Independence* (New York: Alfred A. Knopf, 1984), 331-406; Agnes Whitson, *Constitutional Development of Jamaica, 1660–1729* (Manchester: Manchester University Press, 1929), 70-109; Stephen Constantine, *Community and Identity: The Making of Modern Gibraltar since 1704* (Manchester: Manchester University Press, 2009), 65-92; Desmond Gregory, *Minorca, the Illusory Prize: A History of the British Occupations of Minorca between 1708 and 1802* (Salem, MA: Associated University Presses, 1990), 144-181.

12. This old notion was articulated very clearly in the Proclamation of 1763, which enjoined new legislatures to make laws "as near as may be agreeable to the laws of England." P. J. Marshall, *The Making and Unmaking of Empires: Britain, India, and America, 1750–1783* (Oxford: Oxford University Press, 2007), 187. On the significance of this principle for appellate jurisdiction before the American Revolution, see Mary Sarah Bilder, *The Transatlantic Constitution: Colonial Legal Culture and the Empire* (Cambridge, MA:

Harvard University Press, 2004); and Joseph H. Smith, *Appeals to the Privy Council from the American Plantations* (New York: Octagon Books, 1965). For its use to supervise legislation, see Damen Ward, "Legislation, Repugnancy and the Disallowance of Colonial Laws: The Legal Structure of Empire and *Lloyd's Case* (1844)," *Victoria University of Wellington Law Review* 41 (2010): 381–402; and Aaron Graham, "Jamaican Legislation and the Transatlantic Constitution, 1664–1839," *Historical Journal* 61, no. 2 (2018): 327–355.

13. Lauren Benton and Lisa Ford, *Rage for Order: The British Empire and the Origins of International Law, 1800–1850* (Cambridge, MA: Harvard University Press, 2016), 61.

14. *Campbell v. Hall* came as no shock. See Edward Cavanagh's recent discussion of eighteenth-century crown legal opinions and of the case itself, "The Imperial Constitution of the Law Officers of the Crown: Legal Thought on War and Colonial Government, 1719–1774," *Journal of Imperial and Commonwealth History* 47, no. 4 (2019): 624, 637–639.

15. Harlow describes the attendant shift away from colonies of settlement to garrisons of trade bent on extracting wealth from Indigenous polities. Vincent Harlow, *The Founding of the Second British Empire, 1753–1793,* vol. 1: *Discovery and Revolution* (London: Longmans, Green, 1952).

16. Anthony Anghie, *Colonialism, Sovereignty, and the Making of International Law* (New York: Cambridge University Press, 2005). The imbrication of racism and ethnocentrism into colonial law is foundational to South Asian historiography. See Radhika Singha, *A Despotism of Law: Crime and Justice in Early Colonial India* (New Delhi: Oxford University Press, 2000).

17. Julie Evans, *Edward Eyre: Race and Colonial Governance* (Dunedin: University of Otago Press, 2005); Nasser Hussain, *The Jurisprudence of Emergency: Colonialism and the Rule of Law* (Ann Arbor: University of Michigan Press, 2003); R. W. Kostal, *A Jurisprudence of Power: Victorian Empire and the Rule of Law* (New York: Oxford University Press, 2005).

NOTES TO PAGES 9-10

18. Paul D. Halliday, *Habeas Corpus: From England to Empire* (Cambridge, MA: Belknap Press of Harvard University Press, 2010), 247-258. Regarding the increasing use of military violence in Britain in the Age of Revolutions, see Anthony Babington, *Military Intervention in Britain: From the Gordon Riots to the Gibraltar Incident* (London: Routledge, 1991), esp. 1-97.

19. E. Neville Williams, ed. and comp., *The Eighteenth-Century Constitution, 1688–1815: Documents and Commentary* (Cambridge: Cambridge University Press, 1960), 423-425; Halliday, *Habeas Corpus,* 215-258.

20. Benton and Ford, *Rage for Order;* Lisa Ford, *Settler Sovereignty: Jurisdiction and Indigenous People in America and Australia, 1788–1836* (Cambridge, MA: Harvard University Press, 2010).

21. June Starr and Jane F. Collier, eds., *History and Power in the Study of Law: New Directions in Legal Anthropology* (Ithaca, NY: Cornell University Press, 1989); Sally Merry, "Anthropology, Law and Transnational Processes," *Annual Review of Anthropology* 21 (1992): 357-379.

22. Kathleen Wilson, "Introduction: Histories, Empires, Modernities," in *A New Imperial History: Culture, Identity and Modernity in Britain and Empire, 1660–1840,* ed. Kathleen Wilson (Cambridge: Cambridge University Press, 2004), 1-26; Wilson, *The Sense of the People: Politics, Culture and Imperialism in England, 1715–1785* (Cambridge: Cambridge University Press, 1995); Antoinette Burton, *At the Heart of the Empire: Indians and the Colonial Encounter in Late-Victorian Britain* (Berkeley: University of California Press, 1998); Tony Ballantyne, *Webs of Empire: Locating New Zealand's Colonial Past* (Wellington, NZ: Bridget Williams Books, 2012); Catherine Hall, *Civilising Subjects: Metropole and Colony in the English Imagination, 1830–1867* (Cambridge: Polity Press, 2002). For a very useful overview, see Tony Ballantyne, "The Changing Shape of the Modern British Empire and Its Historiography," *Historical Journal* 53, no. 2 (2010): 429-452.

23. Compare very recent research emphasizing the importance of metropolitan politics and policy over colonial controversy: Steven

Pincus, Tiraana Bains, and A. Zuercher Reichardt, "Thinking the Empire Whole," *History Australia* 16, no. 4 (2019): 610-637. Note that recent work in a similar vein emphasizes constitutive exchange between "men on the spot" and the metropole as a corrective to the literature's excessive emphasis on East India Company autonomy. See, for example, James Vaughn, *The Politics of Empire at the Accession of George III: The East India Company and the Crisis and Transformation of Britain's Imperial State* (New Haven, CT: Yale University Press, 2019), 18-20.

24. Muller, *Subjects and Sovereign,* 5, 17-33.

25. Muller, *Subjects and Sovereign,* 45-79.

26. Wilf Prest, *Albion Ascendant: English History, 1660-1815* (Oxford: Oxford University Press, 1998), 62; and Halliday, *Habeas Corpus,* 11-18, 231-246. Note that Halliday argues compellingly that habeas corpus was not a right but a prerogative that allowed the crown to investigate jailors.

27. Muller, *Subjects and Sovereign.*

28. For a rich, recent exploration of the limited subjecthood of the Québécois after conquest, see Nancy Christie, *The Formal and Informal Politics of British Rule in Post-Conquest Quebec, 1760–1837: A Northern Bastille* (Oxford: Oxford University Press, 2020).

29. This is a point long since made in the foundational work of Elsa V. Goveia, *The West Indian Slave Laws of the 18th Century* (Barbados: Caribbean Universities Press, 1970); and Diana Paton, *No Bond but Law: Punishment, Race, and Gender in Jamaican State Formation, 1780-1870* (Durham, NC: Duke University Press, 2004).

30. Aaron Graham, "The Colonial Sinews of Imperial Power: The Political Economy of Jamaican Taxation, 1768-1838," *Journal of Imperial and Commonwealth History* 45, no. 2 (2017): 188-209. Note, however, that during the American Revolution, king and Parliament made many concessions to Caribbean self-governing colonies to keep them quiescent. See Jack P. Greene, "Liberty and Slavery: That Transfer of British Liberty to the West Indies,

1627-1865," in *Exclusionary Empire: English Liberty Overseas, 1600-1900,* ed. Jack P. Greene (New York: Cambridge University Press, 2000), 67-74; and Andrew Jackson O'Shaughnessy, *An Empire Divided: The American Revolution and the British Caribbean* (Philadelphia: University of Pennsylvania Press, 2000).

31. The imminence of rebellion was a key strand in James Stephen Senior's arguments for withholding a legislature from Trinidad. For a broader discussion, see Benton and Ford, "Island Despotism," 21-46.

32. Brooke Newman, *Dark Inheritance: Blood, Race, and Sex in Colonial Jamaica* (New Haven, CT: Yale University Press, 2018).

33. See Robert Travers's very useful discussion of relative liberty in Bengal. Robert Travers, "Contested Despotism: Problems of Liberty in British India," in Greene, *Exclusionary Empire,* 191-219.

34. On the complexities of sovereignty in Bengal, see Robert Travers, *Ideology and Empire in Eighteenth-Century India: The British in Bengal* (Cambridge: Cambridge University Press, 2007), esp. 43-47; 195-197; 220-23. Contrast Rahul Govind, "The King's Plunder, the King's Justice: Sovereignty in British India, 1756--76," *Studies in History* 33, no. 2 (2017): 151-186.

35. Halliday, *Habeas Corpus,* 65.

36. Prest, *Albion Ascendant,* 62-64.

37. For an elegant exposition of the slippage from king to crown in Blackstone's *Commentaries,* see Paul D. Halliday, "Blackstone's King," in *Re-interpreting Blackstone's Commentaries: A Seminal Text in National and International Contexts,* ed. Wilf Prest (Oxford: Hart, 2014), 169-187. See also the useful discussion in D. Alan Orr, *Treason and the State: Law, Politics and Ideology in the English Civil War* (Cambridge: Cambridge University Press, 2002), 31-57. See also Quentin Skinner, *The Foundations of Modern Political Thought,* vol. 2: *The Age of Reformation* (Cambridge: Cambridge University Press, 1978), 355.

38. S. Max Edelson, *A New Map of Empire: How Britain Imagined America before Independence* (Cambridge, MA: Harvard University Press, 2017), esp. 4-10, 46-53.

39. C. A. Bayly, *Imperial Meridian: The British Empire and the World, 1780–1830* (London: Longman, 1989).

40. See also Benton and Ford, *Rage for Order*.

41. Zoë Laidlaw, *Colonial Connections, 1815–45: Patronage, the Information Revolution and Colonial Government* (Manchester: Manchester University Press, 2014); Alan Lester and Fae Dussart, *Colonization and the Origins of Humanitarian Governance: Protecting Aborigines across the Nineteenth-Century British Empire* (Cambridge: Cambridge University Press, 2014); David Lambert and Alan Lester, eds., *Colonial Lives across the British Empire: Imperial Careering in the Long Nineteenth Century* (Cambridge: Cambridge University Press, 2006); Paul Knaplund, *James Stephen and the British Colonial System, 1813–1847* (Madison: University of Wisconsin Press, 1953). Of the characters in this story, Cornwallis had fought in Europe and America before his posting to Bengal, while New South Wales governors since 1810 had served as officers or administrators in America, Europe, Egypt, India, Mauritius, Ireland, the Caribbean, and the Cape.

42. James Epstein, *Scandal of Colonial Rule: Power and Subversion in the British Atlantic during the Age of Revolution* (Cambridge: Cambridge University Press, 2012); Benton and Ford "Island Despotism," 21–46; James Millette, *The Genesis of Crown Colony Government: Trinidad, 1783–1810* (Curepe: Moko Enterprises, 1970); Murray, *The West Indies,* 78, 81–84.

43. Mary Sarah Bilder, "English Settlement and Local Governance," in *The Cambridge History of Law in America,* vol. 1, ed. Michael Grossberg and Christopher Tomlins (Cambridge: Cambridge University Press, 2008), 91–92.

44. Benton and Ford, *Rage for Order,* 75–76.

45. For an excellent survey of a series of judicial/gubernatorial tussles throughout the empire that ended in the dismissal of judges in the nineteenth century, see John McLaren, *Dewigged, Bothered and Bewildered: British Colonial Judges on Trial, 1800–1900*

(Toronto: Published for the Osgoode Society for Canadian Legal History and the Francis Forbes Society for Australian Legal History by University of Toronto Press, 2011).

46. The importance of antislavery networks and the proliferation of crown efforts to protect vulnerable subjects in the colonies are discussed, inter alia, in Laidlaw, *Colonial Connections;* Lambert and Lester, *Colonial Lives;* Lester and Dussart, *Colonization;* Benton and Ford, *Rage for Order,* 56–84; Amanda Nettelbeck, *Indigenous Rights and Colonial Subjecthood: Protection and Reform in the Nineteenth-Century British Empire* (Cambridge: Cambridge University Press, 2019); John Edwin Mason, *Social Death and Resurrection: Slavery and Emancipation in South Africa* (Charlottesville: University of Virginia Press, 2003).

47. Bayly, *Imperial Meridian,* 8–12, 193–216.

48. Carl Schmitt, *Political Theology: Four Chapters on the Concept of Sovereignty* (Cambridge, MA: MIT Press, 1985), orig. pub. 1922.

49. John Reynolds, *Empire, Emergency and International Law* (Cambridge: Cambridge University Press, 2017); Marcelo Svirsky and Simone Bignall, eds., *Agamben and Colonialism* (Edinburgh: Edinburgh University Press, 2012).

50. Thomas Poole, *Reasons of State: Law, Prerogative and Empire* (Cambridge: Cambridge University Press, 2015), 5.

51. Anghie, *Colonialism;* Benton and Ford, *Rage for Order.*

1. A PEACEABLE RIOT IN BOSTON

1. Hiller B. Zobel, *The Boston Massacre* (New York: W. W. Norton, 1970), 51–56.

2. Note that sugar had been imported in defiance of the Navigation Acts before this more direct approach. At least three-quarters of New England's sugar supply came from foreign sources, and New England provided rum to the other colonies, including slave colonies in the Caribbean. Zobel, *The Boston Massacre,* 14–15.

3. If successful, Sugar Act taxes threatened the local rum industry. See John Phillip Reid, *In a Rebellious Spirit: The Argument of Facts,*

the Liberty Riot, and the Coming of the American Revolution (University Park: Pennsylvania State University Press, 1979); "Great Britain: Parliament—The Sugar Act: 1764," Yale Law School, The Avalon Project, http://avalon.law.yale.edu/18th_century/sugar_act _1764.asp.

4. Reid, *In a Rebellious Spirit,* 90–99.
5. Francis Bernard to the Earl of Halifax, May 17, 1765, Colonial Society of Massachusetts, *The Papers of Governor Francis Bernard* [hereafter cited as *Bernard Papers*], vol. 2: *1759–1763,* https://www .colonialsociety.org/publications/3111/354-earl-halifax.
6. Now Hanover Street.
7. William Sheaffe and Benjamin Hallowell, deposition, September 24, 1766, National Archives, London [hereafter cited as TNA], Colonial Office Records [hereafter cited as CO], 5/755, pp. 771–775.
8. Regarding "his Castle," see Benjamin Goodwin, deposition, September 24, 1766, TNA, CO5/755, p. 744; regarding the blowing out of brains, see Stephen Greenleaf, deposition, October 1, 1766, TNA, CO5/755, p. 785; deposition of Ambrose Vincent and Lewis Turner, November 14, 1766, in George Wolkins, "Daniel Malcom and Writs of Assistance," in Waldo Lincoln, ed., "October Meeting, 1924. Dr. James Denormandie; Malcom and Writs of Assistance; Henry and Elizabeth Poole; William Whately to Andrew Oliver; Lincoln Newton Kinnicutt," *Proceedings of the Massachusetts Historical Society, Third Series* 58 (1925): 81–82.
9. Regarding the posse comitatus, see Pauline Maier, *From Resistance to Revolution: Colonial Radicals and the Development of American Opposition to Britain, 1765–1776* (New York: W. W. Norton, 1973), 19–20.
10. Sheaffe recalled a crowd of "between 3 or 400 People." William Sheaffe and Benjamin Hallowell, deposition, September 24, 1766, TNA, CO5/755, p. 774.
11. John Tudor, deposition, September 25, 1766, TNA, CO5/755, p. 776.

12. Stephen Greenleaf, deposition, October 1, 1766, TNA, CO5/755, p. 785.

13. William Sheaffe and Benjamin Hallowell, deposition, September 24, 1766, TNA, CO5/755, p. 774.

14. Daniel Malcom, deposition, September 24, 1766 TNA, CO5/755, pp. 765, 769.

15. William Mackay, deposition, September 22, 1766, TNA, CO5/755, pp. 741–742.

16. Enock Rust, deposition, September 24, 1766, TNA, CO5/755, p. 747.

17. Depositions of John Ballard, Moses Tyler, Edward Jarvis, Caleb Hopkins, John Matchett, Samuel Harris, and Samuel Aves, undated, TNA, CO5/755, pp. 749–751, 754.

18. Nathaniel Barber, deposition, October 16, 1766, TNA, CO5/755, p. 764.

19. William Mackay, deposition, September 22, 1766, TNA, CO5/755, p. 741.

20. Benjamin L. Carp, *Rebels Rising: Cities and the American Revolution* (New York: Oxford University Press, 2007), 44–45.

21. Edward Jarvis, deposition, undated, TNA, CO5/755, p. 749.

22. Wolkins, "Daniel Malcom and Writs of Assistance," 5–92. On the writs themselves, see M. H. Smith, *The Writs of Assistance Case* (Berkeley: University of California Press, 1978).

23. Reid, *In a Rebellious Spirit,* 23.

24. Hallowell to the Commissioners of the Customs, November 14, 1766, appendix to Wolkins, "Daniel Malcom and the Writs of Assistance," 78–80.

25. Reid, *In a Rebellious Spirit,* 55–56, 63–85, 100–107.

26. Bernard to Board of Trade, October 10, 1766, TNA CO5/755, p. 799.

27. Gordon Wood, "Conspiracy and the Paranoid Style: Causality and Deceit in the Eighteenth Century," *William and Mary Quarterly* 39, no. 3 (1982): 401–441; following Richard Hofstadter, "The Paranoid

Style in American Politics," *Harper's Magazine,* November 1, 1964, 77–86. See also Bernard Bailyn, *The Ideological Origins of the American Revolution* (Cambridge, MA: Belknap Press of Harvard University Press, 1967).

28. Eric Hinderaker, *Boston's Massacre* (Cambridge, MA: Harvard University Press, 2017), chaps. 8 and 9.

29. In 1926 Hinkhouse claimed that the British Press discussed Indians and Indian Country more often than any other group or colony between 1763 and 1775. F. J. Hinkhouse, *Preliminaries of the American Revolution as seen the British Press, 1763–1775* (New York: n.p., 1926), cited in P. J. Marshall, *The Making and Unmaking of Empires: Britain, India, and America c. 1750–1783* (Oxford: Oxford University Press, 2007), 190.

30. See, for example, Maier, *From Resistance to Revolution,* 53–76.

31. Phrase taken from Hinderaker, *Boston's Massacre,* 29.

32. Reid, *In a Rebellious Spirit,* 30.

33. Stephen Greenleaf, deposition, October 1, 1766, TNA, CO5/755, p. 782.

34. John Tudor, deposition, September 25, 1766, TNA, CO5/755, p. 776.

35. William Sheaffe and Benjamin Hallowell, deposition, September 24, 1766, TNA, CO5/755, pp. 772, 774.

36. Stephen Greenleaf, deposition, October 1, 1766, TNA, CO5/755, p. 785.

37. See Paul A. Gilje, *Rioting in America* (Bloomington: Indiana University Press, 1996), 24–34, for a more fulsome list of riots in colonial North America, especially in Boston before 1765. Gilje also notes that many riots were not directly about empire, but were caused instead by border and land disputes. Imperial taxes added a new and explosive layer of disturbances (36). See for example, land riots in Duchess County, New York, in 1766. Thomas Gage to Henry Conway, July 15, 1766, in *The Correspondence of General Thomas Gage with the Secretaries of State, 1763–1775,*

ed. Clarence Edwin Carter [hereafter cited as *Gage Correspondence*] (Hamden, CT: Archon Books, 1969), 1:99-100. For the Stamp Act riots, see Peter Linebaugh and Marcus Rediker, *The Many Headed Hydra: Sailors, Slaves, Commoners, and the Hidden History of the Revolutionary Atlantic* (Boston: Beacon Press, 2000), 214-216, 231.

38. Gilje, *Rioting in America,* 38; Edmund S. Morgan and Helen M. Morgan, *The Stamp Act Crisis: Prologue to Revolution* (1953; Chapel Hill: University of North Carolina Press, 1995), 150-164.

39. Bernard to Halifax, August 31, 1765, TNA, CO5/755, p. 290.

40. William Sheaffe and Benjamin Hallowell, deposition, September 24, 1766, TNA, CO5/755, p. 772.

41. William Mackay, deposition, September 22, 1766, TNA, CO5/755, p. 742; Reid, *In a Rebellious Spirit,* 13.

42. W. L. Melville Lee, *A History of Police in England* (London: Methuen and Co., 1901), 8.

43. Note that, indeed, the military posse became an important peacekeeping measure in the early American republic. From 1789, when the Judiciary Act enshrined it into federal law, the posse comitatus was used repeatedly to summon America's standing army to keep the peace, from capturing slaves under the Fugitive Slave Law to hunting down brigands in the post–Civil War wild West. Clayton D. Laurie, "Filling the Breach: Military Aid to the Civil Power in the Trans-Mississippi West," *Western Historical Quarterly* 25, no. 2 (1994): 149-162.

44. J. V. Capua, "The Early History of Martial Law in England from the Fourteenth Century to the Petition of Right," *Cambridge Law Journal* 36, no. 1 (1977): 152-173; Rory Rapple, *Martial Power and Elizabethan Political Culture: Military Men in England and Ireland, 1558–1594* (Cambridge: Cambridge University Press, 2009); Henry Reece, *The Army in Cromwellian England, 1649–1660* (Oxford: Oxford University Press, 2013).

45. John Childs, "The Restoration Army: 1660-1702," in *The Oxford History of the British Army,* ed. David G. Chandler (Oxford: Oxford University Press, 1994), 54.

46. Childs, "The Restoration Army," 60.

47. Paul D. Halliday, *Habeas Corpus: From England to Empire* (Cambridge, MA: Belknap Press of the Harvard University Press, 2010), 247-258.

48. John M. Collins, *Martial Law and English Laws, c. 1500–c. 1700* (Cambridge: Cambridge University Press, 2016), 248-275. Collins compares the Riot Act's terms to the powers exercised by Tudor provost martials. He argues that this suite of laws gave post-Glorious Revolution monarchs ample (if legislatively defined) power to keep rebels, rabble raisers and mutinous soldiers more or less in check. These powers derogated considerably, and controversially, from the Bill of Rights.

49. Nicholas Rogers, "Popular Protest in Early Hanoverian London," *Past & Present* 79, no. 1 (1978): 81-82.

50. Riot Act 1714 1 Geo.I c.5, s.1. For Britain, see Max Beloff, *Public Order and Popular Disturbance, 1660–1714* (London: Oxford University Press, 1938). For the use of militia against rioters in America, see John W. Shy, *Toward Lexington: The Role of the British Army in the Coming of the American Revolution* (Princeton: Princeton University Press, 1965), 39-40.

51. Contrast Tony Hayter, *The Army and the Crowd in Mid-Georgian England* (London: Macmillan, 1978), 9-12.

52. Riot Act 1714 1 Geo.I c.5, s.3.

53. Contrast Mansfield's reading after the Gordon Riots in 1780. Hayter, *The Army and the Crowd*, 10.

54. See Shy, *Toward Lexington*, 216-223; Dartmouth to Haldimand, October 14, 1773, Gage Papers, vol. 119, William L. Clements Library, University of Michigan; Gage to Bradstreet, January 15, 1766, Schoff Revolutionary War Collection, box 1, Clements Library.

55. Hayter, *The Army and the Crowd*, 16-19.

56. Hayter, *The Army and the Crowd*, 147-159. Also on the Gordon Riots, the upswing in military involvement in policing disorder

thereafter, see Anthony Babbington, *Military Intervention in Britain: From the Gordon Riots to the Gibraltar Incident* (London: Routledge, 1990).

57. "By the King. A Proclamation" (London: Printed by Charles Eyre and William Strahan, Printers to the King's Most Excellent Majesty, 1780), National Archives, *Black Presence,* http://www .nationalarchives.gov.uk/pathways/blackhistory/rights /transcripts/royal_proclamation.htm. For original, see TNA, WO 34/103, folio 100. It was an assertion immediately qualified by Lord Mansfield, who claimed that "the military had been called in . . . not as soldiers, but as citizens . . . in aid of the laws, not to subvert them or overturn the constitution, but to preserve both." Quoted in 185 *Parl. Deb.,* 3d ser. (1867), cols. 919–920.

58. Maier, *From Resistance to Revolution,* 24–26. For Massachusetts Acts, see *The Acts and Resolves, Public and Private, of the Province of the Massachusetts Bay,* vol. 4 (Boston: Rand, Avery and Co., 1881), 617–618. Note, contrasting Maier, that it was renewed a few months after the Boston Massacre. *The Acts and Resolves, Public and Private, of the Province of the Massachusetts Bay,* vol. 5 (Boston: Rand, Avery and Co., 1886), 86–88.

59. The exchange is printed in *Speeches of the Governors of Massachusetts from 1765 to 1775; and the Answers of the House of Representatives to the Same; with Their Resolutions and Addresses for That Period and Other Public Papers, relating to the Dispute between This Country and Great Britain, Which Led to the Independence of the United States* (Boston: Russell and Gardner, 1818), 202–206.

60. There was some discussion of its renewal, according to Thomas Hutchinson's *History.* He alleged that the act had expired and "the house . . . refused to revive it." This was incorrect according to the legislative record, but it is likely that the house refused, as he went on to say, to make "further provision for preventing riots." Thomas Hutchinson, *The History of the Province of Massachusetts Bay, from 1749 to 1774, Comprising a Detailed Narrative of the Origin*

and Early Stages of the American Revolution (London: John Murray, 1828), 283.

61. Bernard to Halifax, August 15, 1765, TNA, CO5/755, p. 267. Though he complained often of the reluctance of magistrates to do their duty, Gage noted their efforts to quell rebellion in New York in 1766 on the anniversary of Stamp Riots. Gage to the Duke of Richmond, August 26, 1766, in *Gage Correspondence,* 104.

62. Bernard to the Board of Trade, September 3, 1766, TNA, CO5/755, p. 573.

63. Bernard to Halifax, August 15 and 16, 1765, TNA, CO5/755, p. 268.

64. Hutchinson to Hillsborough, March 27, 1770, TNA, CO5/759, p. 144.

65. Gage to Conway, December 21, 1765, in *Gage Correspondence,* 1:79.

66. Bernard to the Board of Trade, May 1, 1765, TNA, CO5/755, pp. 221-228. Gage and Bernard both noted the use of civil suits to harass soldiers and crown officers. See Gage to Richmond, August 26, 1766, in *Gage Correspondence,* 1:104; Mackay to Gage, June 18 and 19, 1769, Gage Collection: American Series, vol. 86, Clements Library; Bernard to Halifax, July 1, 1765, TNA, CO5/755, p. 257-260.

67. For example, Gage to Conway, January 16, 1766, in *Gage Correspondence,* 1:82. Regarding the barracking of soldiers, see Gage to Conway, May 6, 1766, and Gage to the Earl of Hillsborough, October 31, 1768, both in *Gage Correspondence,* 1:89, 1:202.

68. Bernard to Halifax, August 15, 16, and 22, 1765, TNA, CO5/755, pp. 262, 279.

69. Copy of a letter from the Commissioners of the Customs in Boston to Bernard, June 13, 1768, TNA, T1/465, pt. 2, folio 157.

70. John Robinson, Henry Hulton et al. to the Lords Commissioners of His Majesty's Treasury, March 28, 1768, TNA, T1/465, pt. 1, folios. 25-26.

71. Bernard to the Board of Trade, September 5, 1763, *Bernard Papers,* vol. 2: *1759–1763,* https://www.colonialsociety.org/node/2309#ch238.

72. Bernard to the Board of Trade, September 5, 1763, *Bernard Papers,* vol. 2: *1759–1763,* https://www.colonialsociety.org/node /2309#ch238. The Board of Trade, also known as the Lords Commissioners of Trade and Plantations, was a committee comprised of paid official and privy councillors charged with overseeing empire from 1696 until 1779.

73. Bernard to Halifax, August 15, 1765, TNA, CO5/755, p. 265. Note that there is a discrepancy between the archival version and the online version of this letter. The latter lists the addressee as the Board of Trade; but the archive version is addressed to "My Lord" as opposed to "My Lords."

74. Bernard Bailyn, *The Ordeal of Thomas Hutchinson* (Cambridge, MA: Belknap Press of Harvard University Press, 1974), 112.

75. "State of the disorders, confusion & misgovernment which have prevailed & do still continue to prevail in His Majesty's Province of Massachusets Bay in America," TNA, CO5/754, folio. 44.

76. Bernard to the Earl of Shelburne, March 12, 1768, *Bernard Papers,* vol. 4: *1768,* https://www.colonialsociety.org/node/2834.

77. Bernard to Lord Barrington, March 4, 1768, *Bernard Papers,* vol. 4: *1768,* https://www.colonialsociety.org/node/2830.

78. Bernard to Shelburne, March 19, 1768, *Bernard Papers,* vol. 4: *1768,* https://www.colonialsociety.org/node/2838#lt600.

79. Bernard to Shelburne, March 19, 1768, *Bernard Papers.*

80. Bernard to Thomas Gage, July 2, 1768, TNA, CO5/757, folio. 354.

81. Gage to Conway, February 22, 1766, in *Gage Correspondence,* 1:84.

82. Ann Hulton to Elizabeth Lightbody, June 30, 1768, Colonial Society of Massachusetts, *Henry Hulton and the American Revolution,* https://www.colonialsociety.org/node/1897.

83. The arguments of the town and of the historian are both admirably canvassed in Reid, *In a Rebellious Spirit,* 86–126.

84. Hillsborough to Hutchinson, March 24, 1770, TNA CO5/759, folio 53.

85. Reid, *In a Rebellious Spirit,* 6.

86. As Barnard noted in a letter to Lord Barrington, "This was afterwards turned to a Joke & said to be nothing but to intimidate them; but if it was only a Joke it was a very cruel one." Bernard to Barrington, March 4, 1768, *Bernard Papers,* vol. 4: *1768,* https://www.colonialsociety.org/node/2830#lt592.

87. Bernard to the Earl of Hillsborough, July 9, 1768, *Bernard Papers,* vol. 4: *1768,* https://www.colonialsociety.org/node/2884#lt646.

88. William Mackay, deposition, September 24, 1766, TNA, CO5/755, p. 741.

89. See, for example, John Adams's Abstract of Otis's argument, John Adams, "Abstract" appendix J, and James Otis's offering to the *Boston Gazette,* January 4, 1762, appendix M, both in Smith, *The Writs of Assistance Case,* 551-555, 562-566, and see also, in general, 312-386.

90. Zobel, *The Boston Massacre,* 13-14.

91. Advice from London after the Malcom affair suggested that the writ was in fact *ultra vires* the Massachusetts court. The King's attorney, William de Grey, argued that English writ rested on "the Seal of His Majestys Court of Exchequer" and that court had never issued a writ for officers in the plantations. Other legislation that might support search and seizure did not mention a writ. De Grey's opinion was not written until October 17, 1766. Thereafter, writs of assistance were never used again. Reid, *In a Rebellious Spirit,* 26; Opinion of the Attorney General, October 17, 1766, appendix to Wolkins, "Daniel Malcom and Writs of Assistance," 71-73; Wolkins, "Daniel Malcom and Writs of Assistance," 21-23.

92. Reid, *In a Rebellious Spirit,* 30-33.

93. William Mackay, deposition, September 24, 1766, TNA, CO5/755, p. 743.

94. Caleb Hopkins, deposition, undated, TNA, CO5/755, p. 751; William Nickells, deposition, October 20, 1766, TNA, CO5/755, p. 763.

95. John Ballard, deposition, undated, TNA, CO5/755, p. 750.

96. Stephen Greenleaf, deposition, October 1, 1766, TNA, CO5/755, p. 784.

97. Benjamin Goodwin, deposition, September 24, 1766, TNA, CO5/755, p. 745.

98. Stephen Greenleaf, deposition, October 1, 1766, TNA, CO5/755, p. 785.

99. Paul Rivere, deposition, undated, TNA, CO5/755, p. 754.

100. Nathaniel Barber, deposition, September 25, 1766, TNA, CO5/755, p. 778.

101. Reported in Bernard to John Pownall, emphasis in original. January 11, 1766, *Bernard Papers,* vol. 3: *1766–1767,* https://www.colonialsociety.org/node/2352.

102. Bernard to Henry Seymour Conway, December 18, 1765, TNA, CO5/755, p. 411.

103. Bernard to the Board of Trade, January 18, 1766, *Bernard Papers,* vol. 3: *1766–1767,* https://www.colonialsociety.org/node/2353#ch08.

104. Bernard to Pownall, January 11, 1766, *Bernard Papers,* vol. 3: *1766–1767,* https://www.colonialsociety.org/node/2352.

105. Bernard to the Board of Trade, January 18, 1766, *Bernard Papers,* vol. 3: *1766–1767,* https://www.colonialsociety.org/node/2353#ch08.

106. Bernard to Conway, January 25, 1766, TNA, CO5/755, p. 494.

107. Bernard to Shelburne, December 6, 1766, TNA, CO5/756, folio 4.

108. Bernard to Shelburne, December 22, 1766, TNA, CO5/756, folio. 7.

109. Undated, Shelburne Papers, vol. 48, pp. 501–503, Clements Library.

110. Burke, November 8, 1768, in *Proceedings and Debates of the British Parliaments Respecting North America,* ed. R. C. Simmons and P. D. G. Thomas, vol. 3: *1768–1773* (Millwood, NY: Kraus International, 1984), 8.

111. Richard Archer, *As if an Enemy's Country: The British Occupation of Boston and the Origins of Revolution* (New York: Oxford University Press, 2010), 96.

112. Bernard to Hillsborough, July 9, 1768, TNA, T1/465, pt. 2, folio 190.

113. Bernard to Hillsborough, July 11, 1768, TNA, T1/465, pt. 2, folio 192.

114. *An Appeal to the World,* 22.

115. Brendan McConville, *The King's Three Faces: The Rise and Fall of Royal America, 1688–1776* (Chapel Hill: University of North Carolina Press, 2007), 193–219; Richard L. Bushman, *King and People in Provincial Massachusetts* (Chapel Hill: University of North Carolina Press, 1992); Richard L. Bushman, *The Refinement of America: Persons, Houses, Cities* (New York: Vintage Books, 1993); Eric Nelson, *Royalist Revolution: Monarchy and the American Founding* (Cambridge, MA: Harvard University Press, 2014), 1–65; compare Gordon S. Wood, "Revolutionary Royalism: A New Paradigm?," *American Political Thought* 5 (2016): 132–146.

116. *Letters to the Ministry, from Governor Bernard, General Gage, and Commodore Hood: And Also, Memorials to the Lords of the Treasury, from the Commissioners of the Customs. With Sundry Letters and Papers Annexed to the Said Memorials* (Boston, 1768), 35.

117. Benjamin Goodwin, deposition, September 24, 1766, TNA, CO5/755, p. 745.

118. John Tudor, deposition, September 25, 1766, TNA, CO5/755, pp. 776–777; Caleb Hopkins, deposition, undated, TNA, CO5/755, folio. 751.

119. William Wimble, deposition, October 17, 1766, TNA, CO5/755, p. 761.

120. Bernard to Board of Trade, October 10, 1766, TNA, CO5/755, p. 799.

121. *An Appeal to the World; or a vindication of the town of Boston, from many false and malicious aspersions contain'd in certain letters and memorials, written by Governor Bernard, General Gage, Commodore Hood, the Commissioners of the American Board of Customs, and others, and by them respectively transmitted to the British Ministry.* Published by order of the town (Boston, 1769).

122. *An Appeal to the World,* 4.

NOTES TO PAGES 49–53

123. *An Appeal to the World,* 4–5.
124. *An Appeal to the World,* 5.
125. *An Appeal to the World,* 6.
126. *An Appeal to the World,* 13.
127. *An Appeal to the World,* 5–6, 16. At one meeting, "Violent proposals" for keeping the peace declared "every Capt. of a Man of War that came into this Harbour, should be under the Command of the Gen. Court"; and suggested "that if any person should promote or assist the bringing Troops here, he should be deemed a disturber of the peace and a Traitor to his Country." Quoted in Bernard to Hillsborough, June 16 and 18, 1768, *Bernard Papers,* vol. 4: 1768, https://www.colonialsociety.org/node/2870#lt632. These resolutions were reported verbatim in an undated summary sent by the King in Council to the PC for advice about what best to do in Boston. TNA, CO5 / 754, folio 50. These, the town later claimed, were the views of extremists and did not represent the feelings of the crown: "What" they asked, "should we think of the most respectable Corporations at Home—what even of both Houses of Parliament, if they were to be judged by every Motion that has been made, or every Expression that has drop'd from Individuals in the Warmth of Debates." *An Appeal to the World,* 18.
128. *An Appeal to the World,* 6.
129. Hinderaker, *Boston's Massacre,* 134–137.
130. Zobel, *The Boston Massacre,* 213.
131. Stephen Saunders Webb, *The Governors-General: The English Army and the Definition of the Empire, 1569–1681* (Chapel Hill: University of North Carolina Press, 1979); compare Richard R. Johnson, "The Imperial Webb: The Thesis of Garrison Government in Early America Considered," *William and Mary Quarterly* 43, no. 3 (1986), 408–430.
132. Journal of House of Representatives, September 26, 1765, TNA, CO5/755, p. 404.
133. *An Appeal to the World,* 23–24.

134. Morgan to Shelburne, undated, appendix to Wolkins, "Daniel Malcom and the Writs of Assistance," 76.

135. William Knox, "Hints respecting the civil establishment in the American Colonies," Shelburne Papers, vol. 48, p. 501, Clements Library.

136. Sir William Keith, *A Collection of Papers and Other Tracts Written Occasionally on Various Subjects. To Which Is Prefixed, by Way of Preface an Essay on the Nature of a Publick Spirit* (London, 1740), 168–184.

137. Extract of the Commission of Lionel Copley Esq. Governor of Maryland, 1691, August 21–23, 1772, Rosslyn Papers, box 1, folder 30, Clements Library.

138. Edward Northey and Simon Harcourt, Power of the Crown in respect to the Resumption of Government I Charter and Proprietary colonies, ca. 1702–1707, copy filed in August 1772, Rosslyn Papers, box 1, folder 29, Clements Library. There was a policy change in 1707, and the crown abandoned legal efforts to dissolve charters for a time. Sydney V. James, *The Colonial Metamorphosis of Rhode Island: A Study of Institutions in Change,* ed. Sheila L. Skemp and Bruce C. Daniels (Hanover, NH: University Press of New England, 2000), 132–133. Wedderburn compiled similar assertions of the prerogative in the case of the Bahamas (1706) and New York (1699), Rosslyn Papers, box 1, folders 29–30, Clements Library. Note that the various undated advices and commissions in box 31 use war as a pretext for appointing royal governors to New York and Massachusetts and expanding their rights.

139. Untitled, undated, and unsigned, Rossyln Papers, box 1, folder 33, Clements Library. It is not clear from the archive that Wedderburn wrote the draft. It appears first in fair hand, and second in his own. It is followed by annotations for another, longer document, missing from the archive. In those notes, Wedderburn disapproves of key terms in the included draft. Specifically he argues that the governor should not have to consult council at all, wonders whether it will be too burdensome to supervise the

content of town meetings, and thinks that appointing the
lieutenant governor to seat in council might not go beyond the
purpose of bolstering executive power.

140. Untitled, undated, and unsigned, Rossyln, box 1, folder 33,
Clements Library.

141. Curiously, Wedderburn's annotations object specifically to giving
the governor power to declare martial law without the consent of
council. He was not to be the arbiter of the boundary between
riot and rebellion. But his appointed council would certainly
support him in doing so.

142. "Great Britain: Parliament—The Massachusetts Government Act;
May 20, 1774," Yale Law School, Avalon Project, https://avalon.law
.yale.edu/18th_century/mass_gov_act.asp.

143. Lauren Benton and Lisa Ford, *Rage for Order: The British Empire and
the Origins of International Law, 1800–1850* (Cambridge, MA: Harvard
University Press, 2016).

2. A MILITARY ASSASSINATION IN MONTRÉAL

1. Letters from Mrs. Walker to Brigadier Burton, December 8, 1764,
Colonial Office and predecessors: Canada, formerly British North
America, Original Correspondence, The National Archives,
London [TNA], Colonial Office Records [CO], ser. 42, vol. 2
[subsequent TNA citations in the format: TNA, CO42/2], folios
142–143. Some wore blackface, others were "covered with black
Drape." See also The Information of Thomas Walker, Esq.,
December 24, 1764, TNA, CO42/2, folio 153.

2. Copy of Mrs. Walker's Information, undated, TNA, CO42/2, folio
152.

3. "Justice Lambe's accounts of the several examinations &c. relative
to Thomas Walker, Esq.," TNA, CO42/2, folio 158.

4. Examination of William Lewis, January 3, 1765, TNA, CO42/2,
folios 148–150; Examination of George Wall, December 24, 1764,

TNA, CO42/2, folios 150–151; Sgt. Rogers' Examination, December 9, 1765, TNA, CO42/2, folio 151.

5. Examination of Susan Mea, December 25, 1764, TNA, CO42/2, folio 157.

6. Examination of James Coleman, December 25, 1765, TNA, CO42/2, folio 152; Examination of Lieut. Tottenham on his request for bail, December 17, 1764, TNA, CO42/2, folio 155; Copy of Ensign Welch's Examination, December 8, 1764, TNA, CO42/2, folios 154–155; Mr. Baker's Examination, December 8, 1764, TNA, CO42/2, folio 155.

7. Carolee Pollock, "Thomas Walker's Ear: Political Legitimacy in Post-Conquest Quebec," *Lumen* 19 (2000): 203–214.

8. James Murray to the Board of Trade, March 3, 1765, TNA, CO42/2, folios 139–140.

9. Placard from His Excellency General Amherst, September 22, 1760, in *Documents Relating to the Constitutional History of Canada, 1759-1791,* ed. Adam Shortt and Arthur G. Doughty (Ottawa: S. E. Dawson, 1907), 32–33; Ordinance Establishing Military Courts, "by His Excellency Mr James Murray, Governor of Quebec, etc.," in Shortt and Doughty, *Documents,* 35–36.

10. Alfred Leroy Burt, *The Old Province of Quebec,* vol. 1: *1760–1778* (Toronto: Carelton Library, 1968), 22–50, orig. pub. 1933.

11. Roland Viau, "Careful Coexistence: The Canadians and the British in Montréal prior to 1800," in *Montréal: The History of a North American City,* vol. 1, ed. Dany Fougères and Roderick Macleod (Montreal: McGill-Queen's University Press, 2017), 212–213.

12. Frederick Bernays Wiener, *Civilians under Military Justice: The British Practice since 1689, Especially in North America* (Chicago: University of Chicago Press, 1967), 39–41, 55–61.

13. Narda Dobson, *A History of Belize* (Port of Spain, Trinidad: Longman Caribbean, 1973).

14. Wiener, *Civilians under Military Justice,* 47–53.

15. On the mobilization of Protestants in early Quebec, see Nancy Christie, *The Formal and Informal Politics of British Rule in Post-Conquest Quebec, 1760–1837: A Northern Bastille* (Oxford: Oxford University Press, 2020), 29–87. Christie suggests that the Quebec Act saved Canada from revolution by facilitating Carleton's declaration of martial law in 1775. Significantly, the declaration followed the disfigurement of a statue of the king (30).

16. John Coffey, *Persecution and Toleration in Protestant England, 1558–1689* (Harlow: Longman, 2000).

17. Christie, *British Rule in Post-Conquest Quebec*, 3, 9–10, 53.

18. William Henry Atherton, *Montreal, 1535–1914*, vol. 1: *Under the French Regime, 1535–1760* (Montreal: S. J. Clarke, 1914), 219.

19. These estimates are taken from Roland Viau, "The Times and Trials of a Distinctive Colony, 1702–1760," in Fougères and Macleod, *Montréal*, 1:178–179.

20. Burt, *Old Province of Quebec*, 1:22–50.

21. Rory Rapple, *Martial Power and Elizabethan Political Culture: Military Men in England and Ireland, 1558–1594* (Cambridge: Cambridge University Press, 2019).

22. P. J. Marshall, *The Making and Unmaking of Empires: Britain, India, and America, 1750–1783* (Oxford: Oxford University Press, 2007), 163.

23. For an overview of the standing army controversy, see Lois G. Schworer, "The Literature of the Standing Army Controversy, 1697–1699," *Huntington Library Quarterly* 28, no. 3 (1965): 187–212. For the best account of seventeenth-century debates about whether civil or military law governed soldiers, see John M. Collins, *Martial Law and English Laws, c. 1500–c. 1700* (Cambridge: Cambridge University Press, 2016), 135–275.

24. Regarding the impact of radical Whigs in America, see Bernard Bailyn, *The Ideological Origins of the American Revolution: Enlarged Edition* (Cambridge, MA: Belknap Press of Harvard University Press, 1992), 35–54, orig. pub. 1967. By contrast, see my discussion

in Chapter 3 of the very different approach to military power in Jamaica.

25. For another discussion of "the soldier's peace" in a new colonial enterprise, see Lisa Ford, "The Pig and the Peace: Transposing Order in Early Sydney," in *Law and Politics and British Colonial Thought: Transpositions of Empire,* ed. Shaunnagh Dorsett and Ian Hunter (New York: Palgrave Macmillan, 2010), 169–186.

26. This and cases like it are discussed in Wiener, *Civilians under Military Law,* 47–53; Douglas Hay, "Civilians Tried in Military Courts: Quebec, 1759–64," in *Canadian State Trials,* vol. 1: *Law, Politics, and Security Measures, 1608–1837,* ed. F. Murray Greenwood and Barry Wright (Toronto: University of Toronto Press / Osgoode Society for Canadian Legal History, 1996), 114–128.

27. Proceedings of a General Court Martial held in the City of Montréal on Monday the 15th Day of February 1762, TNA, War Office [hereafter cited as WO] 71 / 70, 181–205.

28. Proceedings of a General Court Martial held in the City of Montréal on Monday the 15th Day of February 1762, TNA, WO71 / 70, 194, 205.

29. Lewis H. Thomas, "Walker, Thomas," in *Dictionary of Canadian Biography,* vol. 4: *1771–1800,* http://www.biographi.ca/en/bio/walker_thomas_1788_4E.html; Pollock, "Thomas Walker's Ear," 209–210.

30. Judgement of Military Court, Enclosure in Burton to Gage, February 1, 1764, Gage Papers, American Series, vol. 13, William L. Clements Library, University of Michigan.

31. Pierre Beaumont, deposition sworn at Montréal, January 30, 1964, 13, enclosure in Burton to Gage, February 1, 1764, Gage Papers, American Series, vol. 13, Clements Library.

32. Burton to Gage, February 1, 1764, Gage Papers, American Series, vol. 13, Clements Library.

33. Wiener, *Civilians under Military Law,* 53.

34. Charles Gould to Hector Theophilus Cramahé, August 11, 1763, in Wiener, *Civilians under Military Law,* 250–251. The case and its

aftermath are discussed in detail in F. Murray Greenwood and Beverley Boissery, *Uncertain Justice: Canadian Women and Capital Punishment, 1754–1953* (Toronto: Dundurn Press, in conjunction with the Osgoode Society, 2000), 39–59.

35. Note *Campbell v. Hall* (1774) 1 Cowp 204, 98 ER 1045.

36. See Giorgio Agamben, *State of Exception,* trans. Kevin Attell (Chicago: University of Chicago Press, 2005), 24–26.

37. Nasser Hussain, *The Jurisprudence of Emergency: Colonialism and the Rule of Law* (Ann Arbor: University of Michigan Press, 2003), 1–2.

38. H. W. Halleck, *International Law; or, Rules Regulating the Intercourse of States in Peace and War* (San Francisco: H. H. Bancroft and Co., 1861), 776. Emphasis in original.

39. George M. Dennison, "Martial Law: The Development of a Theory of Emergency Powers, 1776–1861," *American Journal of Legal History* 18, no. 1 (1974): 52–55.

40. *Rules and Articles for the better Government of His Majesty's Horse and Foot Guards And all other His Forces in Great Britain and Ireland, Dominions beyond the Seas and Foreign Parts,* 1749, TNA, WO72/2. See also Hay, "Civilians Tried in Military Courts," 119-121.

41. Stephen Payne Adye, *A Treatise on Courts Martial. Containing, I. Remarks on Martial Law, and Courts Martial in General. II. The Manner of Proceeding Against Offenders. To which is added, An Essay, on Military Punishments and Rewards* (London, 1769), 7.

42. Gould to Cramahé, August 11, 1763, and Gould to Murray, August 11, 1763, in Wiener, *Civilians under Military Law,* 251–253.

43. Gage to Gould, April 10, 1764, TNA, CO5/65, part III, folio 89.

44. Gage to Gould, April 10, 1764, TNA, CO5/65, part III, folio 89.

45. Murray to Gould, November 12, 1763, in Wiener, *Civilians under Military Law,* 252.

46. Murray to Board of Trade, March 3, 1765, TNA, CO42/2, folio 134.

47. S. Max Edelson, *The New Map of Empire: How Britain Imagined America before Independence* (Cambridge, MA: Harvard University Press, 2017), 159-160. For a useful discussion of the proclamation,

see Colin G. Calloway, *The Scratch of a Pen: 1763 and the Transformation of North America* (Oxford: Oxford University Press, 2007), 94-99.

48. Board of Trade to Egremont, August 5, 1763, in Shortt and Doughty, *Documents,* 110-111. Generally, see R. A. Humphreys, "Lord Shelburne and the Proclamation of 1763," *English Historical Review* 49, no. 194 (1934): 241-264.

49. "Proclamation," October 7, 1763, in Shortt and Doughty, *Documents,* 122.

50. Regarding the pacifying ramifications of the Proclamation, see Michael McDonnell, *Masters of Empire: Great Lakes Indians and the Making of America* (New York: Hill and Wang, 2017), 235.

51. "Proposed Extension of Provincial Limits," undated, in Shortt and Doughty, *Documents,* 381.

52. Gage to Halifax, November 9, 1764, Gage Papers, 1754-1807, English Series, vol. 2, Clements Library. For a sense of the saga of occupying the Illinois, see John Shy, *Toward Lexington: The Role of the British Army in the Coming of the American Revolution* (Princeton: Princeton University Press, 1965), 152-154.

53. Jack M. Sosin, *Whitehall and the Wilderness: The Middle West in British Colonial Policy, 1760-1775* (Lincoln: University of Nebraska Press, 1961), 102.

54. Note that Colonel William Eyre, the chief military engineer in America, proposed their wholesale relocation from the interior. Sosin, *Whitehall and the Wilderness,* 72.

55. Regarding the nature of the settlement, see Guillaume Teasdale, "Old Friends and New Foes: French Settlers and Indians in the Detroit River Border Region," *Michigan Historical Review* 38, no. 2 (2012): 35-62. On concerns about the need for government in Detroit, see Peter Hansenclever, "Extract of letter on American Affairs advising that the Salaries of Crown Officers may depend upon the Crown," undated, Shelburne Papers, vol. 50, p. 327, Clements Library.

56. Gage to Halifax, July 1, 1764, Gage Papers, American Series, vol. 12, Clements Library. Regarding the siege and the complicated role of French subjects, see Gregory Dowd, "The French King Wakes Up in Detroit: 'Pontiac's War' in Rumor and History," *Ethnohistory* 37, no. 3 (1990): 261–264.

57. Catherine Cangany, *Frontier Seaport: Detroit's Transformation into an Atlantic Entrepôt* (Chicago: University of Chicago Press, 2014), 113–117.

58. "A Memorial of the foregoing French Petitioners in Support of their Petition," undated, in Shortt and Doughty, *Documents,* 357–359.

59. Tomatle Mingo's address, Gage Papers, American Series, vol. 137, pp. 27–31, Clements Library.

60. Alibamo Mingo's address, Gage Papers, American Series, vol. 137, pp. 33–34, Clements Library.

61. Shy, *Toward Lexington,* 196.

62. Enclosure in Gage to Wellbore Ellis, January 22, 1765, in *The Correspondence of General Thomas Gage with the Secretaries of State, and with the War Office and the Treasury, 1763–1775,* ed. Clarence Edwin Carter (Hamden, CT: Archon Books, 1969) [hereafter cited as *Gage Correspondence*], 2:266.

63. Sosin, *Whitehall and the Wilderness,* 104–105, n15.

64. Gage expressed his concerns to Conway in 1766 about how to work with colonial governments to structure arrests in Indian Country. Gage to Conway, July 15, 1766, in Shelburne Papers, vol. 50, pp. 323–327, Clements Library.

65. Quoted in Matthew L. Rhoades, "Blood and Boundaries: Virginia Backcountry Violence and the Origins of the Quebec Act, 1758–1775," *West Virginia History,* new ser., 3, no. 2 (2009): 7.

66. Lisa Ford, *Settler Sovereignty: Jurisdiction and Indigenous People in America and Australia, 1788–1836* (Cambridge, MA: Harvard University Press, 2010), 19–20.

67. Gage to Conway, May 6, 1766, in *Gage Correspondence,* 1:91; quoted in Sosin, *Whitehall and the Wilderness,* 107. On intercolonial competition

for Indian land and borderlands, see Daniel P. Barr, *A Colony Sprung from Hell: Pittsburgh and the Struggle for Authority on the Western Pennsylvania Frontier, 1744–1794* (Kent, OH: Kent State University Press, 2014), pt. 3.

68. Hillsborough to President Habersham, January 11, 1772, TNA, CO5/676, folio 33.

69. "Proposed Extension of Provincial Limits," undated, in Shortt and Doughty, *Documents,* 381.

70. Gould to General Sir William Howe, June 20, 1777, in Wiener, *Civilians under Military Law,* 265. For a detailed examination of military jurisdiction in New York, see Wiener, *Civilians under Military Law,* 95–140.

71. Wiener, *Civilians under Military Law,* 105–106.

72. Belligerent occupation was the subject of international legal discussion from 1874 (the Brussels Conferences) and was adopted by the Hague Convention in 1899. See Eyal Benvenisti, "The Origins of the Concept of Belligerent Occupation," *Law and History Review* 26, no. 3 (2008): 621–623.

73. Burt, *Old Province of Quebec,* 1:81.

74. "The most proper from their circumstances and understandings to be made Justices of the Peace, were those who had had the most disputes with the Troops." Murray to Board of Trade, March 3, 1765, TNA, CO42/2, folios 133–134.

75. Murray to Board of Trade, March 3, 1765, TNA, CO42/2, folio 134.

76. Memorial of Fowler Walker, Agent on behalf of the Merchants, Traders and others the principal Inhabitants of the Cities of Quebec & Montreal, November 1764, TNA, CO42/2, folio 113–114.

77. Copy of Justice Walker's Letter to his Excellency James Murray, undated, TNA, CO42/2, folio 193–194.

78. Copy of Captains John Fraser & James Mitchelson's Letter to His Excellency Governor Murray, November 7, 1764, TNA, CO42/2, folio 183.

79. Copy of Mr. John Livingston's letter to James Goldfrap Esq., Deputy Secretary at Quebec, November 22, 1764, TNA, CO42/2, folio 190.

80. Copy of Walker to Murray, undated, TNA, CO42/2, folio 192.

81. Copy of Captain Mitchelson's Letter to Brigadier Burton, November 21, 1764, TNA, CO42/2, folio 187.

82. Copy of Walker to Murray, undated, TNA, CO42/2, folio 192.

83. Copy of Justice Livingston's Papers relative to the Complaint made by Justice Walker, undated, TNA, CO42/2, folio 165. There are more examples in the papers referred to by Mr. Livingston in the foregoing complaints, enclosed in Copy of Justice Livingston's Papers relative to the Complaint made by Justice Walker, undated, TNA, CO42/2, folios 166–173.

84. Copy of Mitchelson to Burton, November 21, 1764, TNA, CO42/2, folio 187.

85. Copy of Mitchelson to Burton, November 21, 1764, TNA, CO42/2, folio 187.

86. Copy of Lieut. Jacob Schalcks' letter to Brigadier Burton and witness account of Edward Hasniell, November 21, 1764, TNA, CO42/2, folio 188.

87. Copy of Mitchelson to Burton, November 21, 1764, TNA, CO42/2, folio 187.

88. Copy of Livingston's Papers relative to the Complaint made by Walker, undated, TNA, CO42/2, folio 162–166; also reported in Letter from James Murray to the Board relative to the outrage committed on Mr. Walker, March 3, 1765, CO24/2, folios 132–141.

89. Copy of Fraser & Mitchelson's Letter to Murray, November 7, 1764, TNA, CO42/2, folio 181.

90. Letter from James Murray to the Board relative to the outrage committed on Mr. Walker, March 3, 1765, CO42/2, folio 135.

91. Anon, "Querie humbly proposed to the Consideration of the Publick," undated, 1764, Gage Papers, 1754–1807, vol. 13, Clements Library.

92. Quoted in Philip Lawson, *The Imperial Challenge: Quebec and Britain in the Age of the American Revolution* (Montreal: McGill-Queen's University Press, 1989), 54. Copy of the Petition of British Merchants and Traders, in Behalf of themselves & their fellow Subjects, Inhabitants of Your Majesty's Province of Quebec, undated, in Halifax to Murray, June 10, 1765, TNA, CO42/2, folio 127-129. The claims for an assembly were reiterated in 1773, when merchants at Quebec claimed that "a General Assembly of the People would very much Contribute to its peace, Welfare and good Government." "Petition to Lt. Governor for an Assembly," November 29, 1773, in Shortt and Doughty, *Documents*, 345.

93. "Petition of the Quebec Traders," undated, in Shortt and Doughty, *Documents*, 168-169.

94. David Milobar, "The Origins of British-Quebec Merchant Ideology: New France, the British Atlantic and the Constitutional Periphery, 1720-1770," *Journal of Imperial and Commonwealth History* 24, no. 3 (1996): 382-385.

95. "Presentments of the Grand Jury of Quebec," undated, in Shortt and Doughty, *Documents*, 155.

96. Murray to Board of Trade, June 24, 1765, TNA, CO42/3, folio 278.

97. The Memorial of John Strettell on behalf of Thomas Walker, June 25, 1765, TNA, CO42/2, folio 222.

98. Murray to Board of Trade, June 24, 1765, TNA, CO42/3, folio 278.

99. John Frazer to Lord Shelburne, April 1, 1767, Shelburne Papers, vol. 64, Clements Library.

100. W. Stewart Wallace, "Introduction," in *The Maseres Letters, 1766–1768*, ed. W. Stewart Wallace (Toronto: University of Toronto Library, 1919), 17; *The Trial of Daniel Disney, Esq.* (Quebec: Brown and Gilmore, 1767).

101. Murray to Board of Trade, March 3, 1765, TNA, CO42/2, folio 136.

102. Copy of Letter from Capt. Mitchelson to Brigadier General Burton, December 13, 1764, TNA, CO42/2, folio 145.

103. Murray to Board of Trade, March 3, 1765, TNA, CO42/2, folio 133.

104. Information of David Skene, Esq., Captain of H.M.'s 20th Regiment, February 3, 1765, TNA, CO42/2, folio 215.

105. Examination of James Coleman, February 7, 1765, TNA, CO42/2, folio 221.

106. Hannah Weiss Muller, *Subjects and Sovereign: Bonds of Belonging in the Eighteenth-Century British Empire* (New York: Oxford University Press, 2017), 16–44.

107. Christie, *British Rule in Post-Conquest Quebec,* 5–6. Note that Christie both stresses the radicalism of Protestants *and* argues that metropolitan and local government feared control of government in Quebec by the Catholic majority (6). However, she notes that the disorderly claims of Protestants "galvanised" the Crown in proposing the Quebec Bill (53).

108. Muller, *Subjects and Sovereign,* 123–165. For an excellent account of tenures in preconquest Quebec, see Allan Greer, *Property and Dispossession: Natives, Empires and Land in Early Modern North America* (Cambridge: Cambridge University Press, 2018), 145–190.

109. "Statement by French Jurors in Reference to the Foregoing Presentments," October 26, 1764, in Shortt and Doughty, *Documents,* 161.

110. "Address of French Citizens to the King regarding the Legal System," undated, in Shortt and Doughty, *Documents,* 164–165.

111. Lawson, *The Imperial Challenge,* 55–59.

112. Murray to Board of Trade, October 29, 1764, in Shortt and Doughty, *Documents,* 167.

113. Murray to Shelburne, August 20, 1765, quoted in Reginald Coupland, *The Quebec Act: A Study in Statesmanship* (Oxford: Clarendon Press, 1968), 46, orig. pub. 1925.

114. S. J. Connolly, *Religion, Law, and Power: The Making of Protestant Ireland, 1660–1760* (Oxford: Clarendon Press, 2002), 263–313. Contrast D. W. Hayton, "Early Hanoverian Ireland, 1690–1750," in *The Oxford Handbook of Modern Irish History,* ed. Alvin Jackson (Oxford: Oxford University Press, 2014), 401–416. See also John

Coffey, *Persecution and Toleration in Protestant England, 1558–1689* (Harlow: Longman / Pearson Education, 2000).

115. Lawson, *The Imperial Challenge*, 43.

116. "Opinion of the Attorney General, Sir Edward Northey, as to Roman Catholic Priests in the Colonies," October 18, 1705, in *Cases and Opinions on Constitutional Law, and Various Points of English Jurisprudence: Collected and Digested from Official Documents and Other Sources; with Notes,* ed. William Forsyth (London: Stevens and Haynes, 1869), 35–36.

117. Query and Reply from the Board of Trade to Sir Fletcher Norton and Sir William de Grey, 1765, in William Knox, *The Justice and Policy of the Late Act of Parliament, For Making more Effectual Provision for the Government of the Province of Quebec, Asserted and Proved; and the Conduct of Administration respecting that Province, Stated and Vindicated* (London: 1774), 30–31.

118. Muller, *Subjects and Sovereign*, 123–165.

119. Lawson, *The Imperial Challenge*, 142.

120. Quoted in Lawson, *The Imperial Challenge*, 122.

121. Knox, *The Justice and Policy of the Late Act of Parliament*, 11.

122. Muller, *Subjects and Sovereign*, 123–165. For a more qualified exposition of the politics of this move, see Christie, *British Rule in Post-Conquest Quebec*, 36–39.

123. Murray to Board of Trade, October 29, 1764, TNA, CO42/2, folio 15–17

124. "Petition of French Subjects," December 1773, in Shortt and Doughty, *Documents,* 356.

125. Burt, *Old Province of Quebec,* 1:83–84; R. A. Humphreys and S. Morley Scott, "Lord Northington and the Laws of Canada," *Canadian Historical Review* 14, no. 1 (1933): 42–61.

126. Lawson, *The Imperial Challenge*, 136.

127. Regarding socage, see "Lord Hillsborough's Objections to the Quebec Bill in Its Present Form," undated, in Shortt and Doughty, *Documents,* 389; "Notes on the Third Draught of Quebec Bill," undated, in Shortt and Doughty, *Documents,* 385–386.

128. Anonymous, *Observations and Reflections, on an Act, passed in the Year, 1774, for the Settlement, of the Province of Quebec* (London: J Stockdale, 1782), 19. Emphasis in original.
129. See "Memoranda and Draughts of the Bills Relating to the Subject of the Quebec Act," in Shortt and Doughty, *Documents,* 374-405; see 401-405 for the finalized text of the act.
130. Edmund Burke quoted in *Canadian Constitutional Development: Shown by Selected Speeches and Despatches, with Introductions and Explanatory Notes,* ed. H. E. Egerton and W. L. Grant (London: John Murray, 1907), 49-50.
131. Burke quoted in Egerton and Grant, *Canadian Constitutional Development,* 93-94.
132. Edelson, *New Map of Empire,* 311-313.
133. Quoted in Lawson, *The Imperial Challenge,* 134-135.
134. Alexander Hamilton, *A Full Vindication of the Measures of the Congress, from the Calumnies of their Enemies; In Answer to A Letter, Under the Signature of A. W. Farmer. Whereby His Sophistry is exposed, his Cavils confuted, his Artifices detected, and his Wit ridiculed; in a General Address To the Inhabitants of America, And A Particular Address To the Farmers of the Province of New York* (New York: James Rivington, 1774), https://founders.archives.gov/documents/Hamilton/01-01-02-0054.
135. [Philip Livingston], "The Other Side of the Question: or, A Defence of the Liberties of North-America. In Answer to a Late Friendly Address to All Reasonable Americans, on the Subject of Our Political Confusions," in *The American Revolution: Writings from the Pamphlet Debate,* vol. 2: *1773-1776,* ed. Gordon S. Wood (New York: Library of America, 2015), pamphlet 28.
136. Christie, *British Rule in Post-Conquest Quebec,* 32.
137. Dartmouth to Carleton, July 12, 1775, quoted in Christie, *British Rule in Post-Conquest Quebec,* 30.
138. Christie, *British Rule in Post-Conquest Quebec,* 32.

139. The Earl of Abingdon (Willoughby Bertie), *Thoughts on the Letter of Edmund Burke, Esq; to the Sheriffs of Bristol on the Affairs of America* (Oxford, 1780), lxiii.

140. Anonymous, *Observations and Reflections,* 27.

141. See, for example, Anna Haebich, *Broken Circles: Fragmenting Indigenous Families, 1880–2000* (Fremantle: Fremantle Arts Centre Press, 2000); Margaret Jacobs, *White Mother to a Dark Race: Settler Colonialism, Maternalism, and the Removal of Indigenous Children in the American West and Australia, 1880–1940* (Lincoln: University of Nebraska Press, 2009).

142. Philip Lawson, "A Perspective on British History and the Treatment of Quebec," *Journal of Historical Sociology* 3, no. 3 (1990): 253–271.

143. Edelson, *New Map of Empire,* 4–10, 46–53.

144. Muller, *Subjects and Sovereign,* 217–219. See also Lauren Benton and Lisa Ford, *Rage for Order: The British Empire and the Origins of International Law, 1800–1850* (Cambridge, MA: Harvard University Press, 2016), 85–116.

145. Muller, *Subjects and Sovereign,* 126.

3. WAR AND PEACE IN TRELAWNY TOWN

1. So much was clear to a reviewer criticizing Robert Charles Dallas's *History of the Maroons* in the Edinburgh Review in 1803: "The letter of the treaty was observed, and its spirit completely disregarded," justifying the Maroons' protest. *Edinburgh Review, or Critical Journal: For April 1803 to July 1803* 2 (1803): 386. Though Bryan Edwards defended Jamaica's actions in the war and asserted that even a white man could be subject to such a whipping, he noted that the court erred in its judgment in the case of the Maroons. Bryan Edwards, *The Proceedings of the Governor and Assembly of Jamaica: In regard to the Maroon Negroes* (London: John Stockdale, 1796), xliv.

2. John Stewart, *A View of the Past and Present State of the Island of Jamaica; with Remarks on the Moral and Physical Condition of the Slaves, and on the Abolition of Slavery in the Colonies* (Edinburgh, 1823), 11, quoted in Diana Paton, "Punishment, Crime, and the Bodies of Slaves in Eighteenth-Century Jamaica," *Journal of Social History* 34, no. 4 (2001): 939.

3. Note more details in J. Vaughan Junior to Col. Swaby, July 17, 1795, Crawford Papers, a Private Collection, National Library of Scotland [hereafter cited as NLS], ACC9769, 23/11/185. According to one account, the men were freed but went on to "Quarrell" with the people of Montego Bay with "two loaded Guns." Trelawny townsfolk visiting Montego Bay were arrested and released on the promise that the offenders would be arrested and delivered for another trial. They later refused, claiming that they would be punished under Maroon justice. See also Ruma Chopra, *Almost Home: Maroons between Slavery and Freedom in Jamaica, Nova Scotia, and Sierra Leone* (New Haven, CT: Yale University Press, 2018), 27–28.

4. Helen McKee, "From Violence to Alliance: Maroons and White Settlers in Jamaica, 1739–1795," *Slavery & Abolition: A Journal of Slave and Post-Slave Studies* 39, no. 1 (2018): 36–37.

5. See below for fears of Maroon complicity with French revolutionaries. Supporting the truth of these reports, see Bryan Edwards, *Proceedings of the Governor and Assembly of Jamaica,* xlv–li. However, critics dismissed such tales as paranoid rumor. For critique, see Robert Charles Dallas, *The History of the Maroons: From Their Origin to the Establishment of Their Chief Tribe at Sierra Leone,* vol. 1 (London: T. N. Longman and O. Rees, 1803), 167–168. Note that while they had good relationships with some planters, the Trelawny Maroons were distrusted in Montego Bay. Carey Robinson, *The Fighting Maroons of Jamaica* (Kingston: William Collins/Sangster Jamaica, 1969), 73–90. See also Helen McKee who argues (contra

Craton) that Maroon towns were not hemmed in by plantations in 1795, McKee, "From Violence to Alliance," 34.

6. Edwards, *Proceedings of the Governor and Assembly of Jamaica,* xlvii–xlviii; Dallas, *History of the Maroons,* 170–171.

7. Trevor Burnard, *Mastery, Tyranny, and Desire: Thomas Thistlewood and his Slaves in the Anglo-Jamaican World* (Chapel Hill: University of North Carolina Press, 2004), 33.

8. Bryan Edwards, *An Historical Survey of the French Colony in the Island of St. Domingo* (London: John Stockdale, 1797), 11. Emphasis in original.

9. Edward Long, *The History of Jamaica or, General Survey of the Antient and Modern State of that Island: With Reflections on its Situation, Settlements, Inhabitants, Climate, Products, Commerce, Laws, and Government,* vol. 2 (London: T. Lowndes, 1774), 493–505. For a nuanced discussion of the centrality of fear as a weapon wielded to keep slaves at peace in Jamaica, see Trevor Burnard, *Jamaica in the Age of Revolution* (Philadelphia: University of Pennsylvania Press, 2020), esp. 27, 32.

10. Diana Paton, *No Bond but the Law: Punishment, Race, and Gender in Jamaican State Formation* (Durham, NC: Duke University Press, 2004), 68; Else Goveia, *The West Indian Slave Laws of the 18th Century* (Barbados: Caribbean University Press, 1970), 9–10.

11. Burnard describes this as a kind of absolutism, and notes that "Jamaica was not, at bottom, a civil society," *Jamaica in the Age of Revolution,* 36.

12. See Edward B. Rugemer, *Slave Law and the Politics of Resistance in the Early Atlantic World* (Cambridge, MA: Harvard University Press, 2018); and, more generally, John M. Collins, *Martial Law and English Laws, c. 1500–c. 1700* (Cambridge: Cambridge University Press, 2016).

13. For an excellent overview of the legislature's early struggles with the crown, see Agnes Whitson, *The Constitutional Development of Jamaica, 1660–1729* (Manchester: Manchester University Press, 1929).

14. Frederick G. Spurdle, *Early West Indian Government: Showing the Progress of Government in Barbados, Jamaica and the Leeward Islands, 1660–1783* (Palmerston North: F. G. Spurdle, 1961), 59–62; Collins, *Martial Law and English Laws,* 207–247. For a recent exploration of this dependence and debates in Jamaica in this period, see Burnard, *Jamaica in the Age of Revolution,* esp. 67, chaps. 4 and 8.

15. James Stephen Sr., *The Crisis of the Sugar Colonies, or, An Enquiry into the Objects and Probable Effects of the French Expedition to the West Indies* (London: J. Hatchard, 1802), 133–135. For more on Stephen's discussion of the common good, see Lauren Benton and Aaron Slater, "Constituting the Imperial Community: Rights, Common Good and Authority in Britain's Atlantic Empire, 1607–1815," in *Revisiting the Origins of Human Rights,* ed. Pamela Slotte and Miia Halme-Tuomisaari (Cambridge: Cambridge University Press, 2015), 140–162; and Lauren Benton and Lisa Ford, "Island Despotism: Trinidad, the British Imperial Constitution, and Global Legal Order," *Journal of Imperial and Commonwealth History* 46, no. 1 (2018): 21–46.

16. Petley points out that many would not have minded French conquest after a decade of agitation against the slave trade. Christer Petley, "Slaveholders and Revolution: The Jamaican Planter Class, British Imperial Politics, and the Ending of the Slave Trade, 1775–1807," *Slavery & Abolition* 39, no. 1 (2018): 61–64.

17. David Patrick Geggus, *Slavery, War, and Revolution: The British Occupation of Saint Domingue, 1793–1798* (New York: Oxford University Press, 1982).

18. Rugemer, *Slave Law,* 148.

19. Paton, "Punishment, Crime," 926; Burnard, *Mastery, Tyranny and Desire,* 18.

20. Burnard, *Mastery, Tyranny and Desire,* 16–18. For a detailed examination of early Jamaica, see Trevor Burnard, "A Failed Settler Society: Marriage and Demographic Failure in Early Jamaica," *Journal of Social History* 28, no. 1 (1994): 63–82.

21. Philip D. Morgan, "Slavery in the British Caribbean," in *The Cambridge World History of Slavery,* ed. David Etlis and Stanley L. Engerman (Cambridge: Cambridge University Press, 2011), 386; and Trevor Burnard, *Planters, Merchants, and Slaves: Plantation Societies in British America, 1650–1820* (Chicago: University of Chicago Press, 2015).

22. Christer Petley, *Slaveholders in Jamaica: Colonial Society and Culture during the Era of Abolition* (London: Pickering and Chatto, 2009), 7.

23. Burnard, *Tyranny, Mastery and Desire,* 88.

24. Sally Hadden, "The Fragmented Laws of Slavery in the Colonial and Revolutionary Eras," in *The Cambridge History of Law in America,* vol. 1: *Early America (1580–1815)* (Cambridge: Cambridge University Press, 2008), 260; Rugemer, *Slave Law,* 35-36.

25. Rugemer, *Slave Law,* 48; "An Act for the Better Order and Government of Slaves, 1696," in *Acts of Assembly Passed in the Island of Jamaica; From the Year 1681 to the Year 1768, inclusive,* vol. 1 (Saint Jago De La Vega: Lowry and Sherlock, 1769), 57-65.

26. "An Act for the Better Order and Government of Slaves, 1696," 57.

27. "An Act for the Better Order and Government of Slaves, 1696," 57-65.

28. Paton, "Punishment, Crime," 926-927, 941; Robert Worthington Smith, "The Legal Status of Jamaican Slaves before the Anti-Slavery Movement," *Journal of Negro History* 30, no. 3 (1945): 301.

29. "An Act for the Better Order and Government of Slaves, 1696," 57-65. To "compass" or "imagine" death were words drawn directly from English treason statutes. For a discussion of Elizabethan common law and statutory treason, see D. Alan Orr, *Treason and the State: Law, Politics and Ideology in the English Civil War* (Cambridge: Cambridge University Press, 2002), 11-29, esp. 11-12.

30. Long, *The History of Jamaica,* 2:496.

31. Paton, "Punishment, Crime," 928-929, 935.

32. Quoted in Paton, "Punishment, Crime," 931.

33. Paton, "Punishment, Crime," 943.

34. Vincent Brown, *Tacky's Revolt: The Story of an Atlantic Slave War* (Cambridge, MA: Belknap Press of the Harvard University Press, 2020), 212–216.

35. 21 Geo. 3, c. 17 (1781, Jamaica), "An Act to repeal several Acts and Clauses of Acts respecting Slaves and for the better Order and Government of Slaves, and for other Purposes," *Acts of Assembly passed in the Island of Jamaica from 1770 to 1783 inclusive* (Kingston, Jamaica, 1786). Note that 21 Geo. 3, c. 17 is a standard reference used for colonial and metropolitan legislation: "21 Geo. 3" means that the act was passed in the twenty-first year of the reign of George the third. "c." means chapter, and numbers legislation sequentially each year. This legislation is discussed at length in Smith, "The Legal Status of Jamaican Slaves before the Anti-Slavery Movement," *Journal of Negro History* 30, no. 3 (1945): 293–303. Many of these provisions were carried over into the 1788 Code: *The Code of Laws for the Government of the Negro Slaves in the Island of Jamaica* (London 1789). Regarding famine, see Trevor Burnard, "Powerless Masters: The Curious Decline of Jamaican Sugar Planters in the Foundational Period of British Abolitionism," *Slavery and Abolition* 32, no. 2 (2011): 185.

36. Quoted in Paton, "Punishment, Crime," 927.

37. "An Act for the Better Order and Government of Slaves, 1696," 63.

38. Note that one Jamaican overseer was capitally convicted for whipping five slaves to death, but he escaped before his execution. James Houstoun, "Dr. Houstoun's memoirs of his own life-time," in *The Works of James Houstoun, M.D.* (London, 1753), 353, quoted in James Robinson, "A 1748 'Petition of Negro Slaves' and the Local Politics of Slavery in Jamaica," *William and Mary Quarterly* 67, no. 2 (2010): 322. Indeed, no British slave owner was hanged in any Caribbean colony until 1811. See Lauren Benton, "This Melancholy Labyrinth: The Trial of Arthur Hodge and the Boundaries of Imperial Law," *Alabama Law Review* 64, no. 1 (2012): 91–122.

39. For changes in the slave law, see Smith, "Legal Status of Jamaican slaves," 301–302. For the rapid growth of and minimal public opposition to anti-slavery sentiment, see: Christopher Leslie Brown, *Moral Capital: Foundations of British Abolitionism* (Chapel Hill: University of North Carolina Press, 2006), 22–23; Seymour Drescher, "History's Engines: British Mobilization in the Age of Revolutions," *William and Mary Quarterly* 66, no. 4 (2009): 744–745, both cited in Burnard, "Powerless Masters," 187.

40. Burnard, *Mastery, Tyranny and Desire,* 31.

41. On the worsening, see Burnard, *Jamaica in the Age of Revolutions,* 73.

42. Burnard, *Mastery, Tyranny and Desire,* 3, 31, 103–104.

43. Paton, *No Bond but the Law,* 19.

44. Aaron Graham, "Towns, Government, Legislation and the 'Police' in Jamaica and the British Atlantic, 1770–1805," *Urban History* 47, no. 1 (2020): 41–62.

45. Long, *History of Jamaica,* 2:31.

46. Note protests regarding the costs of defense in the Napoleonic Wars: Neville Archibald Theodore Hall, "Constitutional and Political Developments in Barbados and Jamaica, 1783–1815" (PhD diss., University of London, 1965), 149–150.

47. Aaron Graham, "The Colonial Sinews of Imperial Power: The Political Economy of Jamaican Taxation, 1768–1838," *Journal of Imperial and Commonwealth History* 45, no. 2 (2017): 188–209.

48. Long, *History of Jamaica,* 2:309. When troops were pulled from Jamaica to fight in the American Revolution, the assembly martialized its own police, spending as much as £22,000 per annum funding local patrols for every parish, paid by the day. Governor John Dalling, "Observations on the Present State of Jamaica, 14 May 1774," quoted in Rugemer, *Slave Law,* 186.

49. Whitson, *Constitutional Development of Jamaica,* 70–141; Spurdle, *Early West Indian Government,* 50, 56–57, 60; Burnard, *Jamaica in the Age of Revolutions,* 67.

50. Collins, *Martial Law and English Laws,* 137–206, 254. Collins notes that this forbearance was offset by a marked increase in the use of martial law to govern soldiers in peacetime, a move both regulated and solemnized by Mutiny Acts.

51. Collins, *Martial Law and English Laws,* 210–222.

52. Collins, *Martial Law and English Laws,* 227, 230–231, and 236 regarding the uses of martial law, 232–235 regarding imminent danger.

53. Collins, *Martial Law and English Laws,* 229.

54. Section 7 of Militia Act 1681, *The Laws of Jamaica: Comprehending All the Acts in Force . . . ,* vol. 1 (St. Jago de la Vega: Alexander Aikman, 1802), 29; and Robert Graham to Nicol Graham, June 16, 1760, NLS, Robert Graham Papers, Acc. 11335/117, quoted in Brown, *Tacky's Revolt,* 143.

55. Only 6 percent of the tiny white population (some 1,572 men) voted in the election of 1816. This percentage was less, Graham notes, than in "all but the most rotten boroughs in Britain." Aaron Graham, "Jamaican Legislation and the Transatlantic Constitution, 1664–1839," *Historical Journal* 61, no. 2 (2018): 333. On the power of elites, see Turner, who argues that power in Jamaica was effectively monopolized by "about fifty families." Mary Turner, *Slaves and Missionaries: The Disintegration of Jamaican Slave Society, 1787–1834* (Urbana: University of Illinois Press, 1982), 1–20. Regarding compensation, see Collins, *Martial Law and English Laws,* 240.

56. See "Table of the Public and Private Acts," in *The Laws of Jamaica,* 2:1–81. This authorizing legislation may have been more symbolic that real: though such legislation was passed in 1795, the courts were closed anyway; see boxes 1 and 2, John Tailyour Papers, William L. Clements Library, University of Michigan.

57. Spurdle, *Early West Indian Government,* 59–62.

58. Paul D. Halliday, *Habeas Corpus: From England to Empire* (Cambridge, MA: Belknap Press of the Harvard University Press, 2010), 247–258.

59. For a list of these acts, see *The Laws of Jamaica,* vols. 1–2. Details of these acts can be found in Jamaica Acts MS, 1681–1800, in The National Archives, London, Colonial Office Records [hereafter cited as TNA CO], 139/7–50.

60. Whitson, *Constitutional Development of Jamaica,* 31–38, 58, 128, 135. See, for example, the institution of martial law over Christmas 1791. In justifying its use, reference was made to the Christmas slave holidays, noted as a period during which "the Blacks are very outrageous." Adam Williamson to Henry Dundas, November 27, 1791, TNA CO 137/90, folio 17, quoted in Rugemer, *Slave Law,* 234.

61. See the series of long-suffering letters from Peter Ballantine and David Dick to John Tailyour complaining of their inability to collect debts on the island during prolonged martial law. Peter Ballantine to Tailyour, September 8, October 4 and 27, 1795, box 1, and David Dick to John Tailyour, September 8 and October 7, 1795, February 1, 1796, box 2, Tailyour Papers, Clements Library.

62. Quoted in R. W. Kostal, *A Jurisprudence of Power: Victorian Empire and the Rule of Law* (New York: Oxford University Press, 2005), 7. See also Alexander Dirom, *Thoughts on the State of the Militia of Jamaica, Nov. 1783* (Jamaica: Douglass and Aikman, 1783), 23–24; Dirom noted the centrality of martial law in the 1780s.

63. Whitson, *Constitutional Development of Jamaica,* 135.

64. Petley, *Slaveholders in Jamaica,* 58. In Jamaica every free man between sixteen and sixty was required to serve in the militia and muster quarterly, though their obligations were graded according to racial and financial distinctions. A candidate for the Jamaican legislature proposed in 1791 that shirkers be subjected to corporal punishment for avoiding their duties; he was threatened by an angry mob in Kingston. Hall, "Constitutional and Political Developments," 85, 105.

65. Moore to Lords of Trade, April 17, 1760, TNA, CO127/3, folio 5.

66. Moore to Lords of Trade, June 9, 1860, TNA, CO 137/32, folios 7–8; Resolution, Journals of the Assembly of Jamaica, September 19, 1760, TNA, CO140/40, folio 164.

67. Rugemer, *Slave Law,* 165.
68. See Aaron Graham on the formidable cost and logistics of mobilizing an action against slave runaways (let alone a slave rebellion). Aaron Graham, "A Descent into Hellshire: Safety, Security and the End of Slavery in Jamaica, 1819–1820," *Atlantic Studies* 17, no. 2 (2019): 1–23. Brown speculates that Maroons from Accompong town at very least collaborated with the rebels on account of shared Coromantee roots, though he thinks it unlikely that the rebel leader, Accompong, was "the same man as the maroon captain Accompong" after whom the town was named. Brown, *Tacky's Revolt,* 125–126.
69. Minute of Council, April 17, 1860, enclosure in H. Moore to the Lords of Trade, April 19, 1760, CO137/32, folios 5–6.
70. Moore to the Lords of Trade, June 9, 1760, CO137/32, folios 7–8.
71. Smith, "Legal Status of Jamaican Slaves," 301; Brown, *Tacky's Revolt,* esp. 154, 221, 224.
72. H. Moore to the Lords of Trade, July 24, 1760, TNA, CO 137/32, folio 21. Note that others, including Thistlewood, wanted slaves involved in rebellion to be given no quarter. Brown, *Tacky's Revolt,* 189–191.
73. Smith, "Legal Status of Jamaican Slaves," 298–299.
74. Brooke Newman, *Dark Inheritance: Blood, Race, and Sex in Colonial Jamaica* (New Haven, CT: Yale University Press, 2018), 63–64.
75. *Acts of Assembly, Passed in the Island of Jamaica; from 1681, to 1737, inclusive* (London: J. Baskett, 1738), 236. See also M. Bladen, J. Brudenell, T. Pelham, and P. Dominique, "Recommendation for Repealing an Act Passed at Jamaica in March 1730," July 13, 1731, TNA, CO 138/17, folios 160–161. On the legislative aftermath of Tacky's Rebellion, see Trevor Burnard, "Powerless Masters," 193–194.
76. Long, *History of Jamaica,* 2:321.
77. "Reasons in support of the bill to restrain exorbitant grants to negroes &c, and answers to the protest of three of the Members

of the Council in Jamaica," enclosure in L. Stanhope to J. Pownall, June 13, 1763, TNA CO137/33, folio 34. Discussed in Newman, *Dark Inheritance*, 113-128. In 1802, as the free Black community began to mobilize for equal rights, bills for free Black emancipation were discontinued entirely. Newman, *Dark Inheritance*, 260. By 1825 Jamaica's free Black population outnumbered the white population. Newman, *Dark Inheritance*, 17; Daniel Livesay, *Children of Uncertain Fortune: Mixed-Raced Jamaicans in Britain and the Atlantic Family, 1733-1833* (Chapel Hill: University of North Carolina Press, 2018), 307; Arnold A. Sio, "Race, Colour and Miscegenation: The Free Coloured of Jamaica and Barbados," *Caribbean Studies* 16, no. 1 (1976): 7.

78. Though note that Edwards claimed that if "peace had not been offered" to the Maroons, they "had no choice left but either to be starved, lay violent hands on themselves, or surrender to the English." Edwards, *Proceedings,* xiv.

79. Regarding the lead-up to treaties: "Some Considerations relating to the present state of Jamaica with respect to their runaway negroes, 16 October 1734," enclosure within Martin Bladen to Sir Robert Walpole, October 31, 1734, quoted in Rugemer, *Slave Law,* 144. Martial law was declared October 23, 1734. Rugemer, *Slave Law,* 145-146.

80. Lauren Benton notes that such arrangements were common in European treaties with Maroon communities and mirrored governance arrangements common to the African societies from which many Maroons originally hailed. Benton, *Law and Colonial Cultures: Legal Regimes in World History, 1400-1900* (Cambridge: Cambridge University Press, 2002), 62-63.

81. See, for example, the Treaty of Augusta (1763), which preserved Indian jurisdiction in *inter se* crimes. Lisa Ford, *Settler Sovereignty: Jurisdiction and Indigenous people in America and Australia, 1788-1836* (Cambridge, MA: Harvard University Press, 2010), 19-20. On the link between killing subjects or exposing them to harm as a

hallmark of sovereignty, see Achille Mbembe, *Necropolitics* (Durham: Duke University Press, 2019).

82. The treaty is copied in Edwards, *Proceedings,* xvi–xxii.

83. Leann Thomas Martin, "Maroon Identity: Processes of Persistence in Moore Town" (PhD diss., University of California, Riverside, 1973), 167, quoted in Barbara Klamon Kopytoff, "Colonial Treaty as Sacred Charter of the Jamaican Maroons," *Ethnohistory* 26, no. 1 (1979): 59.

84. Geretius McKenzie, January 9, 1991, quoted in Kenneth M. Bilby, *True-Born Maroons* (Gainesville: University Press of Florida, 2005), 277.

85. Kathleen Wilson, "The Performance of Freedom: Maroons and the Colonial Order in Eighteenth-Century Jamaica and the Atlantic Sound," *William and Mary Quarterly* 66, no. 1 (2009): 73.

86. Colonel Ernest Downer, 1952, quoted in Bilby, *True-Born Maroons,* 277–278.

87. Dallas, *History of the Maroons,* 152–153, quoted in Kopytoff, "Colonial Treaty as Sacred Charter," 50.

88. "An Act for raising Companys in the Several Negro Towns and Encouraging them to reduce Rebellious and Runaway Slaves," June 9, 1744, 17 Geo. 2 c. 3 (Jamaica), TNA, CO 139/16, folio 50

89. Barbara Klamon Kopytoff, "The Early Political Development of Jamaican Maroon Societies," *William and Mary Quarterly* 35, no. 2 (1978): 287–307.

90. The Maroon leader, an obeah woman, Nanny, was a marked exception here. Kopytoff, "Early Political Development," 300.

91. "An Act for the Better Order and Government of the Negroes belonging to the several Negroe Towns and for preventing them from purchasing of Slaves," June 9, 1744, 17 Geo. 2, c. 4, TNA, CO 139/16, folio 51.

92. "An Act for the Better Order and Government of the Negroes," June 9, 1744," 17 Geo. 2, c. 4, TNA, CO 139/16, folio 51.

93. "An Act for the Better Order and Government of the Negroes," June 9, 1744," 17 Geo. 2, c. 4, CO 139/16, folio 51.

94. Thomas Thistlewood, folder 2, box 1, Thomas Thistlewood Papers, James Marshall and Marie-Louise Osborn Collection, Beinecke Rare Book and Manuscript Library, Yale University, quoted in McKee, "From Violence to Alliance," 36.

95. Dallas, *History of the Maroons,* 116, quoted in McKee, "From Violence to Alliance," 36.

96. Long, *History of Jamaica,* 2:348–349, quoted in Wilson, "The Performance of Freedom," 46. See Lady Maria Nugent, journal entry, March 18, 1802, quoted in Bilby, *True-Born Maroons,* 154; Nancy Prince, *A Narrative of the Life and Travels of Nancy Prince* (Boston: n.p., 1853), 59, quoted in Bilby, *True-Born Maroons,* 155.

97. Wilson, "The Performance of Freedom," 46–47.

98. David Geggus, "The Enigma of Jamaica in the 1790s: New Light on the Causes of Slave Rebellions," *William and Mary Quarterly* 44, no. 2 (1987): 274–299.

99. Balcarres, Draft Reply, May 23, 1796, Crawford Papers, a Private Collection, NLS, ACC9769, 23/11/120.

100. Geggus, "The Enigma of Jamaica," 280–282

101. Quoted in Edwards, *Proceedings,* lii–liv. Note that the rumor regarding the attempted assassination of Craskell was disputed: Chopra, *Almost Home,* 28. William Fitch (later killed leading a foray against the Maroons) reported that Trelawny Maroons "want to treat" but worried that their treaty party had been executed: Fitch to Balcarres, September 2, 1795, Crawford Papers, a Private Collection, NLS, ACC9769, 23/11/19.

102. Balcarres to the Duke of Portland, October 27, 1795, TNA CO/96, F15. The behavior of leading men in the vicinity of Trelawny impeded the war effort. See G. Atkinson to Balcarres, September 5, 1795, Crawford Papers, a Private Collection, NLS, ACC9769, 23/11/2; James Stuart to Shirley, October 6, 1795, Crawford Papers, a Private Collection, NLS, ACC9769, 23/11/181.

103. "Some Opinions Respecting the Present State of the Maroon War," Balcarres to the Duke of Portland, December 31, 1795, quoted in McKee, "From Violence to Alliance," 39.
104. Miles Ogborn, "A War of Words: Speech, Script and Print in the Maroon War of 1795-6," *Journal of Historical Geography* 37 (2011): 207.
105. Lawrence to Balcarres, September 26, 1795, Crawford Papers, a Private Collection, NLS, ACC9769, 23/11/36; Ricketts to Balcarres, December 28, 1795, Crawford Papers, a Private Collection, NLS, ACC9769, 23/11/61. Regarding the attack on the soldier's wife, see Courtenay, March 20, 1796, *The Parliamentary Register; or, History of the Proceedings and Debates of the House of Commons . . . During the Sixth Session of the Seventeenth Parliament of Great Britain,* vol. 44 (London: J. Debrett, 1796), 343. Regarding deliberate displays of savagery, see Chopra, *Almost Home,* 51.
106. Ricketts to Balcarres, December 28, 1795, and January 8, 1796, Crawford Papers, a Private Collection, NLS, ACC9769, 23/11/61-62.
107. Macleod, March 20, 1796, *The Parliamentary Register . . . During the Sixth Session of the Seventeenth Parliament of Great Britain,* 44:337-341.
108. "Review of New Publications," *Gentleman's Magazine* 67, no. 1 (January 1797), 49.
109. Barham, March 20, 1796, *The Parliamentary Register . . . During the Sixth Session of the Seventeenth Parliament of Great Britain,* 44:341; Dent, March 20, 1796, *The Parliamentary Register . . . During the Sixth Session of the Seventeenth Parliament of Great Britain,* 44:345.
110. Walpole and Montague James to Balcarres, December 22, 1795, in Edwards, *Proceedings,* 12.
111. Balcarres to Walpole, March 9, 1796; Balcarres to Walpole, March 16, 1796; Resolution of Special Secret Committee, April 20, 1796; Message from Council to the House, April 26, 1796; Vote of the House, April 27, 1796; all in Edwards, *Proceedings,* 79-81, 84-86,

98–101, 103–104. Note that the house vote was divided: 21 for, 13 against.

112. French slaves and free Black people were soon to follow; they were deported to Martinique in 1799 and 1800. Public Notice, May 1799, Crawford Papers, a Private Collection, NLS, ACC9769, 23/12/100; Public Notice, J. C. McAnuff, January 6, 1800, Crawford Papers, a Private Collection, NLS, ACC9769, 23/12/123. See a copy of the petition in Edwards, *Proceedings,* 3–8; Chopra, *Almost Home,* 63.

113. Balcarres to Walpole, February 3, 1796, and Balcarres to Walpole, March 11, 1796, both in Edwards, *Proceedings,* 66, 80.

114. Balcarres, Draft Reply, May 23, 1796, Crawford Papers, a Private Collection, NLS, ACC9769, 23/11/120.

115. Dundas, Sewell and Barham, May 1, 1798, *The Parliamentary Register; or, History of the Proceedings and Debates of the Houses of Lords and Commons . . . During the Second Session of the Eighteenth Parliament of Great Britain,* vol. 6 (London: J. Debrett, 1798), 89, 91, 93.

116. Walpole, May 1, 1798, *The Parliamentary Register . . . During the Second Session of the Eighteenth Parliament of Great Britain,* 6:94.

117. Walpole, May 1, 1798, *The Parliamentary Register . . . Second Session of the Eighteenth Parliament of Great Britain,* 6:87

118. Walpole, May 1, 1798, *The Parliamentary Register . . . Second Session of the Eighteenth Parliament of Great Britain,* 6:95.

119. Mavis C. Campbell, *The Maroons of Jamaica, 1655–1796: A History of Resistance, Collaboration and Betrayal* (Granby, MA: Bergin and Garvey, 1988), 248–249.

120. *Journals of the Assembly of Jamaica,* vol. 11, November 14, 1804, 195–196. Mavis Campbell suggests that the simultaneous presentation of these petitions was not accidental. See Campbell, *The Maroons of Jamaica,* 248.

121. *Journals of the Assembly of Jamaica,* vol. 11, November 15, 1804, p. 196.

122. The relevant law is CAP XXXI, "An Act to Indemnify the Commander in Chief and All Others Concerned in arming the

Maroons During the Late Alarm of Invasion," July 12, 1805, in *The Laws of Jamaica: Comprehending all the Acts in Force, Passed between the Forty-Fifth Year of the Reign of King George the Third, and the Fiftieth Year of the Reign of King George the Third, inclusive* ... (Jamaica: Alexander Aikman, 1824), 30-31. Lt. Governor G. Nugent to E. Cook Esq., December 27, 1805, TNA, CO114/59, folios242-243.

123. Kenneth Bilby, "Image and Imagination: Re-visioning the Maroons in the Morant Bay Rebellion," *History & Memory* 24, no. 2 (2012): 41-72.

124. For details of British slave ownership, see Catherine Hall, Nicholas Draper, Keith McClelland, Katie Donington, and Rachael Lang, *Legacies of British Slave-Ownership: Colonial Slavery and the Formation of Victorian Britain* (Cambridge: Cambridge University Press, 2014).

125. *Edinburgh Review, or Critical Journal: For April 1803 to July 1803* 2 (1803): 389.

126. Burnard, "Powerless Masters," 195-196; Kirsten McKenzie, *Imperial Underworld: An Escaped Convict and the Transformation of the British Colonial Order* (Cambridge: Cambridge University Press, 2016), 68-69.

127. Stephen, *Crisis of the Sugar Colonies,* 133-135, 174.

128. Liverpool to Hislop, November 27, 1810, TNA, CO 296/4, quoted in Helen Taft Manning, *British Colonial Government after the American Revolution, 1782-1810* (New Haven, CT: Yale University Press, 1931), 361. For the best account of the emergence of crown rule in Trinidad, see James Millette, *The Genesis of Crown Colony Government: Trinidad, 1783-1810* (Curepe: Moko Enterprises, 1970). In a candid letter to Chief Justice Smith in Trinidad, Undersecretary Cecil Jenkinson noted that Liverpool avoided asking Parliament to legislate a constitution for Trinidad, because he feared that the West India lobby would insist on its being given a legislature: Jenkinson to Smith, March 13, 1810, TNA, CO296/4.

129. *An Account of the Colony of Sierra Leone, From its First Establishment in 1793. Being the Substance of a Report Delivered to the Proprietors* (London: James Philips, 1795), 80.

130. Padraic X. Scanlan, *Freedom's Debtors: British Antislavery in Sierra Leone in the Age of Revolutions* (New Haven, CT: Yale University Press, 2017), 24.

131. Bhavani Raman, "Law in Times of Counter-Insurgency," in *Iterations of Law: Legal Histories from India,* ed. Aparna Balachandran, Rashmi Pant, and Bhavani Raman (New Delhi: Oxford University Press, 2017), 120-145.

4. A TREACHERY OF SPIES IN HOOGHLY

1. Rajat Kanta Ray, "Indian Society and the Establishment of British Supremacy, 1765-1818," in *The Oxford History of the British Empire,* vol. 2: *The Eighteenth Century,* ed. P. J. Marshall (Oxford: Oxford University Press, 1998), 513-521.

2. Ranjan Chakrabarti, *Authority and Violence in Colonial Bengal, 1800- 1860* (Calcutta: Bookland, 1997), 159-169; Basudeb Chattopadhyay, *Crime and Control in Early Colonial Bengal, 1770–1860* (Calcutta: K P Bagchi and Co., 2000), 17-18; John R. McLane, "Bengali Bandits, Police and Landlords after the Permanent Settlement," in *Crime and Criminality in British India,* ed. Anand A. Yang (Tucson: University of Arizona Press, 1985), 27-29.

3. Quoted in Thomas Ernst to W. B. Bayly, register to the Court of Nizamat Adalat, November 15, 1808, Minto Papers, National Library of Scotland, MS11597, [hereafter cited as Minto Papers], 1:8-13.

4. Ernst to George Dowdeswell, January 1, 1809, Minto Papers, 1:3-7.

5. Ernst to Bayly, November 26, 1808, Minto Papers, 1:15. Note that many of the documents cited here are copied in the British Library [BL], IOR.F.4.410.10202-10294. There are some minor date discrepancies between the sources.

6. Ernst to Bayly, November 15, 1808, Minto Papers, 1:12.

7. Ernst to Bayly, November 26, 1808, Minto Papers, 1:14-17. See also "Petition of the Inhabitants of Hooghly to His Excellency the Right Honble Gilbert Lord Minto," August 25, 1808, in Memorials from Mr. Ernst relative to his removal from the Office Judge & Magis-

trate of Hooghly & Superintendent of the late Foreign Factories to the situation of 3rd Judge of the Provincial Courts of Benares, & to his suspension from the latter Office, Examiners Office, India Office Records and Private Papers, IOR.F.4.410.10202, 1–5.

8. Blaquiere to Dowdeswell, May 2, 1809, Minto Papers, 1:27–28.

9. Blaquiere to Dowdeswell, May 2, 1809, Minto Papers, 1:28.

10. Ernst was not alone in this allegation. The first India Office volume devoted to his case contains a series of extracts of letters from magistrates about the problem of dacoity. Most of them represent the ill-effects of employing goindas: see, for example, BL IOR.F.4.410.10202, 285P-287I.

11. Radhika Singha, *A Despotism of Law: Crime and Justice in Early Colonial India* (Delhi: Oxford University Press, 1998), 1–4; Eric Stokes, *The English Utilitarians and India* (Oxford: Oxford University Press, 1959), 145–146.

12. Stokes, *English Utilitarians and India;* P. J. Marshall, *The Making and Unmaking of Empires: Britain, India, and America, 1750–1783* (Oxford: Oxford University Press, 2007).

13. For an overview of radical Whig and American views of the Company government, see James M. Vaughn, *The Politics of Empire at the Accession of George III: The East India Company and the Crisis and Transformation of Britain's Imperial State* (New Haven, CT: Yale University Press, 2019), 236–242.

14. Vincent T. Harlow, *The Founding of the Second British Empire, 1763–1793,* vol. 2: *New Continents and Changing Values* (London: Longmans, 1964), 7–224; Marshall, *Making and Unmaking of Empires,* 207–272.

15. Regarding the colonies of Minorca and Gibraltar, see Hannah Weiss Muller, *Subjects and Sovereign: Bonds of Belonging in the Eighteenth-Century British Empire* (New York: Oxford University Press, 2017), 80–120.

16. Quoted in Robert Travers, "Contested Despotism: Problems of Liberty in British India," in *Exclusionary Empire: English Liberty*

Overseas, 1600–1900, ed. Jack P. Greene (Cambridge: Cambridge University Press, 2009), 191. Regarding British perceptions of Indian proclivities for despotism, see Marshall, *The Making and Unmaking of Empires,* 201–202.

17. Quoted in Marshall, *The Making and Unmaking of Empires,* 204.

18. Huw Bowen, "A Question of Sovereignty? The Bengal Land Revenue Issue, 1765-1767," *Journal of Imperial and Commonwealth History* 16, no. 2 (1988); 164-165.

19. Edward Cavanagh, "The Imperial Constitution of the Law Officers of the Crown: Legal Thought on War and Colonial Government, 1719-1774," *Journal of Imperial and Commonwealth History* 47, no. 4 (2019): 625-631 Contrast Rahul Govind, "The King's Plunder, the King's Justice: Sovereignty in British India, 1756-76," *Studies in History* 33, no. 2 (2017): 151-186.

20. Warren Hastings, first governor-general under the Act, and George Bogle, Commissioner of Law Suits, noted that the right of government was thereafter "solely under the Act of Parliament." Quoted in Travers, *Ideology and Empire,* 195-196.

21. Travers, *Ideology and Empire,* 183.

22. Travers, *Ideology and Empire,* 183-184. For the latest on the Supreme Court and subjecthood, see Muller, *Subjects and Sovereign,* 166-208.

23. Quoted in Travers, *Ideology and Empire,* 194.

24. These are gathered, summarized, and inquired into in "Report from the Committee on the Petitions of Mr. Touchet and Mr. Irving, Agents for the British Subjects Residing in the Provinces of Bengal, Bahar, and Oriffa, and Their Several Dependencies; and of Warren Hastings, Philip Francis, and Edward Wheler, Esquires; and of the East India Company;—Relative to the Administration of Justice, &c. in India," in *Reports from Committees of the House of Commons. Re-printed by Order of the House,* vol. 5: *East Indies—1781, 1782* (1804), 1-375.

25. Travers carefully charts this halting and inconsistent transition in the Company's own arguments about its sources of authority.

Travers, *Ideology and Empire,* 195–197; 220–223. Halliday notes how Parliamentary legislation in 1781, 1784 and 1797 (prospectively or retrospectively) gave governors-in-council powers to reconstitute courts—a power they had at earlier claimed to exercise on behalf of the Mughal Emperor. Paul D. Halliday, *Habeas Corpus: From England to Empire* (Cambridge, MA: Belknap Press of Harvard University Press, 2010), 290. The king's sovereignty in Bengal was not expressly asserted by Parliament until 1813, and was acknowledge by France and Holland soon after. H.H. Dodwell, "The Development of Sovereignty in British India," *The Cambridge History of India,* vol. 5, ed. H.H. Dodwell (Cambridge: Cambridge University Press, 1929), 605. Contrast Govind, "The King's Plunder."

26. Quoted in Travers, *Ideology and Empire,* 198–199.

27. Further innovations followed. In 1784 the governor's powers were placed under the supervision of a metropolitan board composed of privy councillors, and then the governor-general was given supervisory jurisdiction over subordinate, and equally autocratic, governments established in Madras, Bombay, and Bencoolen. See the introduction to *Indian Constitutional Documents, 1773–1915,* ed. Panchanandas Mukerji (Calcutta: Thacker Spink and Co., 1915), xxiv; and "The East India Company Act, 1773 (13 Geo. 3, C.63)," in *Indian Constitutional Documents, 1773–1915,* 1–9. Note that the scope of the governor-general's legislative authority was questionable: Bankey Bihari Misra, *The Central Administration of the East India Company, 1773–1834* (Bombay: Oxford University Press, 1959), 38.

28. "The East India Company Act, 1784 (24 Geo. 3, Sess 2, C.25)," in *Indian Constitutional Documents, 1773–1915,* 9–27.

29. Misra, *The Central Administration,* 35. Vaughn argues, with others, that crown supervision focused chiefly on revenue extraction: James M. Vaughn, *The Politics of Empire,* 227–228. See also Travers, *Ideology and Empire;* and Dodwell, "The Development of Sovereignty." Contrast, Govind, "The King's Plunder."

30. Singha, *A Despotism of Law,* viii.

31. Scholars have contested the notion that this was a period of uniform decline. See Travers, *Ideology and Empire,* 11n38, for an overview of the literature. Key works include: C. A. Bayly, *Rulers, Townsmen and Bazaars: North Indian Society in the Age of British Expansion* (Cambridge: Cambridge University Press, 1983); Richard B. Barnett, *North India between the Empires: Awadh, Mughals and the British* (Berkeley: University of California Press, 1980); D. A. Washbrook, "Progress and Problems: South Asian Economic and Social History, 1750-1830," *Modern Asian Studies* 22 (1988): 57-91.

32. Ray, "Indian Society," 514; Chakrabarti, *Authority and Violence,* 134. For an overview of the global crisis of imperial rule that encompasses the decline of Mughal power in the subcontinent, see C. A. Bayly, *The Birth of the Modern World, 1780–1914: Global Connections and Comparisons* (Malden, MA: Blackwell, 2004), 86–92.

33. Robert Travers, *Ideology and Empire,* 8-9. The popularity of this mode of thinking was absurdly evident in the free colony of Sierra Leone, in which the abolitionist Sierra Leone Company established government based on the Saxon constitution; see Granville Sharp, *A Short Sketch of Temporary Regulations (Until Better Shall be Proposed) for the Intended Settlement on the Grain Coast of Africa near Sierra Leona* (London: H. Baldwin, 1786).

34. Travers, *Ideology and Empire,* 233-234.

35. Singha, *A Despotism of Law,* 52-53.

36. Chattopadhyay, *Crime and Control,* 19.

37. On the radical shift away from the "ancient constitution" in this period, see Travers, *Ideology and Empire,* 233-249.

38. For a detailed description of reforms, see Anandswarup Gupta, *Crime and Police in India, up to 1861* (Agra: Sahitya Bhawan, 1974), 31-46.

39. Some saw the risk. Since 1772, dissenting voices had argued against eroding the powers of landholders to keep the peace. Singha, *A Despotism of Law,* 33.

40. Singha, *A Despotism of Law,* 37–46.
41. For the use of coercive policing in Peel's Ireland, for example, see Galen Broeker, "Robert Peel and the Peace Preservation Force," *Journal of Modern History* 33, no. 4 (1961): 366.
42. McLane, "Bengali Bandits," 28.
43. Stanley H. Palmer, *Police and Protest in England and Ireland, 1780–1850,* vol. 1 (Cambridge: Cambridge University Press, 1988), 296–315. Regarding empire, see Clive Emsley, "Policing the Empire / Policing the Metropole: Some Thoughts on Models and Types," *Crime, Histoire & Sociétés* 18, no. 2 (2014): 5–25; Georgina Sinclair, "The 'Irish' Policeman and the Empire: Influencing the Policing of the British Empire-Commonwealth," *Irish Historical Studies* 36, no. 142 (2008): 173–187. Note the importance of nuance here; see the essays in David M. Anderson and David Killingray, eds., *Policing the Empire: Government, Authority, and Control, 1830–1940* (Manchester: Manchester University Press, 1991). Also compare Mike Brogden, "The Emergence of the Police: The Colonial Dimension," and John Styles, "The Emergence of the Police: Explaining Police Reform in Eighteenth- and Nineteenth-Century England," both in *British Journal of Criminology* 27, no. 1 (1987): 4–14, 15–22.
44. McLane, "Bengali Bandits," 29, 39–42; Chattopadhyay, *Crime and Control,* 56–57, 64–101.
45. Ranjan Chakrabarti, *Terror, Crime and Punishment: Order and Disorder in Early Colonial Bengal* (Kolkata: Readers Service, 2009), 60–67. Watchmen driven to crime are referred to in No. 14 Judicial Letter to Bengal, November 9, 1814, *Papers Relating to the Police, and Civil and Criminal Justice under the Respective Governments of Bengal, Fort Saint George, and Bombay; from 1810 to the Present Time* (House of Commons, 1819), 50–53. McLane, "Bengali Bandits," 32–33, found that 33 convicted dacoits included "11 cultivators, 7 chaukidars (watchmen and rent collectors), 4 paedas (peons), 3 laborers, 2 beggars, 2 betel sellers, 2 thatchers, 1 lime seller and

1 bearer." Suspected dacoits held in the Burdwan jail included "95 village watchmen, 82 laborers, 31 fishermen, 30 bearers, and 11 milkmen and cowherds."

46. Quoted in Sir John William Kaye, *The Administration of the East India Company: A History of Indian Progress,* vol. 1 (London: Richard Bentley, 1853), 381. Regarding Hastings's insistence that this rule be applied with discretion, adopting the sensibility of Muslim law, see Singha, *A Despotism of Law,* 29–31. For a more fulsome discussion of Hastings's police reforms, see Gupta, *Crime and Police in India,* 19–30.

47. Nancy Gardner Cassels, *Social Legislation of the East India Company: Public Justice versus Public Instruction* (New Delhi: Sage, 2010), 40–42.

48. Cassels, *Social Legislation ,* 42–43.

49. Cassels, *Social Legislation,* 45.

50. For a more detailed discussion of Minto's reforms, see Gupta, *Crime and Police in India,* 62–75. Minto was governor-general from 1807 to 1813.

51. Cassels, *Social Legislation,* 44.

52. Cassels, *Social Legislation,* 44.

53. Governor General in Council to Dowdeswell, December 30, 1808, Minto Papers, 1:3.

54. Blaquiere to Dowdeswell, May 2, 1809, Minto Papers, 1:28–30.

55. Blaquiere to Dowdeswell, April 29, 1809, Minto Papers, 1:21.

56. Town named with variable spelling in Lumsden, June 13, 1809, Minto Papers, 1:224.

57. Testimony of Shykh Rufoo in "Proposed Resolutions Submitted to the Court by Mr. Harington," May 17, 1809, BL IOR.F.4.410.10202 [hereafter cited as "Proposed Resolutions"], 138. Note that Chatterjee says eight or ten men entered his house: Testimony of Chatterjee, in "Proposed Resolutions," 133.

58. Testimony of Ramkomar Ghose, in Proposed Resolutions Submitted to the Court by Mr. Harington," May 17, 1809, BL IOR.F.4.410.10202, 131–132.

59. Testimony of Chatterjee, in "Proposed Resolutions Submitted to the Court by Mr. Harington," May 17, 1809, BL IOR.F.4.410.10202, 133.

60. Ernst to Bayly, May 4, 1809, BL IOR.F.4.410.10202, 114.

61. Ernst to Bayly, May 4, 1809, BL IOR.F.4.410.10202, 115.

62. Testimony of Rugonaut Nundy, Gomastah of the Village, in "Proposed Resolutions," 140.

63. Ernst to Bayly, April 29, 1809, Minto Papers, 1:37–38.

64. Ernst to Blaquiere, April 29, 1809, Minto Papers, 1:33.

65. Ernst to Bayly, May 4, 1809, BL IOR.F.4.410.10202, 117.

66. Ernst to Blaquiere, May 2, 1809, Minto Papers, 1:34.

67. Ernst to Bayly, November 26, 1808, Minto Papers, 1:16.

68. Ernst to Bayly, June 14, 1809, Minto Papers, 2:245. Singha makes a similar point about the introduction of English-style oaths that disregarded standing. Singha, *A Despotism of Law,* 46–48.

69. Guthrie to Bayly, April 9, 1809, Minto Papers, 1:168–169; Richardson to Guthrie, May 12, 1809, BL IOR.F.4.410.10202, 327.

70. Regarding his care, see Extract from the Proceedings of the Nizamut Adawlut, May 17, 1809, BL IOR.F.4.410.10202, 191. Regarding chastisement, see Dowdeswell to Ernst, February 11, 1809, Minto Papers, 1:17–19.

71. Ernst to Guthrie, April 16, 1809, BL IOR.F.4.410.10202, 332.

72. Lumsden Report, June 13, 1809, Minto Papers, 1:223–224.

73. Ernst to Bayly, May 4, 1809, BL IOR.F.4.410.10202, 117.

74. Testimony of Chundee Ghose, "Proposed Resolutions," 125–126.

75. Note that there is some slippage in terminology in the sources. The men are usually called goindas, but sometimes they are called pikes, suggesting that the men sent by Andrew had varied legal status.

76. Testimony of Ramdhun Gwalla, "Proposed Resolutions," 146.

77. Testimony of Chundee Ghose, "Proposed Resolutions," 128–129.

78. Testimony of Ramdhun Gwalla, "Proposed Resolutions," 148.

79. Blaquiere, quoted in "Proposed Resolutions," 158–159.

80. Blaquiere to Dowdeswell, April 29, 1809, Minto Papers, 1:22.
81. Blaquiere to Dowdeswell, April 29, 1809, Minto Papers, 1:23.
82. Blaquiere to Dowdeswell, May 2, 1809, Minto Papers, 1:26-30.
83. Blaquiere to Dowdeswell, May 2, 1809, Minto Papers, 1:27-28.
84. Blaquiere to Dowdeswell, May 2, 1809, Minto Papers, 1:28.
85. Blaquiere to Dowdeswell, May 2, 1809, Minto Papers, 1:28.
86. Blaquiere to Dowdeswell, May 2, 1809, Minto Papers, 1:25.
87. Ernst to Blaquiere, April 28, 1809, Minto Papers, 1:39-40.
88. Ernst to Blaquiere, April 24, 1809, Minto Papers, 1:26.
89. Ernst to Blaquiere, April 29, 1809, Minto Papers, 1:31-32.
90. "Proposed Resolutions," 163-165; Regarding the Board of Control, see No. 12 Judicial Letter to Bengal, October 28, 1814, *Papers Relating to the Police,* 18-32.
91. Ernst to Bayly, May 4, 1809, BL IOR.F.4.410.10202, 110. He is described as a servant in "Proposed Resolutions," 122. This document also makes it clear that none of the men involved in the affray in Hooghly were named in a warrant issued by the magistrate of Nadia for the apprehension of "Bishonaut Koit, Kalee Gwala Mohun Surma, Teetateea and His Aboodeen." The validity of such a warrant in Hooghly is not clear, as it seems only Blaquiere and the superintendent held concurrent jurisdiction (122-123).
92. Blaquiere to Dowdeswell, May 2, 1809, Minto Papers, 1:28-29.
93. McLane, "Bengali Bandits," 43.
94. Testimony of Gopal Pandey, "Proposed Resolutions," 123.
95. Kim Wagner, "Thuggee and Social Banditry Reconsidered," *Historical Journal* 50, no. 2 (2007): 353-376.
96. Ernst to Bayly, June 4, 1809, Minto Papers, 1:187
97. Shakspear to Dowdeswell, June 26, 1809, Minto Papers, 2:275.
98. Kaye, *Administration of the East India Company,* 381.
99. Quoted by Kaye, *Administration of the East India Company,* 381.
100. Edward Colebrooke's proposals for remedying alleged defects in the Muhammadan Criminal Law (includes statistics of the

incidence of crime in the Bengal presidency), 1801–1802, India Office Records and Private Papers, IOR.F.4.128.2391, 18. See also William Paley, *The Works of William Paley, D.D. Archdeacon of Carlisle with a Life and Portrait of the Author in Four Volumes* (Edinburgh: Walker and Grieg, 1825), but note that Paley died in 1805.

101. Edward Colebrooke's proposals for remedying alleged defects in the Muhammadan Criminal Law, 21.

102. Quoted in No. 12 Judicial Letter to Bengal, October 28, 1814, *Papers Relating to the Police,* 23–24.

103. Dowdeswell's Report to the Governor in Council, undated, Minto Papers, 1:195.

104. Blaquiere to Dowdeswell, May 2, 1809, Minto Papers, 1:26–30.

105. Dowdeswell's Report to the Governor in Council, undated, Minto Papers, 1:202.

106. Dowdeswell's Report to the Governor in Council, undated, Minto Papers, 1:207–208.

107. Lumsden's Report to the Governor in Council, Minto Papers, 2:222–224.

108. No. 12 Judicial Letter to Bengal, October 28, 1814, *Papers Relating to the Police,* 25. The defects of this mass imprisonment are amply laid out in a letter from Ernst to Court of Directors of the East India Company, Memorials from Mr. Ernst, BL IOR.F.4.411.10204, 62–75.

109. No. 14 Judicial Letter to Bengal, November 9, 1814, *Papers Relating to Police,* 54.

110. No. 12 Judicial Letter to Bengal, October 28, 1814, *Papers Relating to the Police,* 53.

111. No. 7 Judicial Letter to Bengal, October 20, 1813, *Papers Relating to the Police ,* 12.

112. No. 14 Judicial Letter to Bengal, November 9, 1814, *Papers Relating to Police ,* 54.

113. No. 12 Judicial Letter to Bengal, October 28, 1814, *Papers Relating to the Police,* 19–20.

114. J. Stuart, quoted in No. 14 Judicial Letter to Bengal, November 9, 1814, *Papers Relating to Police,* 54.

115. No. 14 Judicial Letter to Bengal, November 9, 1814, *Papers Relating to Police,* 47.

116. No. 12 Judicial Letter to Bengal, October 28,1814, *Papers Relating to the Police,* 28.

117. Singha, *A Despotism of Law,* 168–228; Kim Wagner, *Thuggee: Banditry and the British in Early Nineteenth-Century India* (Basingstoke: Palgrave Macmillan, 2007).

118. Quoted in G. R. Gleig, "Letters on the Present State of India. No. V," *Blackwood's Edinburgh Magazine,* 18 (July–December 1825), 413.

119. Bhavani Raman, "Law in Times of Counter-Insurgency," in *Iterations of Law: Legal Histories from India,* ed. Aparna Balachandran et al. (New Delhi: Oxford University Press, 2017), 120–146.

120. Antoinette Burton, *The Trouble with Empire: Challenges to Modern British Imperialism* (Oxford: Oxford University Press, 2015); Piyamvada Gopal, *Insurgent Empire: Anticolonial Resistance and British Dissent* (London: Verso, 2019).

121. Dowdeswell's Report to the Governor in Council, undated, Minto Papers, 1:196–197.

122. See Chattopadhyay, *Crime and Control,* 64–101; and Chakrabarti, *Authority and Violence,* 33–131. Note IOR/F/4/410/10200—"Removal of Thomas Hayes from the office of Judge and Magistrate of Burdwan owing to various acts of corruption and extortion on the part of his native officials: for the dismissal of a magistrate for tolerating torture."

123. Trevor Burnard recently dated sustained pro-slavery argument to the *Somerset* Decision: Trevor Burnard, *Jamaica in the Age of Revolutions* (Philadelphia: University of Pennsylvania Press,) 151–173.

124. Report of Commissioners into Malta, War and Colonial Department and Colonial Office: Malta, Original Correspondence, The

National Archives, Colonial Office Records, ser. 158, vol. 19, pp. 113–114.

125. Lauren Benton and Lisa Ford, "Island Despotism: Trinidad, the British Imperial Constitution and Global Legal Order," *Journal of Imperial and Commonwealth History* 46, no. 1 (2018): 21–46; James Epstein, *The Scandal of Colonial Rule: Power and Subversion in the British Atlantic during the Age of Revolution* (Cambridge: Cambridge University Press, 2012).

126. Lord Wilberforce on East India Company Affairs, June 22, 1813, *The Parliamentary Debates from the Year 1803 to the Present Time,* vol. 26: *Comprising of the Time between the 11th of May and the Close of the Session, 22nd of July 1813* (London: T. C. Hansard, 1813), 847–851.

127. Nasser Hussain, *The Jurisprudence of Emergency: Colonialism and the Rule of Law* (Ann Arbor: University of Michigan Press, 2003).

5. BUSH, TOWN, AND CROWN IN NEW SOUTH WALES

1. Henry Bialowas, *Ten Dead Men: A Speculative History of the Ribbon Gang* (Oberon: Henry Bialowas, 2010), 1.

2. Governor Darling to Sir George Murray, October 5, 1830, in *Historical Records of Australia,* ed. Frederick Watson, ser. 1, vol. 15 (Canberra: Library Committee of the Commonwealth Parliament, 1922) [subsequent citations in the format: *HRA* 1:15], 769–770.

3. For the most detailed exposition of this incident, though it is partly fictional, see Jeanette M. Thompson, *Bone and Beauty: The Ribbon Boys Rebellion* (St. Lucia: University of Queensland Press, 2020).

4. Quoted in Bialowas, *Ten Dead Men,* 119–121; Thompson attributes this to Entwhistle and renders it thus: "If he has sent men to the gallows, he will send no more" (Thompson, *Blood and Bone,* 104).

5. *Sydney Gazette,* October 7, 1830, quoted in Bialowas, *Ten Dead Men,* 8; Thompson, *Bone and Beauty,* 114.

6. *Sydney Gazette,* November 11, 1830, quoted in Bialowas, *Ten Dead Men,* 6.

7. Darling to Murray, October 5, 1830, *HRA* 1:15, 770.

8. Lisa Ford and David Andrew Roberts, "Expansion, 1830–50," in *Cambridge History of Australia,* vol. 1: *Indigenous and Colonial,* ed. Alison Bashford and Stuart MacIntyre (Cambridge: Cambridge University Press, 2013), 122.

9. Earl Bathurst to J. T. Bigge, January 6, 1819, *HRA* 1:10, 7.

10. James Boyce, *Van Diemen's Land* (Carlton: Black, 2010), 145–212; Lyndall Ryan, *Tasmanian Aborigines: A History since 1803* (Crows Nest, NSW: Allen and Unwin, 2012), 74–150.

11. Ford and Roberts, "Expansion, 1830–50," 128, 135.

12. David Andrew Roberts, "A 'Change of Place': Illegal Movement on the Bathurst Frontier, 1822–1825," *Journal of Australian Colonial History* 7 (2005): 108–112.

13. Viscount Goderich to Darling, March 23, 1831, *HRA* 1:16, 115.

14. Lisa Ford, *Settler Sovereignty: Jurisdiction and Indigenous People in America and Australia, 1788–1836* (Cambridge, MA: Harvard University Press, 2010), 120–127; K. K. Chaves, "'A Solemn Judicial Farce, the Mere Mockery of a Trial': The Acquittal of Lieutenant Lowe, 1827," *Aboriginal History* 31 (2007): 122–140.

15. John Connor, *The Australian Frontier Wars, 1788–1838* (Sydney: UNSW Press, 2002).

16. On Nunn and Myall Creek, see Roger Milliss, *Waterloo Creek: The Australia Day Massacre of 1838, George Gipps and the British Conquest of New South Wales* (Ringwood, VIC: McPhee Gribble, 1992), 166–203, 274–311; Brian W. Harrison, "The Myall Creek Massacre and Its Significance in the Controversy over the Aborigines during Australia's Early Squatting Period" (BA honors thesis, University of New England, 1966); R. H. W. Reece, *Aborigines and Colonists: Aborigines and Colonial Society in New South Wales in the 1830s and 1840s* (Sydney: Sydney University Press, 1974), 34–48, 145–174; Myall Creek special issue, *The Push from the Bush: A Bulletin of Social History,* no. 20 (1985): 1–88. See also Lyndall Ryan's massacre map for the proliferation of mass violence on the frontiers: *Colonial*

Frontier Massacres in Central and Eastern Australia, 1788–1930, Centre for 21st Century Humanities, University of Newcastle, https://c21ch.newcastle.edu.au/colonialmassacres/map.php.

17. Goderich to Darling, March 23, 1831, *HRA* 1:16, 115.

18. Zoë Laidlaw, "'Aunt Anna's Report': The Buxton Women and the Aborigines Select Committee, 1835-37," *Journal of Imperial and Commonwealth History* 32, no. 2 (2004): 1–28; Elizabeth Elbourne, "The Sin of the Settler: The 1835-36 Select Committee on Aborigines and Debates over Virtue and Conquest in the Early Nineteenth-Century British White Settler Empire," *Journal of Colonialism and Colonial History* 4, no. 3 (2003), http://doi.org/10.1353/cch.2004.0003.

19. Note that the humanitarians had proved themselves extremely attached to mercantile logic in Sierra Leone. Padraic X. Scanlan, *Freedom's Debtors: British Antislavery in Sierra Leone in the Age of Revolution* (New Haven, CT: Yale University Press, 2017), 26–64.

20. Lisa Ford, "Protecting the Peace on the Edges of Empire: Commissioners of Crown Lands in New South Wales," in *Protection and Empire: A Global History,* ed. Bain Attwood, Lauren Benton, and Adam Clulow (New York: Cambridge University Press, 2017), 175–193.

21. Ford, *Settler Sovereignty;* Grace Karskens, *The Colony: A History of Early Sydney* (Sydney: Allen and Unwin, 2009), 439–446.

22. Governor Philip's Second Commission, April 2, 1787, *HRA* 1:1, 2–8.

23. Lauren Benton and Lisa Ford, *Rage for Order: The British Empire and the Origins of International Law, 1800–1850* (Cambridge, MA: Harvard University Press, 2016), 41; Alan Atkinson, "Jeremy Bentham and the Rum Rebellion," *Journal of the Royal Australian Historical Society* 64, no. 1 (1978), 1–13.

24. In this respect New South Wales resembled the garrison government of Gibraltar. Stephen Constantine, *Community and Identity: The Making of Gibraltar since 1704* (Manchester: Manchester University Press, 2009), 75–81.

25. J. M. Bennett, "The Establishment of Jury Trial in New South Wales," *Sydney Law Review* 3 (1961): 473–476. Note, however, a brief hiatus, when Forbes argued that the New South Wales Act facilitated civilian juries for quarter sessions. R v. Magistrates of Sydney, NSWSupC 20, NSWKR 3, October 14, 1824, *Decisions of the Superior Courts of New South Wales, 1788–1899,* published by the Macquarie Law School, Macquarie University, https://www.law .mq.edu.au/research/colonial_case_law/nsw/cases/case_index /1824/supreme_court/r_v_the_magistrates_of_sydney/.

26. Ian Holloway, "Sir Francis Forbes and the Earliest Australian Public Law Cases," *Law and History Review* 22, no. 2 (2004): 216.

27. Forbes to R. Wilmot-Horton, March 6, 1827, in *Some Papers of Sir Francis Forbes: First Chief Justice in Australia,* ed. J. M. Bennett (Sydney: Parliament of New South Wales, 1998), 124–134.

28. Tim Castle, "'Time to Reflect': Earl Bathurst and the Origins of the New South Wales Executive Council," *Journal of Australian Colonial History* 16 (2014): 74–75.

29. For an excellent overview of gubernatorial / court politics in the Forbes period, see C. H. Currey, *Sir Francis Forbes: The First Chief Justice of the Supreme Court of New South Wales* (Sydney: Angus and Robertson, 1968); and J. M. Bennett, *Sir Francis Forbes: First Chief Justice of New South Wales, 1823–1837* (Annandale, NSW: Federation Press, 2001).

30. John Kennedy McLaughlin, "The Magistracy in New South Wales, 1788–1850" (PhD diss., University of Sydney, 1973), 374–404.

31. For an overview of some of the more important judicial review cases, see Holloway, "Sir Francis Forbes," 218–224.

32. Meanwhile, hangings skyrocketed. See Tim Castle, "Watching Them Hang: Capital Punishment and Public Support in Colonial New South Wales, 1826–1836," *History Australia* 5, no. 2 (2008): 43.1–43.15.

33. Lisa Ford and David Andrew Roberts, "Legal Change, Convict Activism and the Reform of Penal Relocation in colonial New

South Wales: The Port Macquarie Penal Settlement, 1822-26,"
Australian Historical Studies 46, no. 2 (2015): 174-190; Lisa Ford and
David Andrew Roberts, "New South Wales Penal Settlements and
the Transformation of Secondary Punishment in the Nineteenth-
Century British Empire," *Journal of Colonialism and Colonial History*
15, no. 3 (2014), http://doi.org/10.1353/cch.2014.0038.

34. An Act to consolidate and amend the Laws for the transportation
and punishment of Offenders in New South Wales and for
defining the respective powers and authorities of General Quarter
Sessions and of Petty Sessions and for determining the places at
which the same shall be holden and for better regulating the
summary jurisdiction of Justices of the Peace and for repealing
certain Laws and Ordinances relating thereto, August 24, 1832 (3
Wm. IV, No. 3); David Andrew Roberts, "The 'Illegal Sentences
Which Magistrates Were Daily Passing': The Backstory to
Governor Richard Bourke's 1832 Punishment and Summary
Jurisdiction Act in Convict New South Wales," *Journal of Legal
History* 38, no. 3 (2017): 231-253.

35. James Mudie, *The Felonry of New South Wales: Being a Faithful Picture
of the Real Romance of Life in Botany Bay* (London: Whaley and Co.,
1837), 15-18.

36. Petition from residents of the District Hunter's River to Governor
Richard Bourke, August 22, 1833, Colonial Office and Predeces-
sors, New South Wales Original Correspondence, The National
Archives, London, Colonial Office Records, 201/238.

37. Ford, *Settler Sovereignty,* 45.

38. Sir Thomas Brisbane to Bathurst, June 18, 1824, *HRA* 1:11, 283.

39. Brisbane to Bathurst, November 8, 1825, *HRA* 1:11, 897-898.

40. Sally Hadden, *Slave Patrols: Law and Violence in Virginia and the Carolinas*
(Cambridge, MA: Harvard University Press, 2001), 6-40; Ford, *Settler
Sovereignty,* 115-120. Note that militias were disbanded in England
after 1815. Stanley Palmer, *Police and Protest in England and Ireland,
1780-1850* (Cambridge: Cambridge University Press, 1988), 59-61.

41. Palmer, *Police and Protest,* 24–31, 83–116.
42. See Galen Broeker, "Robert Peel and the Peace Preservation Force," *Journal of Modern History* 33, no. 4 (1961): 363–373.
43. For a sustained comparison of the mounted police in Australia and Canada, see Amanda Nettelbeck and Russell Smandych, "Policing Indigenous Peoples on Two Colonial Frontiers: Australia's Mounted Police and Canada's North-West Mounted Police," *Australian & New Zealand Journal of Criminology* 43, no. 2 (2010): 356–375.
44. Illan rua Wall, *Law and Disorder; Sovereignty, Protest, Atmosphere* (Abingdon: Routledge, 2021), 85.
45. Palmer, *Police and Protest,* 296–315.
46. Members of the New South Wales Council to Brisbane, September 6, 1825, enclosure in Brisbane to Bathurst, November 8, 1825, *HRA* 1:11, 899.
47. Brisbane to Bathurst, November 8, 1825, *HRA* 1: 11, 897–898.
48. Darling responds to House of Commons debate *inter alia* about policing costs in enclosure to Darling to Murray, December 22, 1830, *HRA* 1:15, 851–852. Murray's pushback regarding the augmentation of mounted police is noted in Darling to Murray, February 3, 1831, *HRA* 1:16, 67–70; Darling to Goderich [?], April 12, 1831, *HRA* 1:16, 235–236; Darling to Goderich, June 6, 1831, *HRA* 1:16, 264. Note that Darling seems to have convinced Goderich of their importance by the time Governor Bourke arrived in the colony. See Goderich to Bourke, September 29, 1831, *HRA* 1:16, 395. Waterloo Creek details some of the more spectacular incidents of settler violence against Aboriginal people. From the late 1820s, military parties were deployed repeatedly to guard surveyors and explorers, and to hunt down Aboriginal people and convicts on the colony's fringes. Milliss, *Waterloo Creek.*
49. I. Northby to E. Lockyer, P. Hill, W. Howe, J. Coghill, G. J. Savage, and H. Walpole, April 17, 1830, State Records of New South Wales [hereafter cited as SR NSW]: Colonial Secretary's Correspon-

dence, 4/7090. 188 troops mentioned in F. Rossi to Colonial
Secretary, April 14, 1830, SR NSW: Colonial Secretary's Correspondence, 4/7090.

50. Various, some undated and not addressed, including Colonial
Secretary to F. Rossi, April 19, 1830, SR NSW: Colonial Secretary's
Correspondence, 4/7090.

51. *An Act to Suppress Robbery and Housebreaking and the Harbouring of
Robbers and House Breakers,* April 21, 1830 (11 Geo 4, No. 10). The
first were Smith and McCormick on June 21, 1830. See R v. Smith
and McCormick, NSWSupC 46, June 22, 1830, *Decisions of the
Superior Courts,* https://www.law.mq.edu.au/research/colonial
_case_law/nsw/cases/case_index/1830/r_v_smith_and_mccormick/.

52. Arthur's government in Van Diemen's Land had mooted similar
measures in 1828. See April 9, 1828, Executive Council Minutes,
Van Diemen's Land, SR NSW EC 4/1/1 285-286, but the result is
not listed in numbered acts of 1828.

53. *Sydney Monitor,* April 21, 1840, p. 4, and April 24, 1830, p. 3.

54. *Sydney Gazette,* June 22, 1830, p. 2; R v. Smith and McCormick,
NSWSupC 46, June 22, 1830, *Decisions of the Superior Courts,*
https://www.law.mq.edu.au/research/colonial_case_law/nsw/cases
/case_index/1830/r_v_smith_and_mccormick/.

55. Bourke to Goderich, March 19, 1832, *HRA* 1:16, 565.

56. Mr. Justice Burton to Bourke, August 24, 1834, *HRA* 1:17,
524-533.

57. An Act for the Punishment of Idle and Disorderly Persons, and
Rogues and Vagabonds, in That Part of Great Britain Called
England, June 22, 1824 [3 Geo 4, cap 40]; Remarks by F. Forbes
on opinion expressed by W. W. Burton, September 15, 1834,
HRA 1:17, 535.

58. Remarks by F. Forbes on opinion expressed by W. W. Burton,
September 15, 1834, *HRA* 1:17, 534.

59. Remarks by F. Forbes on opinion expressed by W. W. Burton,
September 15, 1834, *HRA* 1:17, 534.

60. Robert Stewart to the Colonial Secretary, March 24, 1834, reprinted in *New South Wales: Votes and Proceedings of the Legislative Council during the Session of the Year 1834* (Sydney: Government Printing Office, 1846), 151.

61. Compare Cassandra Pybus, *Black Founders: The Unknown Story of Australia's First Black Settlers* (Sydney: UNSW Press, 2006).

62. Fred A. Hely to Colonial Secretary, March 18, 1834, in *Votes and Proceedings of the Legislative Council (NSW), 1934*, 148. Emphasis in original.

63. On snobbery, see Kirsten McKenzie, *Scandal in the Colonies: Sydney and Cape Town, 1820–1850* (Carlton, VIC: Melbourne University Press, 2004), 1–14, 51–56.

64. Alexander Harris, *Settlers and Convicts; Or, Recollections of Sixteen Years' Labour in the Australian Backwoods* (Parkville, VIC: Melbourne University Press, 1995), 75–84, orig. pub. 1847.

65. Harris, *Settlers and Convicts*, 78.

66. This anecdote is more repeated than demonstrated; see Currey, *Sir Francis Forbes*, 417–418.

67. Harris, *Settlers and Convicts*, 79.

68. Harris, *Settlers and Convicts*, 82.

69. *Sydney Gazette*, October 7, 1830, quoted Bialowas, *Ten Dead Men*, 8. Thompson's evocative fiction fills the gaps: *Blood and Bone*, 70–110.

70. Richard Nagle and Henry Brown, depositions, "Minutes to Inquiry before Mr. Hely and Mr. Plunkett," December 19, 1833, Patricks Plains Court House, in James Mudie, *Vindication of James Mudie and John Larnach, from certain reflections on their conduct contained in letters addressed to them respectively, through the Colonial Secretary of New South Wales, by order of his excellency Governor Bourke, relative to the treatment by them of their convict servants* (Sydney: E. S. Hall, 1834), 25, 27–28, 31. Curiously, Larnach admitted to beating convicts younger than twenty-one on the basis that they fell into the same legal category as child apprentices.

71. Henry Brown and Peter Ponsonby, deposition, in "Minutes to Inquiry," 16, 27; drawn from Lisa Ford and David Andrew Roberts, "The Convict Peace: The Imperial Context of the 1833 Convict Revolt at Castle Forbes," *Journal of Imperial and Commonwealth History* 49, no. 1 (2021): 1–21.

72. James Browne and James Harvey, depositions, in "Minutes to Inquiry," 4, 9–10.

73. Peter Ponsonby, deposition, in "Minutes to Inquiry," 16. See also Henry Browne's deposition, in "Minutes to Inquiry," 30–31; and Ford and Roberts, "The Convict Peace."

74. Grace Karskens, *The Rocks: Life in Early Sydney* (Melbourne: Melbourne University Press, 1997).

75. Harris, *Settlers and Convicts,* 83.

76. Ford and Roberts, "The Convict Peace."

77. An Act to Prevent the Harbouring of Runaway Convicts and the Encouraging of Convicts Tippling or Gambling, January 19, 1825 (NSW).

78. An Act for the More Effectually Preventing Persons from Purchasing or Receiving Clothing Bedding or Rations from Convicts, July 17, 1828 (NSW).

79. An Act for the Better Regulation of Servants Laborers and Work People, July 17, 1828 (NSW).

80. Kristyn Harman, *Aboriginal Convicts: Australian, Khoisan and Maori Exiles* (Sydney: UNSW Press, 2010). The following is drawn from Ford, *Settler Sovereignty.*

81. Lisa Ford and Brent Salter, "From Pluralism to Territorial Sovereignty: The 1816 Trial of Mow-watty in the Superior Court of New South Wales," *Indigenous Law Journal* 7, no. 1 (2008): 67–86.

82. R v. Hatherly and Jackie, SR NSW: Court of Criminal Jurisdiction, Indictments, Informations and Related Papers, 1816–1824, December 18, 1822 (or December 27, 1822, and adjourned until January 1, 1823) [SZ800], reel 1978, 1–19; and R. v. Hatherly and Jackie, NSWKR 10; [1822] NSWSupC 10, January 2, 1823, *Decisions of*

the Superior Courts, https://www.law.mq.edu.au/research/colonial
_case_law/nsw/cases/case_index/1822/r_v_hatherly_and_jackie/.

83. Ford, *Settler Sovereignty,* 173–174; David Andrew Roberts, "Beyond
'the Crossing': The Restless Frontier at Bathurst in the 1820s,"
Journal of Australian Colonial History 16 (2014): 244–259.

84. R. v. Tommy, NSWSupC 70, November 24, 1827, *Decisions of the
Superior Courts,* https://www.law.mq.edu.au/research/colonial
_case_law/nsw/cases/case_index/1827/r_v_tommy.

85. Ford, *Settler Sovereignty,* 158–182.

86. Ford, *Settler Sovereignty,* 174; R. v. Lego'me, NSWSupC 4, February 12, 1835, *Decisions of the Superior Courts,* https://www.law.mq
.edu.au/research/colonial_case_law/nsw/cases/case_index/1835/r
_v_legome/.

87. Ford, *Settler Sovereignty,* 175.

88. R. v. Lego'me.

89. Karskens, *The Colony,* 421–455.

90. "Proclamation by His Excellency Lachlan Macquarie Esquire
Captain General: 4 May 1816," in *Original Documents on Aborigines
and Law, 1797–1840,* available at https://www.law.mq.edu.au
/research/colonial_case_law/nsw/other_features/correspondence
/documents/document_6/.

91. R. v. Ballard or Barrett, NSWSupC 26, April 21, 1829, *Decisions of the
Superior Courts,* https://www.law.mq.edu.au/research/colonial
_case_law/nsw/cases/case_index/1829/r_v_ballard_or_barrett/.

92. R. v. Ballard or Barret, quoted in Ford, *Settler Sovereignty,*
169n40.

93. R. v. Ballard or Barrett.

94. SR NSW: Kinchela to McLeay, February 19, 1834, SB: Attorney-
General [4 / 2221.2].

95. Governor Richard Bourke had also served as acting governor at
the Cape. The man Governor Bourke replaced, Ralph Darling,
had toured as a soldier in the West Indies, Europe, and India
before taking on the role of governor of Mauritius. Brian H.

Fletcher, *Ralph Darling: A Governor Maligned* (Melbourne: Oxford University Press, 1984), 5–69.

96. Regarding Burton's legal importations in the context of his 1838 Protection Act, see Shaunnagh Dorsett, "Burton and the Draft Act for the Protection and Amelioration of the Aborigines 1838 (NSW)," in Shaunnagh Dorsett and John McLaren, *Legal Histories of Empire: Laws, Engagements and Legacies* (Abingdon: Routledge, 2014), 171–185.

97. "Judgement of Mr. Justice Burton in the Case of Jack Congo Morral on a Charge of Murder," February 1836, p. 211, in *Original Documents on Aborigines and Law,* available at https://www.law.mq .edu.au/research/colonial_case_law/nsw/other_features /correspondence/documents/document_47/.

98. "Judgement of Mr. Justice Burton," pp. 211–214 For authority, *inter alia,* he cited Vattel and Blackstone. For a detailed discussion of the case, see Bruce Kercher, "The Recognition of Aboriginal Status and Laws in the Supreme Court of New South Wales under Forbes CJ, 1824–1836," in *Land and Freedom: Property Rights and the British Diaspora,* ed. A. R. Buck, John McLaren, and Nancy E. Wright (Aldershot: Ashgate, 2001), 93–99.

99. "Draft information against Jack Congo Murrell: February 1836," in *Original Documents on Aborigines and Law,* available at https://www.law.mq.edu.au/research/colonial_case_law/nsw /other_features/correspondence/documents/document_42/.

100. Burton, "Arguments and Notes for Judgment in the Case of Jack Congo Murrell, February 1836," in *Original Documents on Aborigines and Law,* 238–239, available at https://www.law.mq.edu.au/research /colonial_case_law/nsw/other_features/correspondence /documents/document_48/. Burton had crossed out the words "loose & vague" and "entitled to be respected as . . . 'in the nature of laws by a Christian Community.'"

101. Burton, "Arguments and Notes," 249. On this point, see Emer de Vattel, *The Law of Nations, or, Principles of the Law of Nature, Applied*

to the Conduct and Affairs of Nations and Sovereigns (London: G. G. and J. Robinson, 1797), 98–101, 168–171.

102. Vattel, The Law of Nations, 102, quoted in Burton, "Arguments and Notes," 238–239, emphasis in original. See also Kercher, "Recognition of Aboriginal Status," 93–99.

103. Burton, "Arguments and Notes," 241.

104. R. v. Merridio, NSWSupC 48, May 14, 1841, Decisions of the Superior Courts, https://www.law.mq.edu.au/research/colonial_case_law /nsw/cases/case_index/1841/r_v_merridio/.

105. Summary of Stephen's argument in Burton, "Arguments and Notes," 220.

106. Blackstone, quoted in Burton, "Arguments and Notes," 261.

107. Burton, "Arguments and Notes," 244. Compare the Sydney Gazette report, in which the attorney general stressed that fact that the crime occurred in "a populous part of the King's territory." R v. Murrell and Bummaree, 1 Legge 72; NSWSupC 35, February 5, 1835, Decisions of the Superior Courts, https://www.law.mq.edu.au /research/colonial_case_law/nsw/cases/case_index/1836/r_v _murrell_and_bummaree/.

108. An Act for the Prevention of Vagrancy and for the Punishment of Idle and Disorderly Persons Rogues and Vagabonds and Incorrigible Rogues in the Colony of New South Wales, August 25, 1823 (6 Will 4, No. 7).

109. Ford, "Protecting the Peace," 185–187.

110. Bill Rosser, Up Rode the Troopers: The Black Police in Queensland (St. Lucia, QLD: University of Queensland Press, 1990); Robert Ørsted-Jensen, Frontier History Revisited: Colonial Queensland and the "History War" (Brisbane: Lux Mundi, 2011). Tim Rowse, with others, has written most recently on the Native Police. See Tim Rowse, "The Moral World of the Native Mounted Police," Law and History 5, no. 1 (2018): 1–23; and for reflections on the ramifications of this "difficult heritage" for military history, see Tim Rowse and Emma Waterton, "The 'Difficult Heritage' of the Native Mounted

Police," *Memory Studies* (2018), journals.sagepub.com/doi/10.1177/1750698018766385.

CONCLUSION

1. George Ricketts to Alexander Lindsay, 6th Earl of Balcarres, December 28, 1795, Crawford Papers, 23/11/61, National Library of Scotland.

2. Nasser Hussain, *The Jurisprudence of Emergency: Colonialism and the Rule of Law* (Ann Arbor: University of Michigan Press, 2003), 6.

3. Regarding rarity, but also the increasing nineteenth-century dependence on emergency legislation, see Charles Townshend, "Martial Law: Legal and Administrative Problems of Civil Emergency in Britain and the Empire, 1800-1940," *Historical Journal* 25, no. 1 (1982): 167-195.

4. Amaresh Misra, *War of Civilisation: India, A.D. 1857* (New Delhi: Rupa and Co., 2008).

5. Lyndall Ryan, "Martial Law in the British Empire," in *Violence, Colonialism and Empire in the Modern World,* ed. Philip Dwyer and Amanda Nettelbeck (Cambridge: Cambridge University Press, 2017), 93-109.

6. Bhavani Raman, "Law in Times of Counter-Insurgency," in *Iterations of Law: Legal Histories from India,* ed. Aparna Balachandran, Rashmi Pant, and Bhavani Raman (New Delhi: Oxford University Press, 2017), 120-146.

7. Julie Evans, *Edward Eyre: Race and Colonial Governance* (Dunedin: University of Otago Press, 2005); Zoë Laidlaw, *Colonial Connections, 1815–1845: Patronage, the Information Revolution and Colonial Government* (Manchester: Manchester University Press, 2005).

8. John Manning Ward, *Colonial Self-Government: The British Experience, 1759–1856* (London: Macmillan, 1976), 38-81.

9. Catherine Hall, *Civilising Subjects: Metropole and Colony in the English Imagination, 1840–1867* (Cambridge: Polity Press, 2002), 338-370, 435-436.

10. Partha Chatterjee, *The Nation and Its Fragments: Colonial and Post-Colonial Histories* (Princeton, NJ: Princeton University Press, 1993), 10.

11. Note Damen Ward's caveat that colonial legislation passed by settler polities was supervised by the colonial office after self-government: Damen Ward, "Legislation, Repugnancy and the Disallowance of Colonial Laws: The Legal Structure of Empire and *Lloyd's Case* (1844)," *Victoria University of Wellington Law Review* 41 (2010): 381–402.

12. Amanda Nettelbeck, Russell Charles Smandych, Louis A. Knafla and Robert Foster, *Fragile Settlements: Aboriginal Peoples, Law, and Resistance in South-West Australia and Prairie Canada* (Vancouver: UBC Press, 2016).

13. Antoinette Burton, *The Trouble with Empire: Challenges to Modern British Imperialism* (Oxford: Oxford University Press, 2015).

ACKNOWLEDGMENTS

This book has been with me for a long time. It brings together archival tendrils I started following while I was doing my PhD from 2000 to 2007. It builds on a much smaller project I planned to write in 2010 when I applied for my first major grant. The project was happily derailed by *Rage for Order,* my collaboration with the wonderful Lauren Benton. It was further delayed by a brief but manic stint in university administration. Eleven years later, I give you *The King's Peace.*

During this book's long gestation, I have incurred many debts. First, I must acknowledge the generous support of the University of New South Wales, which gave me financial support and time to visit archives and test my ideas. This support allowed me to incur a much greater debt to the Australian Research Council and the academics who make it work. This book draws on research I have assembled in the course of three large grants: DP110103832, Convicts, Empire and Order; DE120100593, Protecting the Peace; and FT190100232, Empire of Emergency. ARC support has allowed me to write books that are bigger and bolder than I dreamed of when I started out in academia fourteen years ago.

I thank the many archives I have visited. I give particular thanks to the staff of the National Archives, London, which is the most accessible, generous institution I have ever worked in, and to the British Library, the Massachusetts Historical Society, the William L. Clements Library, the State Records of New South Wales, and the National Library of Scotland. I have been made most welcome and spent a good deal of time in all of these places. I also extend special thanks to the Earl of Crawford and Balcarres for permission to use and cite the invaluable Crawford Papers, a private collection held in the National Library of Scotland.

And thank you to my friends. My career has been enfolded in the kindness and intellectual generosity of others. Thank you to Aparna Balachandran, Lauren Benton, Aaron Graham, Paul Halliday, James Keating, Kirsten McKenzie, Naomi Parkinson, and David Roberts, who have all read and commented on parts of this book. Thanks to Max Edelson, Grace Karskens, and Mike McDonnell for keeping me on the straight and narrow with maps (and of course to Isabelle Lewis for her saintly patience in drawing and redrawing them). Thanks to David Armitage, Adam Clulow, Paul Halliday, Benedict Kingsbury, and Phil Stern for inviting me to share chapters with seminars at Harvard, Princeton, Duke, Virginia, and NYU. Thanks to Jacqueline Mowbray and Tim Sherman, who let me hide from my Associate Deanship in their gorgeous timeshare beach shack to finish the draft in August 2019. Everyone should edit with the Pacific Ocean as a backdrop.

Finally, I thank my family. My big sister, Michele, has caffeinated me wearily while sitting through endless verbal restructures. My people, Craig and Jonathan, endured my comings and goings with good humor, not least because they were being well fed and watered by my beautiful parents, Mary and Alan, and mother-in-law, Margaret, in my absence. Mary also helped to research and proofread the manuscript. I think she has since decided that this is not the best way to spend her retirement. I dedicate this book to her.

INDEX

Figures, maps, and notes are indicated by f, m, and n following the page number.

Bengal, 137-175; capital punishment in, 149, 163-164; courts in, 4, 144-146, 154; due process in, 145-147, 149-151, 158-160, 162-167, 172-175; emergency legislation and powers in, 149-150, 161-169, 224-225, 228-230; governance in, 143-152,169-172, 224-225, 228-229; governors in, 141, 143-145, 147, 148-49; jurisdiction in, 137-138, 145-146, 148, 150, 155, 158-160; legal divergence in, 142-143, 148-151, 169-175; map of, 139m; martial law in, 170, 228-229; Parliament and, 4, 14-15, 143-146, 169-170; police and policing in, 137-142, 148-152, 155-156, 158-159, 164-169, 171, 225; sovereignty in, 4, 15, 144-145; subjecthood in, 15, 145-146, 171-174

Bengal Judicature Bill of 1781 (Britain), 145-146

Benton, Lauren, 9, 280n80

Bernard, Francis (governor of Massachusetts): disorder in Boston and, 24-25, 38-40, 44-48, 47, 250n66, 252n86; on magistrates, 36-37; prerogative powers and, 12, 44-47, 52-53, 219; on use of civil suits to harass crown officers, 250n66

Bigge Report on the State of New South Wales (1822), 190

billeting, 78-83

Bill of Rights (1689), 11-12, 227, 248n48

Blaquiere, William (Bengal), 140-141, 151-161, 159f, 164-165

Bligh, William (governor of New South Wales), 190

Board of Trade (Britain), 18, 72, 75, 117, 251n72

Boston, 24-57; "acts of riot" in, 31-41; map of, 30m; "people's peace" and, 41-48; prerogative power and, 48-56, 219; "return of the king" and, 48-56; riots in, 31-41. See also American colonies

Boston Massacre, 50, 51f

Bourke, Richard (governor of New South Wales), 189, 196, 201, 209, 306n96

Bowdoin, James (Massachusetts), 50

Brahmins, 10, 152-157

Brisbane, Thomas (governor of New South Wales), 191, 193, 204

Brown, Vincent, 279n68

Browne, James (New South Wales), 201

Bummaree, George (Aboriginal Australian), 209-210

Burch, William (Massachusetts), 39

Burke, Edmund, 44, 90, 92, 142, 144

Burnard, Trevor, 102-103, 133, 272n11, 296n123

Burton, Antoinette, 171, 230

Burton, Ralph (Quebec), 60, 78, 80

Burton, William (New South Wales), 184, 196-198, 210-214, 227, 307n101

Bushrangers Act of 1830 (New South Wales), 16, 182, 195-198, 202, 209, 216, 227

Byrne, Patrick (New South Wales), 176, 200

Calvin's Case (1608), 11

Campbell, Mavis, 284n120

Campbell v. Hall (1774), 8, 18, 55, 238n14

capital punishment: in Bengal, 149, 163-164; in Jamaica, 108-109, 111, 116-117, 119; in New South Wales, 177-178, 195-196; in Quebec, 69

Carleton, Guy (governor of Quebec), 13, 62, 91, 94

Castle Forbes uprising (1833), 200-201

Castle Hill Rebellion (1804), 190

Catholics: in Britain, 89; civil rights and subjecthood of, 13, 62, 64, 86, 89-90, 95-97; in Ireland, 89-90, 95, 143; in Quebec, 62, 64, 78, 83, 85-92, 95-97, 220-221, 267n107

Chakrabarti, Ranjan, 149

Charter of Justice of 1814 (New South Wales), 188